RUMORS

The author wishes to thank the Centre HEC-ISA and the Fondation pour l'Etude et l'Information sur les Rumeurs for their support.

RUMORS

Uses, Interpretations, and Images

Jean-Noël Kapferer

Transaction Publishers
New Brunswick (U.S.A.) and London (U.K.)

Copyright © 1990 by Transaction Publishers, New Brunswick, New Jersey 08903
Originally published in 1987 as *Rumeurs: Le Plus Vieux Média du Monde*, by Editions du Seuil, Paris. Revised edition published in English. Translated by Bruce Fink.

Library of Congress Catalog Number: 89-20413
ISBN: 0-88738-325-4
Printed in the United States of America

Library of Congress Cataloging-in-Publication Data

Kapferer, Jean-Noël.
    [Rumeurs. English]
    Rumors : the world's oldest media / Jean-Noël Kapferer : translated by Bruce Fink.
        p.   cm.
    Translation of: Rumeurs.
    Includes bibliographical references.
    ISBN 0-88738-325-4
    1. Rumor. I. Title.
HM291K17613   1990
302.2′4—dc20   89-20413
                                                CIP

Contents

v

Figures and Tables

Figures

Tables

Introduction

In 1981, Procter & Gamble, one of the biggest American producers of mass-consumption articles, received several thousand phone calls every month from worried consumers wanting to know whether the company had dealings with Satan, as rumor had it. The company's emblem—a human face contemplating myriads of stars—was said to hide within it a great many Satanic signs. If one looked closely, the stars traced out the Devil's number: 666. Procter & Gamble was rumored to have made a pact with the Devil in order to increase sales, and was sending 10 percent of its profits to a satanic sect. Flaring up around 1980 in western Mississippi, this rumor spread rapidly, and soon reached the East Coast. It brought on a war for which Procter & Gamble was in no way prepared—a star wars of an unusual ilk. Shaken up by the meaning of these innocent stars, many religious groups even started boycotting products marked with the fatal symbol. A leaflet began circulating telling consumers which brands they should boycott. In 1987, a translation of the leaflet began circulating in France among the country's most religious populations.

Towards the end of 1966 in Rouen, a good-sized town in the northwest of France, rumor accused a well-known dress shop of being a front for white slave trading. The shop's phone rang off the hook with threatening calls. Pursued by the rumor, which no amount of denials succeeded in dispelling, the store's manager opted to give up the fight and leave town. Three years later, the same kind of rumor plagued Orléans in the Loire Valley. Clients deserted six widely known clothing stores run by Jews, word having it that young women were being kidnapped in the dressing rooms. Inspecting the basements of these stores, police were said to have found two or three young girls who had been drugged and were about to be handed over to a white slave trade network. The rumor took on considerable proportions, requiring full mobilization of the Parisian as well as local press to snuff out what came to be known as the "Orléans' rumor," or to at least reduce it to silence.

In January 1973, a rumor ran rife in both majority and opposition political circles. Georges Pompidou, the president of France, was said to be seriously ill, his life being imperiled; he would thus be unable to complete his seven-year term. Word leaked out across the nation, and was relayed by the press and media which spurred on questioning. Though never officially confirmed, the president's illness was in the conversational "top ten." Pompidou in fact succumbed to a terrible disease one year later.

On November 22, 1963, John Fitzgerald Kennedy was assassinated while the presidential cortège paraded through Dallas. The guilty party was almost immediately identified as Lee Harvey Oswald. An official commission was assigned the task of investigating this dark moment in America's history. Its conclusions, spelled out in the famous Warren Report, showed not the slightest uncertainty: President Kennedy was affirmed to have been assassinated by one single person, L. Oswald, acting under his own initiative. Right after the assassination, however, a rumor sprang up to the effect that there had been several gunmen in Dallas that day and thus a real conspiracy. Some people mentioned Fidel Castro, others the CIA, and still others the Mafia. What is clear is that the official hypothesis of one isolated gunman never convinced a certain portion of American public opinion.

All four of the above rumors were widely known. In each and every case, the same process took place. An idea, coalescing out of thin air, started proliferating and circulating. Its movement gained speed, reached a climax before falling off, split into small brush fires, and then faded, in most instances, into total silence. These four examples are, however, quite heterogeneous. The Orléans rumor was utterly groundless. Similarly, Procter & Gamble had nothing to do with the Devil. The rumor concerning President Pompidou's terminal illness was, on the contrary, altogether founded. And as for the rumor challenging the conclusions of the Warren report, uncertainty has never been dispelled, and room for doubt remains.

For the public, the word "rumor" conjures up a mysterious, almost magical phenomenon. An analysis of common terms used is revealing in this respect: rumors fly, crawl, slither, brood, and run rife. Physically speaking, rumors are surprising animals, swift and insatiable, belonging to no known family. Their effect on men seems to be akin to that of hypnosis: they fascinate, subjugate, seduce and set them ablaze.

The main thesis in this book is that this conception is erroneous. Rumors, far from being mysterious, comply with a strict logic whose mechanisms can be demonstrated. We can better answer today the important questions raised by rumors: how do they arise? Where do they come from? Why do they appear on a particular day in a particular group or in a particular place? One can also interpret rumors: why do they always relate misfortune? What rules does a rumor's message obey? Beyond its apparent content, what is its hidden message?

Moreover, one cannot analyze the phenomenon of rumors without speaking of their role in everyday life. How do we live with rumors, how do we use them, for what purposes, and with what expected or unexpected consequences?

And a final question: can one snuff out a rumor? Up until now, most researchers have confined themselves to furnishing a descriptive or explanatory analysis of the phenomenon; but social realities require us to stride beyond analysis on towards prescription. Above all, it is through in-depth study of the problem of rumor control that one pierces to the very heart of its logic—to the fundamental phenomenon of belief.

1

A Fleeting Phenomenon

Introduction

Rumors are everywhere, regardless of our social spheres. Rumors are also the oldest form of mass media. Before writing existed, word of mouth was the only social channel of communication. Rumors transmitted news, made and shattered reputations, set off riots and wars. Yet the advent of newspapers, the radio and, most recently, the audiovisual explosion, have not smothered rumors. In spite of the media, the public continues to glean some of its information from word of mouth. The arrival on the scene of mass media, instead of suppressing talk, has merely made it more specialized: each form of communication now has its own territory. Nevertheless, little is known about rumors. It is unusual for such an important social phenomenon to be so seldomly studied; as mysterious, almost magical events, rumors still constitute a sort of no man's land or *Mato Grosso* of knowledge.

Where does the phenomenon known as "rumors" begin and where does it leave off? Where does it differ from what is commonly called "word of mouth"? The concept in fact slips away just when one believes one has pinned it down. Everyone thinks he can recognize rumors when he comes across them, but very few people have yet managed to provide a satisfactory definition of them. On the whole, whereas everyone feels quite certain that rumors exist, there is no consensus concerning the phenomenon's precise delimitations.

How is the scarcity of works on the subject to be explained? The difficulty of the task is at least partly to blame. It is quite easy to study the press, radio, and television, as their messages are preserved. Anyone can peruse complete collections of magazines and newspapers. Similarly, tape recorders and VCRs allow one to listen to and/or see old broadcasts again. This is not at all the case with rumors. Except in very few cases, social scientists generally only hear of them when it's already too late: when the rumor has faded away or is in its final stages. Only then can they carry out interviews about people's recollections of the rumor, which are subject to forgetfulness, rationalization, and distortion. In doing so, social scientists are not studying the rumor but rather, the trace it left behind in people's memories. The object thus lends itself but poorly to observation. Another reason for the dearth of studies on the subject stems from the fact that more energy has been spent on stigmatizing rumors than on clarifying their mainsprings.

Troubling Information

The first systematic work on rumors was done in America. The large number of rumors circulating during the Second World War, and their deleterious effects on the morale of the troops and population at large, led several research teams to look into the subject.

How did they define rumors? According to Allport and Postman, the founding fathers of the field, a rumor is "a specific (or topical) proposition for belief, passed along from person to person, usually by word of mouth, without secure standards of evidence being present" [6, p. ix] (numbers in brackets refer to works cited in the reference list at the end of this book). According to Knapp, it is "a proposition for belief of topical reference disseminated without official verification" [154, p. 22]. In Peterson and Gist's words, a rumor is "an unverified account or explanation of events circulating from person to person and pertaining to an object, event or issue of public concern" [201, p. 159].

According to these three very similar definitions, a rumor is primarily a piece of information: it provides news about a person or an event important in current goings-on. In that sense, rumors differ from legends, as the latter bear upon past facts. Secondarily, rumors are for believing. People don't generally tell them with the sole intention of amusing others or giving them pause for thought: in that sense they differ from tall tales and funny stories. Rumors set out to convince people.

Having thus defined the concept, the above-mentioned researchers went on to present a series of examples and experiments. Strangely enough, all of their examples were cases of "false" rumors: ideas the public believed which turned out to be groundless. Yet cases of well-founded rumors are by no means in scarce supply: e.g., those concerning the illnesses of Reagan, Brezhnev, Andropov, and Pompidou. Every currency devaluation is preceded by rumors. In the business world, rumors foretell layoffs and transfers. In politics they antedate ministerial changings of the guard. In 1985, a few weeks before the news was officially confirmed, rumor announced a great success on the part of French industry: the Americans were going to opt for Rita, a transmission system perfected by Thomson CSF, in equipping their land-based military forces. As it turned out, Rita was ultimately chosen over its British competitor.

The examples used by the above-mentioned researchers are tendentious, comprising only cases in which rumors have proven to be unfounded. And yet their definitions of rumors make no reference whatsoever to the truth-value of the information transmitted by rumors. Nowhere is it stated that a rumor is "false information"; rather they claim that a rumor is a piece of "unverified" information. Nothing is ever said concerning the verdict of subsequent verification.

Although researchers are aware that rumors aren't necessarily false, it seems that they nevertheless feel they have to discourage this form of expression. Allport and Postman only present cases of "false" rumors. Moreover, just in case their readers might not understand the dangers involved, they demonstrate the process by which rumors inevitably lead to error. Their experiments are well known: a person looks at a photograph of a street scene for a few seconds, and then tells what he has seen to a second person, who goes on to tell what he has heard to a third person, and so on. After the sixth or seventh relay, the information passed on bears but a vague resemblance to the original photograph.

Allport and Postman's experiment set out to show that rumors inescapably lead to error: as they spread, they get farther from the truth—in both literal and figurate senses—thus constituting a distortion of reality. We will see further along that this experimental simulation does not correspond to rumors' functioning in everyday life. There are cases where the message is carefully preserved in going from one person to the next; and, more importantly, rumors do not *take off from* the truth but rather *seek out* the truth. Let us dwell for a moment on this crucial point.

Rumors and Reality

In their experiment on the word-of-mouth chain, Allport and Postman attempt to demonstrate that as a message is passed farther and farther along, one gets farther and farther from the reality seen at the first relay. Word of mouth is thus presented as leading to a distortion of reality.

In everyday life, rumors rarely arise out of "reality"; they spring, rather, from raw, confused facts. A rumor's purpose is precisely that of explaining these raw facts, i.e., to posit a reality. Between 1980 and 1989, ten young men

called up for military duty disappeared near the Mourmelon military base in
eastern France. So much for the raw facts. What really happened? No one
knows. These facts spurred on two parallel processes [143]:

1. A police investigation, which to this day has come up with nothing.
2. Collective discussions among people living near Mourmelon attempting to
    explain the facts and uncover a reality, which could be agreed upon by the
    majority of them, that would account both for the disappearances and the
    failure of the official investigation. Rumors thus seek out a reality that
    does not await the verdict of official investigations. In any case, reality is
    not at the *origin* of a rumor; it is more likely to be a product of the rumor.
    In effect, there is no *a priori* theoretical reason why the interpretation
    provided by the rumor (involving a mad soldier hiding on the military
    base) necessarily differs from the reality that will someday be provided by
    a complete investigation. Rumors obviously involve collective invention
    of explanations at a distance, whereas detectives stick to the terrain and
    follow up even the slightest clues; their explanations could, nevertheless,
    very well coincide. Were that the case, the rumor would not suddenly stop
    being a rumor. As long as an official reality has not been prescribed by the
    police investigation, explanations going around must be taken for what
    they are worth and nothing more: popular beliefs which spread, not
    because they are true, but because they are popular (i.e., pleasing to the
    people).

FIGURE 1.1

The External Validity of Word-of-Mouth Chains

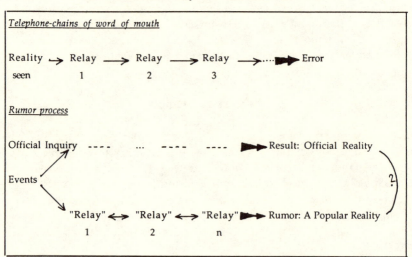

Figure 1.1 illustrates the differences between the laboratory simulation and the rumor process as it took place in our example. In the rumor process, the word "relay" is inappropriate, as no information is passed on unidirectionally. All concerned parties converse with each other, the rumor being the final consensus of their collective deliberations seeking out a convincing, encompassing explanation. As we shall see further along, rumors entail a subjective construction of reality.

Morale or Science?

By selecting only examples of false rumors, and stressing the dangers of word of mouth in their progressive distortion of reality, the aforementioned investigators reflected the concerns of their time. Working for the Office of War Information—one of their jobs being to stem the flow of rumors—such American social scientists took great pains to discredit this form of communication. While their concept of rumors was itself neutral, they carefully selected the examples they needed to prove their point. But there was a contradiction in their approach: were rumors always "false," why would one need to worry about them? After all, in time and with experience, the population would have long since learned not to trust them.

In reality, rumors are bothersome because they may turn out to be true. During wartime, the enemy and its mythical ear (the fifth column) may discover a hidden truth through rumors—clear proof that they are not always unfounded. So as to avoid the risk of confidential information leaks, the Office of War Information undertook poster campaigns claiming that good citizens don't spread rumors ("Shush, the walls have ears"). Unfortunately, this recommendation neglected an essential problem: that of teaching the public how to recognize a rumor. This brings us back in a very concrete way to the problem of definition. Now the three definitions examined above are of no use whatsoever to the public: for what exactly is "unverified information"? In everyday life, we rarely verify the information we get from others. Didn't Jesus Christ himself scold Saint Thomas who felt seeing was believing, by saying, "Happy are those who believe without seeing"? Social life is based on confidence and on the delegation of the task of verification. When we tell others about something we read in the papers, we assume that it has been verified, though we have no proof that it has.

The notion of verification is thus indissociable from the person assumed to have done the verifying. If we have no confidence in him, we suspect that the information may be unverified. In this respect, the Warren Report is open to question in the minds of many Americans: they feel that the hypotheses laid out therein have never been checked, and thus do not believe that the assassination was the isolated act of one single man. As we see, the criterion of verification reintroduces a serious dose of subjectivity.

Lastly, defining rumors as circulating through "unverified" information hinders the public from realizing that rumors generally present themselves with all the trappings of ideal verification, e.g., an eye-witness who states: "I have a friend who saw the ambulance coming out of the White House with his own eyes!" Rumors always reach us through a friend, colleague, or relative who was not himself the first-hand witness of the event in question, but a friend of that witness. Who is more believable than a first-hand witness? What better proof can one expect? A first-hand witness has the status of a spontaneous and disinterested reporter: his narrative is motivated only by an altruistic desire to communicate to his friends what he has seen and/or heard.

Hence every definition of rumors based on their supposedly "unverified" character leads to a logical dead end and an inability to distinguish rumors from plenty of other kinds of information spread by word of mouth or the media. Returning to the concrete problem raised by the Office of War Information, how is one thus to discourage rumors? It was impossible to stop Americans from communicating, especially during wartime, when anxiety (at an all-time high) was leading people to talk in order to dissipate some of it. The five "recommendations" made by Knapp to discourage the proliferation of rumors are particularly interesting. They unwittingly reveal why, in every era, rumors have been troublesome [154].

1. In the first place, the public must have total confidence in the *official media* (press, radio, and television) so as not to be tempted to seek information elsewhere.
2. In the second place, the public must have *total faith* in its leaders, and confidence that its government is doing its best to solve problems brought on by crisis and war. Everything possible must be done to avoid distrust and suspicion which only serve to feed rumors.
3. When something happens, a *maximum of information* should be disseminated as quickly as possible. Rumors arise from spontaneous questions the public asks itself to which no answers are provided. They satisfy the need to understand events, in the cases where events do not speak for themselves.
4. Broadcasting information provides no guarantee that it will be received; one must thus ensure that official reports be heard by everyone. *Pockets of ignorance must be eliminated.* (Knapp cites, for example, an at that time recent initiative on the part of the British army: "educational meetings" at which soldiers could touch on all subjects and receive correct answers in the clearest possible way.)
5. As boredom gives rise to interest in the slightest little rumors that dispel

monotony, it is important to secure the population from *idleness* through work and the organization of free time.

In the context of the Second World War, Knapp's recommendations seemed legitimate, motivated by concern for the national war effort. Reconsidered during peacetime, they seem to outline a totalitarian regime. His first recommendation aims at instilling in the public a distrust of unofficial sources: in seeking information elsewhere, people are likely to come across a version of the facts that does not correspond to the version broadcast by the official media. His second recommendation is a hymn to the respect of one's leaders: the public must have total confidence in those who rule their nation, city, business, trade union, and political party. The third and fourth recommendations are there to ensure that the whole population has clearly understood the official version, i.e., that no pockets of ignorance remain. Unaware of the official account, such pockets could come up with their own accounts. Knapp's fifth recommendation requires that the population's time be as structured as possible: free time and idleness must be done away with.

We have thus seen that definitions of rumors which stress the "unverified" nature of the information they contain stem from a historical era in which mistrust of rumors was at its height. Such definitions are unsatisfactory, for, as mentioned above, the "nonverification" criterion is subjective and cannot distinguish rumors from word-of-mouth transmission of information found, for example, in one's morning paper. We delegate verification, but don't always have formal proof that it has been carried out. Presenting themselves as stories told by eyewitness observers, rumors enjoy the same semblance of verification as every other media.

Definitions based on the criterion of "unverified" information, and *a fortiori* those based on the criterion of "false" information, are in fact ideological definitions manifesting a bias against rumors and a moralizing tendency. Knapp's recommendations seem like caricatures during peacetime, but have the advantage of clearly indicating the roots of the bias. Rumors are not troubling because they are "false": were that the case, no one would pay any attention to them. They are believed precisely because they often turn out to be "true," as in the case of information leaks and "political secrets" that are a secret to no one. Rumors are troubling because they constitute a source of information that is not controlled by the powers that be. Turning their backs to the official version, other versions spring to life—to each his own truth.

Collective Deliberation

Is every case of news that spreads by word of mouth tantamount to a rumor? If that were so, every bit of news going around in society would be dubbed a rumor, even if it concerns what the president, in the course of his usual duties, said that very morning at city hall. Now one would have reservations about qualifying such simple repetition as a rumor. It seems obvious that when someone asks, "What rumors are going around?" he does not expect to be supplied with official information or the text of the president's speech. An acceptable definition of rumors must exclude legitimate retransmission of official information by word of mouth.

The best-known definition of rumors in terms of their dynamics must be accredited to the American sociologist, T. Shibutani: rumors are improvised news resulting from a process of collective discussion. According to Shibutani, important, ambiguous events are what give rise to rumors. To provide an example: late one night, a great many tanks roll through a Tunisian village. There being tight control over information in Tunisia, the population begins wondering what is going on. Rumor constitutes a "putting together of the group's intellectual resources to arrive at a satisfactory interpretation of the event" [239]. A rumor thus entails both an information-spreading procedure and a process of interpretation and commentary. Shibutani understands rumors as collective action that aims at giving meaning to unexplained facts: "Do the tanks mean that Kadhafi is back in Tunisia? Has there been a revolt because of price hikes? Or are the tanks merely indicative of ordinary maneuvers? Did the president die?" In spreading and commenting upon the facts, the group arrives at one or two explanations. Changes in a rumor's content are not taken, in this view, to be due to distortions in human memory, but rather to the evolution and contribution of commentaries made throughout the rumor's process.

Shibutani's argument can be summarized in a simple formula:

$$R = \text{Importance} \times \text{Ambiguity}$$

There is a geometrical or multiplicative relation at work here: were the event of no importance whatsoever or totally devoid of ambiguity, there would be no rumor. The energy behind the group's mobilization would be lacking. For example, it is often thought that it is easy to start rumors in marketing, but this is incorrect. Indeed, most people are barely interested in their toothpaste or yogurt: few products really stand out in their minds. Moreover, consumer items are generally unambiguous and seem totally transparent [238].

It is no accident that advertising is of the utmost importance in the realm of consumption. The public isn't very interested in talking about insignificant goods. The mainspring of word of mouth is missing. It is a significant finding that rumors about trivial consumer products make them more important or mysterious: e.g., there is opium in Camel cigarettes, three Ks in the red designs on the Marlboro pack (only fitting, as Marlboro finances the Ku Klux Klan), and a well-known cheese is carcinogenic.

Generally speaking, all mysterious symbols provide an ideal springboard for rumors: they are ambiguous and thus fertile ground for speculation. What Frenchman, for example, hasn't noticed at some point, near the door of his home, geometric signs drawn with a pencil or chalk? A leaflet started going around explaining the symbols as "signs of recognition used by gypsies and thieves" (unusual bedfellows, to say the least): a circle, for example, means "No point trying," a triangle "A woman who lives alone." The letters N, D, and DM supposedly indicate the best time to break in. The leaflet, very unprofessionally typed on ordinary white paper, lays claim to managerial authorship—it is supposedly written by a city police chief in Hauts-de-Seine near Paris. It blithely circulates in businesses and administrative offices.

Whenever the public endeavors to understand but receives no official answers, rumors arise. They constitute an informational black market.

As we see, Shibutani's definition of rumors implies a theory about their genesis and temporal development. It deals with rumors as they form in the aftermath of an event. This definition is too specific. Not all rumors relate to an event which must be explained: certain rumors literally create events. And there is no reason not to call them rumors. In January 1985, for example, for no apparent reason, and without even the flimsiest factual basis, a gruesome story went around Strasbourg and its outlying areas according to which unthinking parents had left their young child in the car while they were out skiing in the area. Both the child's legs were said to have frozen and had had to be amputated (*Dernières Nouvelles d'Alsace,* January 27, 1985). Were we to follow Shibutani's lead and limit the concept of rumors to only those rumors born of real events, we would be obliged to create other concepts to account for rumors stemming from other sources. Certain people already tend, for instance, to call stories that are based exclusively on "fantasy," "modern urban legends" (Mullen 1972). But a proliferation of concepts is undesirable when the latter do not correspond to clearly distinct phenomena. We take these two stories to be cases of rumors: unofficial information circulating in society.

The Psychiatrization of Rumors

Morin, on the other hand, applies the appellation "rumor" *only* to the story of the frozen child. For it exactly fits the two criteria he provides for the detection of rumors in their purest form: (a) the existence of no real child who froze in the area ("no fact which could serve as a point of departure or basis for the rumor"; (b) "information circulating exclusively by word of mouth, neither the press, posters, leaflets nor graffiti playing a role" [186]. The book Morin wrote on an exemplary case of such a rumor (the white slave trade in Orléans in May of 1969) was widely read, and his acception has become dominant in France. In an issue devoted to the study of rumors, a journal defined them from the outset as follows: "Rumors have no foundations, and that is perhaps their most basic definition" [106].

Structurally speaking, this approach is symmetrical to Shibutani's: it involves taking some of the narratives spun and transmitted by word of mouth and erecting them as the only representatives of the rumor phenomenon. But then how should rumors born of events be qualified when a social group puzzles over the events, engendering and transmitting its own explanations for them? Reserving the label "rumor" for only those narratives arising out of thin air obliges one to create other names for phenomena which are no different from such narratives in terms of concrete manifestation.

Morin's definition confining rumors to stories lacking in factual basis has had a pernicious side effect: rumors have acquired a reputation as a mental illness affecting the social body. It is worthy of note that his analysis of the Orléans rumor relied heavily on medical vocabulary: germs, pathology, infectious zones, incubation phases, and metastasies. Rumors were thereby associated with disease, "psychological cancer." Pierre Viansson-Ponté, an editorialist for *Le Monde,* wrote that "We have but barely examined another form of contagious illness related to opinion, which particularly affects the political class . . . , an illness which could be called the political rumor" (*Le Monde,* September 28, 1977).

This association of rumors with illness and even madness is logical. Indeed, if rumors are but beliefs that circulate without any grounds whatsoever for their existence, i.e., without reason, they must be unreasonable, i.e., a sign of madness: the sociological counterpart of hallucination. Consequently, rumors can only be explained by psychiatrists in this manner: if people believe rumors, it's because they are mad.

The psychiatrization of rumors has a considerable practical advantage, allowing one, as it does, to stigmatize all those who do not adhere to "official reality." If they don't believe in it, it's not their *fault:* it is merely a question of delirium.

The psychiatrization of rumors is thus the direct consequence of a refusal to recognize a crucial fact: once false information has penetrated into the social body, it circulates just like true information. Its circulation has nothing to do with collective madness or hallucination, but quite simply with the rules which ground social life. As has already been mentioned, we do not hear rumors from strangers, but, on the contrary, from those who are close to us. Social life is based on confidence: we do not, in principle, assume that our relatives are inventing or concocting things, or are subject to hallucinations.

Once it had been proven that the Orléans rumor was unfounded, it was easy to reproach the town's residents for having believed and transmitted it. But the truth-value of information is not like a label that comes attached to it. Why thus should Orléans residents have immediately perceived, guided by a kind of revelation, that the idea of white slave trade in certain stores was necessarily groundless? The idea conveyed by the rumor was not impossible *a priori*.

One forgets all too easily that a piece of information's truth-value is above all a product of convention and delegation—it is not recorded somewhere in a dictionary of true and false that everyone can consult by flipping open their handy old Webster's. The notions of truth and verification stem from a social consensus: reality is, hence, essentially social. For a *Pravda* reader, what the *New York Times* sustains is not reality, and vice-versa. There is not one sole and unique reality, i.e., some kind a standard of truth, but rather multiple realities. To form an opinion of one's own, one draws upon one's immediate environment and one's own group or clan [259].

There are thus two sources of knowledge: what the media tells one and what is spread by word of mouth within one's group. Rumor is the group's voice. Now in many circumstances the group's voice—manifested by a particular rumor—is way ahead of the media. To claim that only the reality conveyed by the Orléans press should have counted is to completely dismiss our second source of knowledge: what people around us think and say. What the group takes to be true *is* true. This truth is expressed in rumors.

Truth and Falsehood

At the Fondation pour l'Etude et l'Information sur les Rumeurs (Foundation for the Study of Rumors), a permanent telephone number was installed to allow the public to clue us in to the latest rumors. "Allô Rumeurs" (a rumor call line) answering machine showed that in general people called to tell us stories they didn't believe. As these stories were in circulation and believed by part of the public, these callers expected the Foundation to publish formal disclaimers and expose the truth. Other phone calls came in from people wishing to know whether a particular story they'd heard should be believed or not.

It is significant that callers phoned to warn us about stories going around that they did not believe. In doing so, the "rumors" they did believe (and thus did not take to be "rumors") were not recorded by "Allô Rumeurs." This shows that, for the public, the watershed between information and rumors is not objective. They take as "information" what they believe to be true and as "rumors" what they believe to be false or, in any case, unverified.

Thus it is not the nature of the message conveyed nor of the media in question (press versus word of mouth) which makes us decree in one case that we are dealing with information, and in another with a rumor. The dividing line between information and rumor is subjective, resulting from our own conviction. When someone is convinced by a message recounted by a friend or acquaintance, he believes that it is information that he has at hand. Should he be seized by doubt, however, he will quickly qualify the same message as a rumor. There lies the paradox. Once a rumor is qualified as a "rumor" by the public, it stops spreading. On the other hand, when the public does not recognize it as such, it can go on spreading. One would thus be mistaken to ask "But how can people believe such rumors?" In reality, it is because they believe them that they retransmit them and that thus there are rumors. Rumors do not precede persuasion, they are rather its visible manifestation. The labels "information" and "rumor" are not attributed before believing or disbelieving: they are consequences of belief or disbelief. What is at stake here is an altogether subjective value judgment.

One can thus understand why rumors seem more easily grasped in terms of their existence than of their essence. This is because the recognition of a rumor is but the reflection of one's own doubt. Hence different people run the risk of coming up with opposite diagnoses: one will call rumor what the others call truth.

A first conclusion must be drawn here: while this popular definition of rumors is not acceptable as a scientific definition, it is fundamental in the explanation of rumors' persuasive impact.

Generally speaking, any definition of rumors involving the criterion of truth or falsehood is doomed from the outset, hindering as it does the explanation of rumor dynamics. A logical examination of the opposition between truth and falsehood shows that the dividing line between information and rumor is particularly vague. On the whole, the public is unable to distinguish truth from falsehood when news arrives by word of mouth.

While the question of truth or falsehood is always the first one raised whenever rumors are discussed, in reality it is of no use in understanding rumors. A rumor process gets underway because people believe information and consider it to be sufficiently important to pass on to those around them. This says nothing about its real status. Later, with all the elements at one's disposal, one can proceed to examine the rumor's grounds or lack thereof. A rumor's dynamics are thus independent from the problem of determining whether it is authentic or not. Introducing the notion of truth and falsehood into the scientific definition of rumors, as Morin does, means introducing a useless and obfuscating parameter. One example suffices to illustrate this point.

During their lifetimes, François Mitterrand, Georges Pompidou, and Leonid Brezhnev were rumored to be serious ill. With hindsight, we recognize that the rumors were well-founded in the latter two cases, though official corroboration only came later. Thus, at the time the rumors were circulating, the spreading and belief processes were the same for all three of the presidents. One cannot define whether such and such a message is a rumor on the basis of posterior official confirmation. To say that Mitterrand's supposed illness alone deserves to be called a "rumor," would be to run the risk of having to change labels should archives reveal, twenty years up the road, that Mitterrand truly had cancer in 1981, refuting the claims of official communiqués. Running counter to traditional views equating rumors with false information, in this book the word "rumor" in no way, shape, or form constitutes a forecast as to its correctness or incorrectness.

Hearsay Is What Goes Unsaid

As we have seen, the classical definition of a rumor is that of "a proposition for belief of topical reference disseminated *without official verification.*" This definition is unsatisfactory: in effect, rumors often subsist even when official verification declares them false.

What characterizes a rumor's content is not its correctness or incorrectness, but rather *its unofficial source.* Assume for a moment that due to an information leak, the president is claimed to have cancer. If he denies it, is the claim that he does not have cancer thereby verified and the opposite claim disqualified? Verification is indissociable from the person who verifies and the confidence we have in him. This is an overly subjective criterion upon which to ground a definition. On the other hand, at any particular moment in a society or group, there is a consensus concerning the identity of so-called "official" sources: even if one denies them any credibility whatsoever, they remain "official" sources, i.e., sources that are qualified to pronounce.

We shall thus label "rumor" the emergence and circulation in society of information that is either not yet publicly confirmed by official sources or denied by them. "Hearsay" is what goes "unsaid," either because rumors get the jump on official sources (rumors of resignations and devaluations) or because the latter disagree with the former (e.g., the rumor about the "true" culprits in the assassination of John F. Kennedy).

Thus the phenomenon of rumors is as political as it is sociological. The notion of an "official" source is a political notion: it is governed by a consensus about who has the juridical authority to speak, even if his moral authority henceforth fails him. *A rumor constitutes a relation to authority*: divulging secrets, suggesting hypotheses, it constrains authorities to talk while contesting their status as the sole source authorized to speak. A rumor is a spontaneous vie for the right to speak, no previous invitation having been made. It often involves oppositional speech: it remains unconvinced by official disclaimers, as if "official" and "credible" did not go hand in hand. It attests thus to a questioning of authorities, of "who has the right to speak about what." As information that runs alongside and at times counter to official information, rumors constitute a counter-power, i.e., a sort of check on power.

Rumors in the business world best illustrate this point. When someone is assigned to a position—even with the greatest secrecy—well before information has circulated through the organizational and hierarchical channels, from the manager to the assistant manager and on to the assistant's assistant, those at the bottom have already been clued in. In every organization, alongside the legitimate communication channels and procedures, rumors set up fantom, alternative, and invisible channels. They allow interested parties to keep abreast of things. In the life of any organization, surprise is important in bringing about or forcing change. A company's board of directors may suddenly inform several of its employees and executives that they are being laid off; the rumor already going around defuses the board's *fait accompli* tactic, providing the targeted employees with some means to plan and organize their reaction.

In disclosing what is not suspected—certain hidden truths—rumors reestablish the transparency of power, and further counter powers. Rumors, a kind of disrupting speech, are tantamount to a people's first free, unregulated radio station. When official sources disappear (as in Romania), rumors flourish.

Let us now illustrate the new light shed on the question by abandoning the usual conception and defining rumors as unofficial information. Being unofficial, rumors necessarily begin circulating outside of traditional channels (*viz.* the major medias) by word of mouth or leaflets. One of rumors' characteristic features is their speed. Isn't it often said that they run rife? But why do rumors spread like wildfire? Because they have value.

Being unofficial, rumors propose a reality that the group should have known nothing about. That is precisely why everyone is on the look out for rumors and hurriedly speaks about them with friends and family. Rumors reveal secrets; they are rare and thus highly prized—that is the very basis of their value. But it doesn't explain why they spread. Indeed, gold too is rare and thus highly prized: but instead of spreading it around, people hoard it up. There is a fundamental difference between gold and information: information's value doesn't last. It thus must be used as quickly as possible. To spread a rumor is to reap profits from its value, as long as the latter lasts. By taking others into his confidence and sharing a secret with them, the transmitter's personal importance is magnified. He comes across as the holder of precious knowledge, a sort of front-runner scout—creating a favorable impression in the minds of those he informs [107].

A rumor's speed quite logically results from the ineluctable impoverishment of information's value. This same process also explains other facets of rumors. For example, rumors almost always relate recent events. Even when it is a question of repetitive rumors that have been going around for ten years, the teller always presents himself as having a scoop, something really new. The continual attempt to make information current is one of rumors' structural features. It is necessary and logical: by erasing time—turning the clock back to zero—each individual recreates value.

Rumors, Gossip, and Legends

How can rumors be situated in relation to closely related phenomena: gossip, slander, legends, and word of mouth? Gossip refers to the rumor's focal object: certain people in our group [101]. It relates the good and bad fortune of the great and small people around us. In general, gossip is not nasty, exhausting itself in the pleasure of chewing it over: it is very fleeting and must thus often be replaced by fresh gossip which still has all its flavor. When it concerns the latest fight between George Bush and his wife, it's "macro-gossip"; when it relates a high school headmaster's diurnal and nocturnal frolics, it's "micro-gossip."

Up until recently, the distinction between rumors and legends was clear: rumors concern people and recent events, presenting themselves as information whose vocation it is to be believed. Legends, in the traditional sense, refer to past facts accepted to be fictitious that often stage fantastic characters: gods, heroes, etc. Now in recent years, modern folklorists have come up with a new concept, that of the "contemporary legend" or "modern urban legend" to cover "narratives involving recent happenings to real persons," told with the intent of being believed [72]. Many urban legends have been published and are now widely known: the hook, the stolen grandmother, the alligators in the sewer, the K-Mart snake, etc. Aside from the fact that these contemporary urban legends are often neither contemporary nor urban [29], we find this proliferation of concepts—referring to realities which, empirically speaking, are barely distinguishable—unwanted. Such stories are part of the general family of rumors. Indeed, there is not *one* kind of rumor but *several* different kinds that show similar behavior while allowing for variations in their mode of creation and narrative structure. They will be examined below.

Word of mouth is but one form of media. It encompasses a great many phenomena: conversations between two people, group discussions, confidential talks, harangues, and so on. When news from an unofficial source is transmitted by word of mouth alone, showing a characteristic process of chain spreading and large-scale propagation, then we are dealing with a case of "pure rumor." If the medias take up the torch in spreading the news—without warning the public that it is a rumor—they ennoble it: they turn it into information, giving it the *Good Housekeeping* seal. The rumor phenomenon is then no longer pure: it has been "informationalized" and "mediatized." Only "pure" rumors allow us to observe the movement of progressive growth, which starts from virtually nothing and lapses in the end into silence. Indeed, rumors have a life cycle of their own: they are not spontaneously generated, but rather develop by stages from start to finish.

PART I
The Life and Death of Rumors

2

How Rumors Are Born

Beside the Point?

What are the sources of rumors? What kinds of events, facts, and people do they use as springboards? These are always among the first questions asked in taking up the subject of rumors.

As fascinating as it may be, the question of the source is, paradoxically enough, not the most interesting. To search for sources is to lend credence to the myth that rumors are generally started with a specific intent. Certainly there are notorious cases of rumors whose appearance in the right place at the right time clearly cannot be accidental, e.g., those about the private lives of candidates in gubernatorial, state, and national elections, which generally coincide with impending trips to the ballot box. But rumors are most often spontaneous social productions, devoid of ulterior motives and underlying strategies.

The myth of hidden sources is terribly persistent, being both pleasing and useful—pleasing as it catapults us into an imaginary universe of conspiracy, manipulation, misinformation, and economic and political warfare. Rumors are seen as crimes committed by third parties. They are perfect crimes that leave not the slightest trace and require no weapons whatsoever—the defense is left without a leg to stand on. Admittedly, rumors sometimes kill: ministers Roger Salengro and Robert Boulin committed suicide, the former in 1936 and the latter in 1979, because of campaigns against them coupled with unbearable rumors.

The source continues to be embued with mythical importance because it has social utility. In order to hush up rumors among the allies during World War II, the power and efficiency of the so-called "fifth column"—the enemy hidden behind our walls—were exaggeratedly made out to be the source of defeatist rumors.

Furthermore, detection of the source exonerates those who had believed the "false" rumor. Their pursuit and accusation of the source is tantamount to a refusal to recognize that *they themselves* had made a mistake, quite frankly declaring that they had been fooled *by someone else*. Projecting responsibility for rumors outside of the group (traitors can be their only possible source, as they mislead) is not a fortuitous act: it dissimulates true responsibility. There was a rumor—a collective act of talking—because the group seized upon certain information. At every moment, innumerable potential sources send out innumerable signals and messages that have no effect. Now and then, one of them sets off a rumor process. It would be erroneous to think that it is some intrinsic property of the signal or message that accounts for its motor force. At a certain moment, people grabbed hold of the signal or message because it took on meaning for them.

Most facts, signals and messages are mute or neutral: they acquire the meaning we give them. Not dreaming for a minute that the Japanese would attack Pearl Harbor, the Americans didn't pay enough attention to the "signals" of preparation or "suspicious" naval concentrations.

On the other hand, during the tumult accompanying the French Revolution—while the foundations of the secular order were being shaken, though it was not known by what it would be replaced—in the countryside, small groups of people travelling by foot were immediately taken to be brigands and beggars recruited by the nobles to take vengeance on the people. The proliferation of such generally groundless alarm was dubbed the "Great Fear" by historians [163]: insecurity felt by villagers cast ominous shadows on the most insignificant events. The rumors and panic engendered attest to the group's state of uncertainty and the era's psychological situation.

Sources are, in the end, of but little importance. What must be explained in the genesis of a rumor process is the group's adherence and mobilization. Even if there is an initial speaker, it is the other people who found the rumor for, having heard it, they *pass it on*.

To look for the person who started the rumor is to reduce the rumor phenomenon to a purely individual problem that is external to the group, falling into the category of individual pathology: that of an intentional or unintentional pyromaniac, a sorcerer's apprentice, a practical joker who went too far, or someone who tried to get even with someone else. Such scenarios make for good films, but whereas in a film the public plays the role of spectator, in the case of rumors, the public steals the limelight: the public is the main actor.

After such a proviso, it may seem strange to certain readers to devote several pages to the sources of rumors. The intent is to provide a systematic account of rumors, and the examples that follow attest to the fact that what is fascinating about them is not their sources, but what the public does with them. All pretensions to exhaustiveness aside, we shall review a number of processes that are typical in the starting up of rumors.

What the Experts Say

Since 1978, some of the best-known American companies have had to face up, one after another, to terribly tenacious rumors to the effect that large portions of their capital being controlled by the very powerful Moon sect, or that they were out and out possessed by the Devil. Procter & Gamble, a world leader in household products (Pamper's, Ariel, Bonux, etc.), McDonald's, the world's largest hamburger chain, and Entenmann's, a giant in the food industry [131] all served as grist for the rumor's mill. The rumors were, as it turned out, started by pastors of fundamentalist religious communities in the southern United States, i.e., the Bible Belt. Those communities' worldview is ruled by intense fundamentalist religious faith. In their sermons, their pastors warned the faithful about these companies. Just as in the Middle Ages, the Church became the rumors' media [234].

FIGURE 2.1

Procter & Gamble's   **The Emblem as Interpreted**
Emblem   **by the Rumor**

These rumors were based on the deciphering of signs which could not fool these fundamentalist "experts"; according to them, the signs were virtual avowals. Procter & Gamble's emblem, mentioned in the preface, showed the face of an old Jupiter-like man in the form of a crescent moon gazing at thirteen stars (in honor of the thirteen American states existing at the time the emblem was designed). The rumor focused first on the crescent moon: an obvious allusion to the Moon sect and its founder, the Antichrist incarnate. The rumor next attacked other parts of the emblem thought to be far more revealing: the thirteen stars were claimed to "trace out" the number 666, Satan's number according to one interpretation of a verse found in chapter 13 of the book of Revelation. This number was also detected in the curls of the old man's beard, the man himself being revealed to be a ram, Satan's animal form. In April 1985, in order to try to snuff out this persistent rumor, Procter & Gamble decided to take its emblem off all its products—its emblem having appeared on them since the founding of this highly Puritan company more than a century before.

As specialists able to read signs that are undecipherable for common mortals, experts are classic sources of rumors. Entitled to judge, prognosticate, and predict, they have an immediate echo chamber: the people who take them to be experts, i.e., the reporters whose job it is to diffuse their opinions.

On October 12, 1969, Russ Gibb, a disk jockey on a Detroit radio station, WKNR-FM, specializing in pop music, received a phone call during a live broadcast from a young man introducing himself as Tom [216]. Tom detailed a few extraordinary coincidences: if, for example, one played the Beatles' song "Revolution Number 9" backwards, one heard that the refrain "Number 9, number 9, number 9" became "Turn me on, dead man!"; similarly, at the end of the song "Strawberry Fields" on the *Magical Mystery Tour* album, if one listened carefully and eliminated the background noise, one heard John Lennon murmur "I buried Paul!" According to Tom, this explained why Paul McCartney hadn't been seen in public for quite some time.

Two days after Russ Gibb's radio show, the University of Michigan's newspaper, the *Michigan Daily,* announced in large print: "McCartney is dead: further clues found." A long article detailed the panoply of undeniable indications of the hidden truth. Its author, Fred Labour, editor of the paper's pop section, wrote that "Paul McCartney was killed in a car accident in early November 1966 after leaving the EMI studios tired, sad, and depressed." The article was "documented" with a few "facts." On the inside cover of the *Sergeant Pepper* album, Paul McCartney is wearing on his arm a badge bearing the letters OPD, standing for "Officially Pronounced Dead." On the back cover, we see all the Beatles face-on except Paul McCartney. The Beatles were also said to have sprinkled clues on the *Abbey Road* album cover. John Lennon is dressed like a clergyman, Ringo Starr is wearing black like an undertaker, and George Harrison, appearing in workman's garb, stands ready to dig a grave. As for McCartney, we see him crossing a street, barefoot, and everyone knows that in Tibetan burial rituals (very much in vogue at the time) dead people are barefoot. Moreover, the license plate of the Volkswagen parked in the street bears the inscription "28 IF," that is, the exact age Paul McCartney would have had "IF" he had lived.

That was more than enough to get the rumor going. The experts, taking advantage of the newspaper's wide circulation, had brought the subject to the attention of quite a number of readers who hurriedly told their friends and family, spurred on by the news' important implications for Beatle fans. Was McCartney really dead? It is not clear whether the majority believed he was, as no survey was ever carried out (the hypothesis seeming too dreadful); in any case, people seriously wondered for several months. But even after Paul McCartney appeared in *Life* magazine to clarify the situation, the rumor continued its course: the guy in the magazine was said to be a look-alike or something of the sort. Moreover, on the back of the page upon which McCartney's picture appeared, there was an advertisement for a car—if one looked through the page, the car could be seen to be cutting McCartney's head off. McCartney's denial backfired: rumor reread it as it saw fit, reversing its meaning.

Confidential Information

As mentioned above, rumors arise when information is scarce. We see in the exchange of information constituted by rumors the principles ruling all exchange [107]. Information circulates because it has value, i.e., because it is worth its weight in gold! In our localities, many rumors stem from secrets that have been more or less intentionally leaked. We are very attuned to what happens at the end of banquets and receptions when, because of general high spirits, a deputy or councilman comes out with confidential information or an aparté on some subject of importance to the town. When one overhears a conversation between two people, unbeknownst to them, in a train, at a restaurant, or on the phone, for example, one gains access to confidential information.

Psychologists have for a long time wondered whether the fact of hearing a message in such a way was more persuasive than hearing it directly from people's mouths. They designed experiments to find out [256]. Two people went, for example, into a subway car at rush hour, a crowded elevator, or a long line at a movie theater, and made sure they were not right next to each other so that their conversation could quite naturally be overheard by those between them. Their experiments showed that messages overheard unbe-knownst to the speakers were superior if the overhearer was already concerned by the subject discussed and if the message confirmed his already formed opinions. In overhearing conversations, we do not think anyone is attempting to persuade us, and thus unconsciously consider the conversation to reflect perfectly the speakers' opinion—to be authentic. The procedure can of course be reversed if one wants to start a rumor. In the United States, for example, a public relations agency, W. Howard Downey and Associates, built its reputation on its ability to get teams of specialists to a particular place within hours to get rumors started [11].

Confidential statements can thus be intentional or unintentional. The former contributes to important political affairs. In the United States, a secret informer nicknamed "Deep Throat," was behind the Watergate leaks which eventually led to President Nixon's downfall. In France, in 1971, *Le Canard enchaîné* (a weekly newspaper) published Prime Minister Jacques Chaban-Delmas' tax return. How did the paper get hold of it? Chaban-Delmas was then working at the Matignon address, and had his personal mail forwarded to his private residence. But the postal system erroneously sent his tax return to another ministerial office. There an office worker noticed that the sender was the French equivalent of the Internal Revenue Service; overcome with curiosity, he opened it and discovered that the prime minister was paying no more taxes than an ordinary country doctor (*Le Canard enchaîné*, No. 3410, March 5, 1986, supplement, p. 13). He passed it on to a friend who sent it to the newspaper.

A Troubling Fact

The source of many a rumor is a troubling event or fact. A rumor consists in the mobilization of the group's attention: in the course of successive exchanges, the group tries to reconstruct the puzzle made up of scattered pieces gathered here and there. The fewer the pieces they have, the greater a role the group's unconscious plays in their interpretation; the more pieces they have, the closer their interpretation is to reality. The most satisfactory interpretation circulates and is, in general, passed on to posterity. It's the only one that is remembered. Let us examine a recent example.

On November 20, 1984, fighting and commotion broke out in New Delhi: "Have you heard the news? It seems the President has been assassinated ..." (*Le Monde*, November 23, 1984). At eleven o'clock a.m., at the embassies alerted by their Indian employees, commotion was at its height. "It's impossible! Check it straightaway through your informants!" By noon, telephone operators at press agencies were overwhelmed by anxious telephone calls: Is it true? Isn't it true? At one p.m. in several neighborhoods, shopkeepers (Sikhs and non-Sikhs) pushed their customers out and quickly closed up. "Haven't you heard? President Zail Singh has been killed. All hell is going to break loose!" In the middle of the afternoon, bureaucrats and bank employees requested to leave early. School teachers sent their pupils home before the bell. At seven p.m., overwrought New Delhi was talking about nothing else. At nine, on TV network news, the announcer annihilated the rumor without repeating it (as many people would probably have thought that he was announcing that the president *was* dead): "Mr. Zail Singh is doing fine. He spent the whole afternoon with a number of visitors." On the screen, the president appeared.

Behind those "eight hours of cold sweat" there was an ambiguous fact considered important by those who were present, whether right near by or further away. Someone had in fact died that very day at the presidential palace: an assassinated gardener. Still affected by Indira Gandhi's assassination, Indian public opinion remained feverish and on the verge of panic. In such a state of mind, the most plausible interpretation of an assassination at the palace seemed to be that the head of state had been its victim. When anxiety is high, it always seems more likely that the worst of all possible events has occurred than the best [202].

In France, a rumor broke out on the Riviera a few years ago: special firefighting planes, known as Canadairs, were said to have inadvertently scooped up swimmers as they were filling up on water. The unfortunate innocent swimmers were claimed to have been directly dumped into the fire blazing in the forests. One of our informants, an airline pilot, remembered having read the news in an aviation journal. The article in question mentioned that a dead man had been found in a bathing suit in a charred area where Canadairs had been working. His presence, in bathing attire, so far from the sea was intriguing; the hypothesis was put forth—alongside other more realistic ones—that he had been sucked up by a Canadair and dropped to an atrocious death.

The vague recollection of such real but trivial events announced in the news often provides a ready-to-use scenario to explain some troubling event which has taken place close to home. In a working-class neighborhood in Metz, for example, a rumor sprang up in November 1984: "An unfortunate child has been devoured by a dog. It seems that all that remained were his legs" (*L'Est Républicain,* November 3, 1984). At its origin was the real death of a three-month old girl due to respiratory failure. Her family did in fact have a German shepherd, but the only thing he devoured that day was his usual can of Pedigree or Haines dogfood. The rumor was not surprising: the press had often spoken of outbursts of instinctual aggressiveness in German shepherds, especially directed against young children. Such happenings are not just in the papers—why couldn't they happen right next door?

Testimony

Believing that there is a grain of truth in certain rumors involves a risk that many take lightly: they conclude that, on the whole, rumors are grounded. In reality what one calls the grain of truth is the ambiguous fact (taken to be important) that rumors echo. Now facts do not exist: only the reporting of facts, i.e., testifying that one has seen or heard, has any real existence. In other words, rumors start less from facts than from their perception. The study of rumors inescapably leads to that of the psychology of testimony. Criminologists and jurists have shown for many years how much we overestimate our perceptual abilities [47]. Many laboratory experiments have proven this beyond the shadow of a doubt.

A classic type of experiment involves creating an artificial incident for a group of unsuspecting people; one then asks them to write up a report testifying to what they have seen. One of the founders of legal psychology, Claparède, for example, organized the following scenario: the day after the famous mascarade festival held in Geneva every year, a disguised person burst into the auditorium where Claparède was conducting his class on legal psychology to an audience of students. The intruder began gesticulating and mumbled a few more or less incomprehensible words. Claparède threw him out of the auditorium [86]. The incident lasted all of twenty seconds.

Claparède immediately passed around a questionnaire with eleven questions to be answered by all present: the mean number of correct answers was but four and a half. Moreover, the students' errors were very significant. The individual chosen to provoke the incident was wearing a long gray cotton coat, dark slacks that were virtually invisible under his long coat, white gloves, and a light-brown and white scarf around his neck; his hair was hidden under a grey felt hat. In one hand he was holding a cane, and in the other a pipe; over his arm hung a blue apron. Most students mentioned the following four elements: the coat, cane, hat, and scarf. But according to certain students, the hat was made of straw, while to others it was a top hat. Some mentioned checkered pants, and his hair was said to be black, brown, blond, grey, and even white. The majority of students sustained that the scarf was red, that he was not wearing gloves, and so on.

Claparède was one of the first people to show that witnesses testify more in accordance with the *degree of probability* of things than with what they have observed. Thus the anarchy set off in the classroom by this individual could but have been the work of a revolutionary, and everyone knows that when a revolutionary wears a scarf, it has to be red. Durandin, specializing in the study of lies, summarized the results of this and related experiments as follows [86]:

1. Altogether exact testimony is most unusual.
2. Witnesses provide false information with the same self-assurance as they provide true information, and with the same good intentions.
3. What we sustain sometimes reflects more our mental stereotypes than what we have really seen;
4. Consequently, when the testimony of several different witnesses converges, it is not necessarily an indication of the truth of their declarations. It can mean that, having the same stereotypes and mental scenarios, they perceived the facts identically but nevertheless erroneously [117].

The factors favoring error are movement (as in the case of car accidents), the fleetingness of the perceived object or scene, the witness' physical state, the extent of his biases, and his stress level at the moment the scene takes place.

Fantasies

The preceding discussion shows how much the imagination, in the form of typical mental scenarios, can influence the perception of events we witness. In the example of the intruder bursting into the classroom, there was nonetheless an event, i.e., a fact to be perceived. Imagination structured the perception of the original fact. Something offered itself up "to be seen." The examples of the rumors in the cities of Laval, La Roche-sur-Yon and Orléans go well beyond that: in all three cases, there was nothing "to be seen," no originating incident or fact. The rumors created the facts.

Twenty years ago, an activist opposing white slave trade organized a city hall circuit in France: at meetings in each town, she warned of the invisible danger, alerting parents and young girls, and accused the authorities of indolence. Just before or very shortly after her stay in Laval, a rumor of white slave trading shook the town. A few years later, the popular magazine *Noir et Blanc* (Black and White), which has since closed up shop, presented the following scenario as a real "recent" event (in fact taken from the erotic novel, *L'Esclavage sexuel* [Sexual Slavery]):

> In Grenoble, a businessman was driving his young wife to an elegant clothing store in town. He waited in the car for half an hour, then three-quarters of an hour, and finally grew impatient. He went in to look for his wife and was told "We've never seen her here." As he was absolutely sure he'd seen her go into the store, he became suspicious but carefully hid his suspicions. He apologized to the salesmen, got back in his car and drove straight to the nearest police station. The police officers, having reasons of their own to be suspicious of the store, soon surrounded the building the store was in, and began carrying out a thorough search. They were said to have found the young woman in the back of the store in a very deep sleep.

On her right arm the police found the mark of a needle: she had been drugged. (*Noir et Blanc*, May 6–10, 1969.)

A week after this article came out, the Orléans rumor, with the very same scenario, broke out. It surfaced once again, almost word for word, later in March 1985: its target this time was a well-known women's clothing store in La Roche-sur-Yon.

The source of such rumors is the pure and simple projection of a typical scenario: "someone" imagined that the scenario was being played out right next door, or in the downtown shopping area, and many people believed it. Who was the "someone"? It is of little importance whether it was Miss X or Miss Y. Edgar Morin and his co-workers [186] located the rumor's incubation site in all-girls' classes (in religious junior highs and high schools). This adolescent population, isolated from social reality and closed off from the rest of the world, is fertile ground for the production of sexual fantasies— imaginary scenarios embodying repressed desires—that one girl tells her friends as if they had really happened to her, and that the friends in turn envy and make into their own experiences. In Laval and Orléans, it would have sufficed to have heard the anti-white-slave-trade activist or to have come across the article in *Noir et Blanc* to have a ready-to-use sexual fantasy, certified as more than plausible. Within several days, in the echo chambers known as boarding school and junior high, every girl had been taken into confidence, knew, believed, and trembled, stories being all the more believed when they play off the attraction of sexual prohibitions [112].

Catherine Lépront, a novelist [164], described the process of fantasy creation and incubation in Saint-Julien Junior High School in a very quiet little town in the French provinces:

[On his way back from horseback riding] a man brushes past an adolescent girl. "Oh excuse me!" he says. She is half drunk with excitement. She is upset, he touched her. She begins inventing a story for, after all, something must have happened to her! She tries the story out on her immediate entourage and her mother cries out, "Our daughters aren't safe anywhere!" [Back at the junior high] the adolescent girl, mixing with a crowd of girls her own age, tells them what happened to her the day before. "After going horseback riding, Jean-Pierre Suzini didn't just brush up against me, he pushed me up against one of the stable walls, with that smile everyone knows so well at the store . . . as I resisted, he drew me to him. He smelled good. He always left his shirt open, and so. . . . The bell began ringing, drowning out the girl's last words, and her friends' shouts, muffled laughter, and their "Stop! Stop! I suspected as much from the start, just from the look of his face." [A few days later] the story swelled in the assembly hall. . . . No one any longer knew who had started it. . . . "It" hadn't happened to them . . . , but rather to their neighbor or girlfriend. The guy had gone into the dressing room, supposedly to help her with her zipper.

Thus what had been but an adolescent girl's narcissistic fantasy had come true, right next door. The incarnation of fantasies in reality is not rare. Carl Jung drew attention to a rumor which had arisen in a girls' boarding school [134]. A teacher was accused of having had sex with one of the students. In fact, it had all started with an adolescent girl telling a dream she had to three girlfriends. Jung called such rumors grounded exclusively in the imagination, "visionary rumors," in order to distinguish them from "ordinary rumors" [135].

Contemporary Urban Legends

This same process of anchoring a myth in reality also explains the regular and unpredictable reappearance of rumors that have been called "exemplary stories" by sociologists [50], and "urban legends" by folklorists [46, 242]. These stories seem like short moral tales, and their appearance seems linked to no tangible fact. For example, in July 1982, all the mothers in Wittenheim (Mulhouse, in the Alsace region of France) were upset: at the Cora supermarket, a small child was said to have been bitten by a tiny snake hiding in a bunch of bananas; though rushed to the hospital, he was claimed to have died. The supermarket—one of the only ones that offered a babysitting service—was quickly deserted by one and all. The same rumor had already stirred up trouble in several other French towns, starting in 1981. It had also sprung up in the United States, going by the name of the "K-Mart snake," and circulated widely in Europe [118, 152]. It closely resembles parents' warnings to their children not to eat too much candy or touch anything on store shelves. Were such warnings suddenly taken seriously by a child who attributed them to a store next door? His school would have provided him with the necessary echo chamber and a large number of relays. Recess is the crucial period for the spreading of rumors among children [97].

Once over, a rumor becomes migratory [150] and slowly moves from one town to another. From time to time in the course of its existence, the rootless story can be "brought up to date" by someone who tells it: "Yes, I think it happened in the supermarket this past summer!" Then people start imagining that it just happened yesterday, and things speed up from one conversation to the next. The story thus has an underground existence as a semi-legend, with no spatial or temporal reference. It is a contemporary urban legend. On a certain day, in a certain discussion, it anchors itself in reality: "it's happening here and now." One day it breaks out in Nice, and the next day in Glasgow; still later it erupts in Liège in Belgium or in Evanston. Who transformed it from a timeless, city-less narrative into today's news? No one knows anymore. Such insignificant details are easily forgotten.

What's more, let us recall that they are besides the point. They explain the initial mechanism, but not that of the rumor's rapid spreading throughout a town. What is important is that a town adopts this rumor: as we shall see further along, the seemingly innocent story of the child and the tiny snake symbolically says (as in a dream, though out loud in this case) what towns secretly think to themselves.

Generally speaking, though one could possibly find facts that might someday, in some other place, give rise to such exemplary stories, what remains the most astonishing is their persistence. Even if every exemplary story, like every legend, is but the deformed echo of a true but distant fact, one must still explain why collective memory holds on to it so dearly. What truth lies hidden in its breast [15]?

The rumor about mice found in Coca-Cola is an example of a rumor based on real facts. According to the rumor—one of the most prevalent rumors of poisoning in the United States—consumers found bits of mice in bottles of Coke. Indeed there are facts proving that this has happened [99]. If one examines the judicial annals, one finds that a first suit was set off and won by a consumer in 1914 in Mississippi. Since that time, forty-four other cases have led to suits against companies that bottle Coca-Cola. Though these suits have gotten very little publicity, the facts must have seriously fired imaginations, setting the rumor going across the whole country. The anecdote is now a part of the American oral tradition, belonging to the series of stories now told about Coca-Cola; it is a sort of warning concerning the power of the mysterious drink whose recipe is kept such a secret.

Similarly, anyone who has ever lived in New York City has at one time or another heard that the city's sewer system was infested with alligators. How did such animals find their way to such an unlikely place? According to certain versions of the rumor, it all started with a family that had brought back baby alligators from their vacation in the Florida Everglades. Having tired of them, they decided to get rid of them by flushing them down the toilet bowl. Living on detritus and rats, the saurians were said to have survived and even thrived. The rumor was often denied by the city sewer department. But though no sewer worker has ever declared seeing an alligator, many New Yorkers believe the city's underworld to have returned to the jungle state, portending an ominous future for the seemingly booming metropolis.

Loren Coleman, an anthropologist, managed to find about seventy articles in American newspapers and magazines reporting untimely encounters with alligators, in the most unexpected of places, between 1843 and 1973 [61]. In only one article, that appearing in the *New York Times* in 1935, are sewers ever mentioned, and they are Manhattan sewers, as it turns out. That such an event may have occurred changes nothing in our diagnosis. Very few

Americans have ever even heard of the article: belief in the rumor stems from other sources. The fact that this trivial item was handed down for more than fifty years—and is now part and parcel of current folklore, i.e., of the repertoire of contemporary urban legends—shows to what extent it struck imaginations, fascinated by the shrouded mysteries of the underworld. Moreover it bears within it several symbolic messages which affect us deeply (see chapter 10). It is a sort of parable or moral tale not confined to Americans alone. In September 1984, police officers and authorities of the Dordogne region in France had to track down a crocodile "seen" in river waters in Castelnau-la-Chapelle and Beyssac, in vain (*Sud-Ouest*, December 9, 1984).

The fact that real encounters with alligators in public and unlikely places did take place—encounters detailed by the press—should not obscure a fundamental point concerning these "urban legends," which would better be called "exemplary stories." Rumors always add a detail that is not contained in the true stories covered by the media. In the rumors of alligators in the sewers, it is significant that the reptiles were always said to have been "flushed down the toilet" [55]. Of the seventy articles listed by Coleman, only one mentioned a sewer (the baby alligator had been dumped down storm drains). The intangible persistence of these two details has an essential meaning in the rumor's lasting vogue. Similarly, while it is true that cargos brought mygales and snakes back from their tropical trips, it is worth pointing out that in the rumors of snakes at local K-Marts, the animal found its way right up to the customer, the snake was most often associated with a bunch of bananas, and the victim was always a child. There is thus systematically a legendary addition that persists around the kernel of truth.

It is the process of anchoring urban legends in the reality of a particular time and place that explains the perennial appearance of rumors like that of the fantom hitchhiker and other secular myths [44, 45]. In May 1982, for example, people in the Vendée region (along France's Atlantic coast) suddenly began speaking about the mystery of the hitchhiking monk. The tale told was always the same. The scene takes place in the evening or at night; on the side of a road a monk stands hitchhiking. A driver stops and invites him to get in the car, he sits in the back seat. According to the various witnesses, he is alone and says very little until he makes several statements that sound like predictions: "We'll have a hot summer, and a bloody fall." Intrigued, the driver or passenger in the front seat turns around. But there is no one in the back seat: the monk has disappeared without the vehicle having ever stopped. Dumbfounded drivers were said to have reported the incident to police squads who informed them that others had had the same experience (*Ouest-France*, May 24, 26, and 29, and June 1, 1982).

In reality, an investigation showed that no one had reported any such thing at police stations [83]. Moreover, as usual, the supposed eye-witnesses—the drivers said to have picked up the strange passenger—always turned out to be but intermediate relays. The story had been told to them by someone else.

Only two things are certain: monks travel throughout France, and can thus be seen in the Vendée region. The story of the hitchhiking monk is part of a general category of stories well known to folklore specialists: the fantom hitchhiker. Such stories were isolated and classified starting back in 1942, and regularly give rise to highly localized outbursts in both Europe and the United States [46]. A few centuries ago, the same story spread from parish to pub: the car back then was a simple carriage.

Misunderstandings

Rumors often arise due to faulty interpretations of messages. Misunder-standings relate to one person's report on what another person reported, and to a difference between what was transmitted and what was decoded.

In mid-February 1984, the inhabitants of Algiers were worried that a "cyclone" was going to wreck havoc in the capital (*Le Monde,* February 25, 1984). Over the preceding two weeks, a rumor had been gaining force that a cyclone was expected in the region, far as may be from the Tropics. It was the Japanese, well known to be experts on natural disasters, who supposedly informed the local authorities. Furthermore, and this is what proved that the warning was to be taken seriously, doctors had been advised to ready hospitals for the weekend. As a matter of fact, in certain hospitals an order had been sent around: "Due to atmospheric disturbances, the staff is to remain on duty February 23rd and 24th." Was the longest weekend about to begin? Shopkeepers were assailed with orders for bottled mineral water. Concerned city dwellers decided to get away from the capital for a few days. On Tuesday, September 21, the newspaper *El Moudjahid* dispelled the rumor. It seemed that an ORSEC (a rescue organization) emergency plan was going to be tested, but that the orders had been misunderstood, no doubt because they were ambiguous.

In January 1986, a rumor hit the Savoy region: "Haroun Tazieff has announced on television that six (or ten) meters of snow were going to fall, and that the town of Chamonix was in danger of being wiped off the map." According to other people, the forecast came from the star weatherman on French television's channel 2, Alain Gillot-Pétré. The rumor spread as far as Dijon, where over five feet of snow were supposed to drop. The secretary of state for natural disasters, a famous volcano specialist by the name of Haroun Tazieff, does in fact often appear on television: a mistake in comprehension is not unlikely. Moreover, the so often announced return of Halley's comet must have impressed certain TV watchers: they were unconsciously expecting some sort of fallout. An avalanche of snow seemed still more believable.

Turkish immigrant workers who read an article in the journal *Turceman* in April of 1980 couldn't believe their eyes. Their fondest hope, their lifelong dream seemed to have come true: in Mulhouse, authorities were granting residence and work permits to those who did not have any. Within days, 3,500 illegal Turkish immigrants had converged on Mulhouse (*Alsace,* May 31, 1980). May was a Turkish month in the Alsace region. What had in fact happened was that *Turceman* had published an article by its Frankfort correspondent about a clandestine immigrant in Colmar who was given a receipt for a request for papers in order to be able to undergo an operation he needed, i.e., a humanitarian question. The article showed a picture of the Turk as well as a facsimile of the receipt. In the article, the journalist was already asking: what will happen when the receipt, good for only three months, expires? But for the Turkish readership, the only thing that stuck out in their minds was that a clandestine worker had received "a paper." Nothing more was needed to set off a trans-European race to Mulhouse.

A famous historical case illustrates how the process of misunderstanding can be repeated: as the new message passed on remains ambiguous, the following hearer is justified in making his own interpretation. In the present case, it was a question of transformations undergone by a newspaper article when taken up by other papers. During World War I, a German newspaper, the *Kölnische Zeitung,* was the first to announce the fall of the city of Anvers into German hands. The title given to the article was: "Upon proclamation of the fall of the city of Anvers, bells were rung." As the newspaper was German, it was self-evident that bells were rung in Germany in honor of the victory. The information was taken up by the French paper *Le Matin:* "According to the *Kölnische Zeitung,* Anvers' clergy was forced to ring the church bells when the fortress was taken." The information reported in *Le Matin* was then repeated by the *London Times*: "According to *Le Matin,* taking its information from Köln, priests in Belgium who refused to ring church bells upon the fall of Anvers were removed from office." The fourth version appeared in Italy in the *Corriere de la Sera:* "According to the *Times,* citing information from Köln (via Paris), the unfortunate priests who refused to ring the church bells when Anvers was taken were condemned to hard labor." The paper, *Le Matin,* then repeated the "news": "According to information reported by the *Corriere de la Sera,* (via Köln and London), it has been confirmed that Anvers' barbaric conquerors punished unfortunate priests for heroically refusing to ring church bells by hanging them in the bells head down like human gongs."

That was how the last paper fed the rumor of the Germans' barbaric behavior in Anvers. Several facts stand out here: on the one hand, while the difference between the first and last version is enormous, the shift from one version to the next is not surprising. It conforms to a logic of clarification of ambiguous words or of selective perception of words. On the other hand, each reporter added something new: faced with the paucity of information, he tried to reconstruct a complete picture, ready and willing to create the missing pieces. Each addition reflected the prevailing mood: World War I was almost a holy war. France wanted to take its revenge on the Germans for the affront it suffered at their hands in 1870. Now one is an even greater hero when one's enemy is depicted as barbarian. This distortion confirmed popular stereotypes of the Germans and justified the population's latent anxiety as well.

Thus it was not a question of bungled readings. Error in fact consists in constructing information according to a plausible scenario, and rumors reflect images and stereotypes that have gained currency. Someone we interviewed mentioned a rumor that sprang up in his village after the disappearance of her brother. The latter had simply gone to Great Britain. To one question she replied that he was "*à Londres*" (in London). The rumor made a prisoner of him, as someone thought he heard "*à l'ombre*" (locked up); it seems not to have surprised him, nor the other villagers for that matter; it corresponded to their image of him.

Manipulation and Disinformation

In November 1968, a rumor sprang up and spread that very seriously slandered the wife of Georges Pompidou, the former French prime minister who later became president [174]. The rumor, related to the Stefan Markovic assassination, arose from a letter dated October 10, 1968, that was addressed to movie actor Alain Delon by a young Yugoslav, held prisoner in Fresnes, who was a friend of Markovic's. The letter made slanderous accusations and was seized by the penitentary administration. Though the prisoner declared that his letter to Delon was spontaneous, i.e., that no one had told him to write it, subsequent investigation attributed its writing to one of his fellow prisoners, convicted for forgery and the use of forgeries.

In February 1976, a simple typewritten page began circulating bearing a list of food additives, dividing them into three groups: carcinogenically toxic, possibly harmful, and innocuous. According to this flyer, a great many common products and brands were altogether lethal. Where did the flyer come from? Who typed the first copy? No one ever found out. It was, nevertheless, copied and recopied by thousands of volunteers struck by the seriousness of the accusations and the ominous spectre of the word "cancer." It is estimated that since that time, seven million people have seen the flyer and been "poisoned" by the rumor [144].

Indeed, an in-depth reading of the flyer quickly revealed to specialists its dubious character. Most of the food additives prohibited in France, and thus not used in currently available products, were placed in the innocuous category. Entirely harmless substances, on the other hand, were claimed to be carcinogenic. The flyer listed E330, for example, as the most dangerous of all. This "mysterious" code in fact refers to everyday citric acid, naturally found in oranges and lemons, which most people consume more or less daily in ample quantities. As Professor Maurice Tubiana, worldwide cancer specialist and director of the Gustave-Roussy Institute in Villejuif (near Paris), put it, "The flyer lists as dangerously carcinogenic a whole series of extremely innocuous substances found in everyday food. . . . Every scientist who has read it has burst out laughing at its load of inanities."

In the course of being copied and recopied, an explicit reference to the Villejuif Hospital showed up on the flyer, suggesting that the flyer had been authorized by the hospital. The Gustave-Roussy Institute repeatedly denied having anything to do with the alarming list, but could not put a stop to it: in 1986 the leaflet was still going around. Persuaded that it was authentic, individuals passed it on in elementary schools, social organizations, hospitals, and medical and pharmacy schools particularly responsive to references to the illustrious hospital. Newspapers printed it verbatim, without checking its accuracy. Still worse, in 1984, a doctor writing a book on cancer for a wide-reading public, included the list of carcinogenic products without looking into them, thus adding the weight of the medical establishment to the false information, making people suspicious of innocent products like "La Vache-qui-Rit" (Laughing Cow) cheese and Amora brand mustard. What was the intention of those who first wrote the flyer?

The emergence of a rumor without any other apparent motive than sheer pleasure can be seen in the case of Leonid Brezhnev's illness a number of years back. At that time, rumors ran rife in the chancelleries and were repeated in the press. An important but ambiguous event was taking place: the head of the Soviet Union hadn't been seen in public for five weeks. According to the ever "well-informed" sources, his illness ran the gamut from a tooth-ache to leukemia. The rumor that Brezhnev was coming to Massachusetts to be treated in a world-renowned cancer clinic sprang up in Boston [216]. The widely read local daily paper, the *Boston Globe*, even officially announced his arrival.

What had in fact happened was that someone had fed the name "L. Brezhnev" into the clinic's computer, putting it on the list of expected patients. He had then contacted various sources, like the *Boston Globe* and the city police. The paper requested more information from Washington, and when no denial was forthcoming and the fact was repeated by the police, it published the information.

This example is related to the warning mentioned at the beginning of this chapter. What made for the success of this scam was the extraordinary sensitivity of opinion relays at that precise moment to anything concerning Brezhnev's health. What in effect makes a rumor is not its source but the group.

Innocent Publication of Unverified Facts

On October 5, 1985, in a shopping center in Créteil (a suburb of Paris), volunteers handed out leaflets to passers-by doing their shopping. The leaflet was signed by the very serious, well-known MRAP (Movement against Racism and for Friendship amongst Peoples). To pressure the Pretoria regime and fight apartheid, in accordance with the United Nations' recommendations, the humanitarian movement was calling for a boycott of "fruit and drink tainted with blood" and mentioned several brand names. One drink was specifically targeted: under the heading "Juicy Apartheid," the leaflet mentioned that "Pampryl fruit juices are made from fruit grown in South Africa."

Now the J.F.A. Pampryl Company had, in fact, been buying its fruit from Israel and Morocco. Meetings between Pampryl's managing director and the secretary-general of MRAP showed that the latter had not checked his information. One of MRAP's members had claimed that Pampryl was supplied by South Africa, and that was enough for them to publish it without any further question.

This example illustrates, as if illustration were necessary, to how small an extent checking one's information is natural. If one must teach reporters and historians to verify their sources, it is no accident. For while we only rarely verify what we learn from third parties and word of mouth, those responsible for informing thousands of others should not do the same. Many rumors still get off the ground in articles in local and amateur newspapers, written with the best of intentions and plenty of good will, but often omitting to verify their authenticity.

Where There's Smoke There's Fire?

The above examples clearly show that the proverb "where there's smoke there's fire" is absurd. It is meaningless unless we call "fire" the passion and sometimes fertile imagination of witnesses, message receivers and people who deliberately start and spread rumors. In reality, attachment to this proverb constitutes the royal road to manipulation by rumors. The public's mental program is quite explicit: every wisp of smoke veils a grain of truth. With that in mind, strategists have adopted a well-known rule for action: slander all you like—something will stick.

A Typology of Rumors

To summarize this chapter, it appears that there is not one kind of rumor but rather several, and that they vary as to their etiology. One can identify six basic types of rumors (see figure 2.2 below).

FIGURE 2.2
The Six Types of Rumors

		Origin of Rumor		
		Event	Detail	Exclusively Fantasy
Birth Process	Spontaneous	1	2	3
	Provoked	4	5	6

These types depend first of all on rumors' factual grounds. On the one hand, many rumors are the result of an event whose meaning is uncertain or ambiguous. If, say, eleven young soldiers disappear from a military camp, this is certainly an event that will set off rumors, especially if the official investigation turns up nothing. Shibutani primarily focused on this first type of rumor. The second type starts from a detail or sign, i.e., something very tenuous that had hitherto gone unnoticed. Such was the case of the rumor concerning the mysterious meaning of food additives. Near nuclear plants, the birth of an abnormal calf or chicken prompts rumors about leaks or excessive radioactivity. Thus some people's selective attention unveils a previously hidden "reality." The third type of rumor, known as "exemplary stories" or "modern urban legends" are stories that regularly crop up here and there without any precipitating fact. Most "snake in the K-Mart" rumors develop from scratch: in a suburb where it springs up, one finds not the slightest event that could have been misinterpreted and thus fired off the rumor. The fact that these floating stories typically become "true," somewhere or other, shows that some people make no distinction between fantasy and reality. This trait, known as mythomania, is not rare. In studies of the Orléans' rumor, for instance, its origin was traced to groups of female junior high students, twelve to thirteen years old. At their age—bordering on puberty—fantasies hold sway and some girls indulge in make-believe. Once the story is convincingly told as if it were true, it takes on a life of its own.

In all three categories, rumors may arise spontaneously; they reflect natural processes within social groups. Now rumors can also be provoked, their objectives varying from deliberate misinformation to a search for sensationalism. For example, when Pope John Paul I died on September 28, 1987, thirty-three days after he was elected to office, the event shocked Rome's inhabitants. A journalist suggested that his death was "surprising": it seemed odd that he had died so soon after taking office. The most likely explanation seemed to be that he had been poisoned.

The Procter & Gamble case provides an example of the fifth type of rumor. No one had really paid attention to the corporate emblem on Tide, Pampers, Ivory, Mr. Clean, and Head and Shoulders packaging before a fundamentalist religious community not only drew attention to it but also engendered its Satanic explanation. Leaks and confidential information also fall under this category of rumors. Insiders who wish to remain anonymous call attention to some detail and in the meantime provide an explanation. This is quite frequent in politics and in the stock exchange. Lastly, one cannot preclude the possibility that some urban legends are deliberately concocted in a certain place at a certain time. Reading books about urban legends, someone might well play the "sorcerer's apprentice." This typology of rumors is based on their etiology. As we shall see in the fourth part of this book, rumor control presupposes a diagnosis of the nature of the rumor; such a typology is a first step in that direction.

Facts and Fantasy

All rumors are the product of both fact and imagination. Different types of rumors reflect the prevalence of either realism or imagination and subjectivity in the production of a rumor's content. Some rumors dwell almost exclusively on the "imaginary phreatic layer", i.e., the collective data bank of symbols and unconscious mythical motives. That is the case of "modern legends" or "exemplary stories," which have attracted folklorists' attention in recent years [30]. At the other pole, that of rumors with a predominantly realistic slant, one cannot eliminate the influence of the imaginary. Thus on the stock market, the interpretation of a bond's unexpected rise or fall remains subjective even if it is subject to the censorship of rational filters.

In the above typology, where can we situate the sightings of UFOs, and the stories of kidnappings by extraterrestrial beings? Theoretically speaking, these are not rumors for, unlike rumors, there is an initial witness who saw or said he was kidnapped [182]. In the case of rumors, the word always comes from the FOAF (friend of a friend), disclosing a story that was not previously known. The story bears upon a third person who can either remain silent, deny, or confirm the story. Thus rumors take the form "it's been said that . . ." The person by whom "it's been said," even if he is in a position to know (being a close friend of the star, president, businessman, or city governor in question) is not an "official" source. In the case of UFO sightings and kidnappings, the original witness speaks for himself; he is the official source about what he saw or what happened to him. Unlike rumors—which are what we might call [70] "proto-memorates" (memories via a third person: "I heard that the following happened to someone")—the UFO story originally begins with a "I personally saw a flying saucer." Here we have an authentic subjective experience that is totally imaginary, but which was taken to be real by the original witness, who officially proclaims it to those around him by word of mouth or mass media. Let us recall that rumors are what is left unsaid, i.e., things which official sources have not (yet) confirmed.

3

Rumors Run Rife

Introduction

Even though there may be an originator, what makes a rumor is other people: those who, having heard it, spread it around. A rumor is first and foremost a type of behavior. At a certain moment, a group mobilizes and starts "rumoring": speaking becomes contagious. Not every story told sets off a rumor. The first question is this: Why do we spread some of them and not others?

Why We Spread Them

What information is worth spreading around? Why do we want to tell it to others? These same questions arise every evening in the minds of the editors-in-chief of daily papers. On their desks, the telexes, reports, official statements, and notes pile up. Which of them should be printed, i.e., communicated to the public? What should they retransmit?

Rumors are News

The head of a newspaper once said, "News is what makes people talk." This definition is not satisfactory, but it is instructive. Information that isn't news cannot give rise to a rumor.

The editor-in-chief can't await tomorrow's discussions to know what was or wasn't news in the morning paper. He needs to identify news right now in the mountains of information piling up on his desk. As the proverb has it, what happens is always unexpected [199]. As the news announces what just happened, one must conclude that news is what is unexpected and uncommon. In fact, more innocuous events—from the moment they stray ever so little from routine and habit—have a good chance of winding up in the papers.

The task of an article's title is to synthetically and surprisingly summarize the unexpectedness of what is related therein. Whereas "a dog bites a man" is no big news, "a man bites a dog" is.

As we see, what makes news is not its intrinsic significance. A man's being bitten by a dog is more important than the other way around. Similarly, announcing that there will be twenty thousand deaths from car accidents in 1990 is significant information, but it is not news, it is part and parcel of the order of things. It is grounded in normality, i.e., the drawbacks of our civilization. What makes the information about a man biting a dog into "news" is that it is so uncanny, uncommon and out of the ordinary that it is guaranteed to amuse, surprise, or excite the reader, who will be sure to remember it and repeat it to others in order to share his feelings.

If, to take up the proverb once again, it is always the unexpected that happens, an attentive examination of the press shows that it is the "not entirely unexpected" that in fact goes into the news. There are births and deaths, marriages and divorces, the weather, and so on. These are events that have already taken place and have already been in the news—they are thus no longer unexpected. What is of the essence in "news" is that it relates expected things which were at the same time totally unforeseeable: the winning and losing numbers in the lottery of life, for example. The news presents accidents and incidents for which the public is prepared; things people fear or hope for form the stuff of news and, by that very token of rumors.

News is neither a narrative nor an anecdote; it is, first and foremost, information having *pragmatic interest*. It almost always concerns events that can lead to sudden, important changes. It is information that is full of implications for oneself and those one holds dear; one expects immediate consequences from it, whether positive or negative. News is pragmatic information: it plays the same role for the public as does perception for an individual. It does not inform, it orients. In learning what's new around, for example, in one's building or in town, one can have a better sense of one's environment and act accordingly.

A reader's first reaction to news is to repeat it to someone else: it becomes the subject of conversation, sparking off commentary and debate. But in doing so, one always finds that discussion quickly moves from the fact related (the news) to its implications, the questions it poses, and the lessons to be drawn from it. Thus on the basis of news (a fact) found in the papers, a discussion is born which bears not on the fact itself but rather on what is to be made of it; from this debate of feelings, hypotheses, and certainties, a sort of consensus emerges—called "public opinion"—as to the interpretation to be made of the event in question.

News we repeat is about people we feel close to, whether emotionally or geographically, e.g., Isabelle Adjani, Caroline of Monaco, Ronald and George (the American presidents), the village celebrity, and those who ventured into the fashionable boutiques in a nearby shopping district. This is normal. Information has more pragmatic interest and personal implications when it concerns an individual or state of affairs close to home. But discussion also seizes on news from afar whose range is general, not involving heroes but normal people, laymen, youths, college girls in the next town over, etc. It usually involves an "exemplary story" (one type of rumor): e.g., the news of a man going home late at night who, noticing someone in his house, shoots him with a gun. The "someone" was his son who had come home on a surprise visit after several years overseas. The story is exemplary in that, even without stating a moral, it has one. It overflows with implications not only for oneself but for the collectivity as a whole—like La Fontaine's and Aesop's fables, it speaks to us regardless of the precise historical era, place, and characters involved in the particular adventure related by the press. Even if it does not reflect *the* truth, it expresses *a* truth. Its moral implications for the group constitute the mainspring of its repetition by readers and its regular and perennial resurgence in the form of rumors; it highlights the dangers of self-defense.

Thus the public spontaneously repeats but that information transmitted by the media which enjoys the status of "news." Attention shifts very quickly from repeating to interpreting—drawing conclusions from the original raw facts and thereby defining public opinion, that is, what the group subjectively thinks. The same process occurs when information is transmitted not by the media but by someone, by word of mouth. This information must nevertheless be expected, and answer to more or less conscious hopes, fears, and forebodings. It must also be unforeseen and have immediate, significant consequences for the group. If these three conditions are fulfilled, then we have "news" capable of sparking off the same process of repetition-discussion described earlier in this book that is characteristic of rumors.

First on the list of rumor-engendering information is everything that upsets the state of things and leads people to react, such as news with direct pragmatic interest such as warnings of danger (whether physical, nutritional, or sexual), breaches in moral conduct, social changes, transformations of the physical environment, etc. Rumors about natural catastrophes, for example, spread instantaneously; in Nice, as in California, tidal waves are periodically predicted. In Aix-en-Provence, a rumor announced that an earthquake would occur in June of 1976. Chamonix (in the French Alps) was to be wiped off the face of the earth between January 7 and 14, 1986. Information that indirectly affects people also travels quickly, since the public identifies with others who are more or less removed from them, such as stars and public figures, whether politicians, artists, or athletes.

Rumors always run rife when it is physically or symbolically dangerous not to know the news, whether it be true or false. But aside from warning people, rumors must also determine what is to become of the news, what one should make of it. That is the second function of repetition: speaking in order to know.

Speaking in Order to Know

The comparison between newspaper readers and those who heed stories they are told has a sizable limit: to the reader, the facts related are authentic and verified, he has confidence in the media. The story listener cannot be so certain, even if he believes they may possibly be true. He must find some assurance and also wants to know what to think.

Humans are social animals. This statement has been so often repeated that it now sounds banal. Nevertheless, it draws our attention to several phenomena at the crux of rumors. The American social psychologist Leon Festinger [94] has heavily stressed the concept of social comparison. We seem to have a permanent tendency to compare ourselves to others; we feel a need to situate and evaluate ourselves in relation to others. This concerns each individual's capacities; knowing, for example, that one can jump four and a half feet in the air is fine, but one would still like to know whether that is a good performance or not. Naturally, one doesn't compare oneself with just anyone; one chooses one's reference group among those in one's general proximity.

The same is true of our opinions. We want to know whether our opinions are good or bad. Abilities can be assessed by comparison with a standard, i.e., objective reality—jumping higher than five feet. Opinions, however, don't always correspond to a "reality" against which they can be checked. How do we thus know whether they are correct or not? By comparing them to those of the group with which we identify, this group being taken as our reference group [128].

In other words, the fact of speaking about information reveals what kind of consensus there is about it in the group to which we belong. Other means are trickier. How can we know whether our town's notables are involved in fraud or adultery (typically rumor material in medium-sized towns)? We obviously cannot go ask them. Moreover, the source of many a rumor is not within hand's reach: there is always at least one more link between it and the person from whom we hear it. As already stated, the criterion of truth is thus a purely social one: *what consensus takes to be true is true*. To speak is to start up a process of discussion and elaboration on the basis of news, with the aim of arriving at a collective definition of reality.

The fact that we speak in order to know clearly shows that at the beginning of a rumor process, those who talk about it don't necessarily believe it. It is through rumors that the group communicates to us what we must think if we are to continue to be part of it. Rumors are an efficient medium of social cohesion: all the discussions that spring up express the opinion of the group with which we identify. *To talk about rumors is to take part in the group.* Many readers will find it surprising that people want to hear what others think (their reference group) before forming their own opinions. It is true that appearances run counter to this view. Moreover, we are often pleased to think that our opinions are intimately and exclusively personal. Experiments show, however, that conformity to the group exerts considerable influence on our opinions: it sometimes leads us to say the opposite of what we think and to doubt our own convictions.

In the course of every conversation about rumors, we shape a consensus by contributing details, additional elements, and personal hypotheses. The consensus that forms is not foreign to us: we are all its collective craftsmen. Like a collective report resulting from an international convention, consensus implies the involvement of each of the group's participants. Not to ally oneself with it is to remove or isolate oneself from the group, i.e., to choose another reference group.

Speaking in Order to Convince

For certain people, transmitting rumors is like starting a crusade or spreading the good word. They feel totally committed to their content, which they see as a kind of revealed truth. This happens when rumors play on their personal anxieties or resolve conflict. The first people to spread accusations of debauchery are those who, having seriously repressed their sex drive, derive pleasure from lascivious anecdotes, all the while playing the part of denunciators and scandalized moralists [217, 226]. Now, one is never right all by oneself, nor does one preach in a desert. Rumors become an attempt to convert people to one's own views: the more the circle of believers expands, the more one feels one is right. One must not simply transmit the rumor—one must convince. Identification between a proselytizer and his message is so great that rejecting or being skeptical of the rumor is tantamount to rejecting him. Thus in every rumor there are active relays who are totally one with the rumor's content: they derive satisfaction therefrom, and their individual tension is relieved by gaining social approval. "If people believe me it's because I'm right."

Speaking in Order to Free Oneself

Rumors are a first step to blowing off steam. Many rumors announce anxiety-producing situations, e.g., "The Germans are committing atrocities as they penetrate into conquered territories" and, "There's going to be a massive arrival of immigrants in Lorient coming up from Marseille" (*Liberté du Morbihan*, November 7, 1984). Speaking about them is the first step towards reducing anxiety, for our interlocutors may prove to us that the rumors are groundless or meaningless. If, on the other hand, they turn out to be grounded, collective action to deal with the danger eliminates each individual's isolation: "everyone is endangered, not just me." The danger is subjectively cut down to size. What's more, speaking of an event perceived to be threatening is to take a step towards its control or extinction: in Amiens, Laval, Rouen and all the other towns where talk spread of the white slave trade, accusatory speech was a prelude to other forms of liberation.

Rumors thus constitute a socially acceptable safety valve for repressed aggressiveness. And as hearsay has a guilt-diffusing function—always supposed, as it is, to come from someone else—it allows for the freest expression of repressed and heretofore unavowable drives. One thus understands why they arise in situations and environments with a high degree of moral censorship: rumors are anonymous letters that anyone can write with total impunity. The desire to do harm or slander has been stressed in the case of many rumors. We shall thus not emphasize this function, which has led researchers to neglect others [183].

Speaking in Order to Please

Many rumors go around not because the people who spread them believe them lock, stock, and barrel, but rather because they are amusing and surprising objects of curiosity. The rumor monger is assured of having an effect on the group of friends assembled to whom he announces the news. The motor force behind joke telling is very similar [41, 81]. One tells them in order to consume them, i.e., for the pleasure they provide—pleasure that is not always innocent. Humor is another convenient way to let out what is repressed. But rumors are not funny stories: they claim to reflect reality—"it happened at such and such a place at such and such a moment." He who unveils rumors enjoys greater prestige than a simple public entertainer [126]. He provides information that is scarce, exciting, and moving; he has at his disposal an object of value to exchange. In return he reaps the pleasure of pleasing others and of being attentively listened to. In revealing the rumor, he proves that he has close contact with well-informed sources, i.e., that he himself is part of the inner circle. He is a step ahead of the others and in the know; he's on to the latest news—the news no one else knows, and thus the most important news.

Considering the benefits he reaps in transmitting it to those who are not already in the know, it is understandable that rumors encounter no dearth of mouths to pass them on. The delight one finds in troubling one's astounded audience (and the certainty one has that this desired effect will be achieved), explains the incredible persistence of certain rumors. Lacking in current-event status, they stir up no noticeable commotion, enjoying instead peaceful and imperturbable circulation. The reader will certainly recognize, in the sample provided below, bits of "information" he has already heard and probably believed:

- A worker fell into a vat of Martini or wine. No one realized it until the vat was emptied one day.
- When one places a rusty coin in a glass of Coca-Cola, the rust disappears (the same being true for copper). Coke is an excellent spermicidal contraceptive.
- Hip bartenders polish up their bar counters with Martini.
- When one buys a Rolls Royce, one signs a sales contract prohibiting one from using it in an automobile race (it would be unthinkable if such a symbol of excellence were to come in second).
- A female singer pretended to be pregnant by putting a pillow under her dress, in order to hide the fact that she is an hermaphrodite.
- A particular singer is in fact the son of X and Y, well-known celebrities.
- To make some pocket money, one can clean cadavers at the morgue—one is paid forty bucks a stiff.

That is why "urban legends" last so long: they are savored at the end of a meal, or in a bar while sipping on an after-dinner drink. They provide a certain momentary pleasure in consuming. They are a sort of collective chewing gum. The private lives of the famous and the names of their most recent conquests circulate because of the pleasure and excitement to which they give rise. Each individual acts like a mini editor-in-chief; the newspapers also transmit certain news because of its surprising incongruity which is sure to attract attention. Whether it's true or not is of little importance: the effect it makes suffices to justify its being printed.

There is an exemplary case of this kind of rumor: the cabbage joke (and later that of manually operated foghorns) [121]. This American rumor was the subject of a study. The rumor has lasted since 1950, and is regularly repeated by some paper which resuscitates it in the form of a short article: "The prayer 'Our Father' is made up of 66 words, the Ten Commandments of 297 words, and Lincoln's 'Gettysburg Address' of 266 words. A recent administrative order fixing the price of cabbage contains 26,611 words." Every reader spontaneously attributed the "recent order" to the Carter or Reagan administration. Only a small number of people recall that there haven't been any price controls in the United States since the Korean War. The study in fact showed that every paper that has printed the rumor has copied it from another paper, and that this has been going on since 1950. The rumor was even used in several "double or nothing" radio games. Listeners had to guess how many words were contained in the "recent administrative order fixing the price of cabbage."

What is remarkable is that the Office of Price Stabilization (OPS) had never published anything whatsoever related to cabbage. Since the rumor's first appearance, around one hundred large-circulation newspapers and magazines have, from time to time, drawn people's attention to this incredible incongruity on the part of the administration. The latter, justifiably sensing that it was under attack, has continually demanded that the papers and magazines in question print rectificatory errata. The "double or nothing" sort of games refused to announce the correction; it didn't seem to them wise to let it be known that their answers were at times erroneous (and their questions misleading).

The cabbage rumor has a variant that dates back to more or less the same time. A newspaper that wanted to print the anecdote about the price of cabbage checked the information and noticed that no such order had ever existed. As the story was too good to drop, they sought another order that could do the trick. And they found one concerning 375 manufactured products. The paper published the information in selecting a particularly unusual product: the article made fun of "a 12,962 word regulation concerning the ceiling price of manually operated foghorns and other products." To create a still more striking effect, subsequent publications of the information naturally dropped the "and other products." Thus was born the joke about the manually operated foghorn regulation.

The extraordinary longevity of this rumor stems from several causes: it is amusing and produces a sure effect by the contrast it mentions in the length of the different texts. But the humor is not gratuitous: it is derived at the expense of American business' traditional whipping boy—the government. In the country of free enterprise, anything that suggests that the administration is a useless, wasteful, and corrupt institution is received with open arms. Stories about cabbage or manually operated foghorns seem quite trivial to all editors-in-chief, but are delectable enough not to be passed up.

What's more, no one ever (to our knowledge) sought to check the veracity of the information before printing it (to put it more precisely, verification was systematic, but bore only on the number of words in the Ten Commandments, the "Our Father" and Lincoln's "Gettysburg Address"!). When a story is entertaining, seems inconsequential and confirms our opinions, it is rarely verified.

Once started, such rumors are uncontrollable. They acquire the status of patented facts, and constitute but another illustration of the administration's stereotypical ineptitude. The number of newspapers, journals, and radio and television stations is so great that any attempt at denial remains in vain. The rumor goes underground only to suddenly resurface a year or two later, brought out of hibernation by some paper here or there. *Se non é vero, é bene trovato!* (If it isn't true, at least it is nice.)

Talk for Talk's Sake

The savory side of rumors and the prestige one derives from telling them are not the only reasons why rumors run rampant even though people don't necessarily believe them. There is another reason for this: one has to have something to talk about with one's friends, neighbors, and relatives. There is a continual void to fill. By definition, we see those who are close to use quite often: they know everything about us and vice versa. Talking exclusively about oneself is soon tiring for one's listener. Discussion is thus threatened by the worst of dangers, silence. Having nothing to say to each other is tantamount to an avowal of vacuousness. Rumors and gossip marvelously fill up the empty space: they allow us to continue to talk. When silence supervenes during meals between friends, it's in general a signal that the time has come for the ritual exchange of gossip and rumors.

Why were former communal washing places, and contemporary markets, hairdressers, hallways, and cafeterias the hubs of rumors? Because there people create or transmit a host of information, whether false or true, born of the need to arouse interest, converse, or say something entertaining. As one hesitates to speak of oneself, one speaks about others: starting with the slightest little trifle, one improvises and a rumor takes shape.

But rumors are also an invitation. Speaking means speaking with others. Gregory Bateson is one of the thinkers who has shown that all communication proposes a certain type of relationship between two people conversing together. To speak about a rumor with someone is to invite him to "rumor" with oneself: it implicitly tells him that "You and I, instead of engaging solely in small talk and remarks about the weather, will tell each other rumors". Now rumors are a form of emotional communication: they incite moral commentary, personal opinions and emotional reactions. Telling a rumor therefore means that one wishes to start up or pursue a relationship with one's interlocutor in which each person learns more about himself, exposing his feelings and values, while not talking about himself. On the whole, rumors furnish an occasion not to exchange information, but rather to express oneself [181].

As they often concern a third person, rumors favor the establishment of such a relationship: evaluating someone else together, two people implicitly recognize the similarity in their views and are brought closer at the expense of this third person. Overall, rumors and gossip are a stepping-stone to closer social relations and the strengthening of friendships, neighborly feelings and kinship ties.

The Speed of Rumors

On November 22, 1963, the president of the United States was shot down in Dallas, Texas at 12:30 p.m. He died at 1:00 p.m. By that time, 68 percent of the American people had already heard the news; by 2 p.m. the percentage had risen to 92 percent and by 6 p.m. to 99.8 percent. In less than two hours, almost everyone in the country knew. Half of the population received the news by radio or television, and the other half by word of mouth. 54 percent of the people immediately felt the need to talk about it with those around them [236]. Why does some information travel quickly and other information slowly, without ever really snowballing? What factors explain a rumor's speed? Such questions constantly crop up. The very fact that they are posed comes of no surprise: they reflect the ascendancy of the mythical image of rumors. In effect, our ways of talking about rumors makes them into independent subjects that are uncontrollable and endowed with fantastic properties: they "run rife," "break out," "take off like rockets," and "explode like bombshells."

Faced with such out of the ordinary, mysterious beings, the public looks to a guru for the key to understanding. But, in fact, the public bears the key within itself. Rumors become what we make of them. They are not endowed with magical circulatory virtues—they depend on us. In the habit of receiving without cross-examining the media, the public has forgotten that it is itself a transmitter. A rumor's speed is determined by our answer to the following question: when does one drop everything to talk about something with someone?

Sources of Eagerness

A rumor's speed is nothing but the result of people's eagerness to talk about it with those around them. A rumor exists in the first place because there is news concerning the group: its consequences are not limited to some particular person, but rather, concern the whole group. Moreover, it is news, and is thus perishable over time. That is why rumors about past and permanent facts travel more slowly than rumors about what just happened. The latter, like fresh produce, must be consumed quickly, otherwise they become less delectable or valuable. The rapid circulation of the rumor-object aims at preserving its value.

Like alarm signals, rumors are warnings. Emergency information must be communicated: it has too many implications for people to take the time to check its accuracy before transmitting it. Even if they are not sure it is true, the fact that it calls for an immediate response justifies passing it on: "Pay attention to what your children eat! It seems that the latest candy they've fallen for, 'Pop Rocks', can explode in their stomachs!"; "It will soon be election day: it seems that candidate X is not at all what he's cut out to be."

Close Relations

The more tightly knit a group is, the more structured it is by an efficient exchange network linking people together, and the easier it thus is for news to spread to all members. If, on the contrary, it is but a grouping of people with no communication amongst them, rumors necessarily take time to reach all parties. One often hears, for example, that doctors, reporters, and antique dealers work in rumor-prone fields where news travels very quickly. In a short time, the whole medical community, for example, is in the know—precisely because there is a community. The same is true of provincial towns and villages. On the contrary, in recently built urban housing projects, and in early stages of so-called "new towns," rumors circulate with great difficulty. Their inhabitants' physical proximity to each other is not enough: individuals are juxtaposed therein, but there is no true group. Each inhabitant has far more to do with people outside of the town than inside: internal communication doesn't exist.

The French expressions for what we in English call "the grapevine"—"the

Arab telephone" and "the bamboo telephone"—are quite telling. Communities around the Mediterranean basin, like those in Asia, show a high level of cohesion. The speed at which news travels reflects the efficiency of a communication system whose function is precisely that of perpetuating such cohesion.

In the Western world, up until but a few years ago, markets were not simply the places where one purchased goods, but also where one exchanged information; people took the time to talk, comment, and discuss. The same was true of fairs, parades, patron saint festivals, and even Sunday mass after which people would walk together and maintain social links. All of these have now more or less become places and occasions for solitary consumption. Former collective clothes-washing areas in villages were social places where women communicated with each other while washing. Our modern automatic laundromats are nothing more than waiting rooms where people watch each other in silence.

Rumor as Commodity Exchange

A rumor is above all a behavior. How do analysts in fact learn about the existence of a rumor? They observe that, within a social group, people speak and exchange information. A rumor appears as a sort of contagious exchange behavior. An economic model should thus prove helpful in understanding such exchange behavior: what do people trade in this exchange?

FIGURE 3.1
A Commodity Model of Communication Exchange

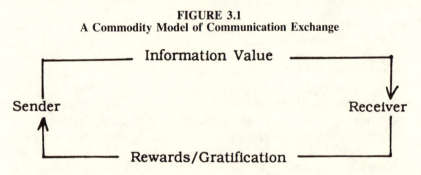

In structural terms, the rumor-diffusion process is a sequence of dyadic interactions between a sender and a receiver. This interaction is initiated by the sender, unlike other types of word-of-mouth phenomena where receivers ask for advice [11]. As all behavior is motivated, it is assumed that the sender expects to receive gratification, i.e., rewards for transmitting information. His information thus has value, for otherwise he would not receive rewards. We shall not elaborate on the nature of these rewards here; they have already been indicated by the various functions rumors serve: prestige enhancement, group affiliation, reduction of anxiety, catharsis, and reduction of cognitive dissonance.

From an economic standpoint, the main question is: what is the source of the rumor-commodity's value? Knowing that what is scarce is expensive and is endowed with value, one can deduce that a rumor is valuable because its information content is scarce. What kinds of information are scarce?—those withheld from the public, whether deliberately or not. Structurally speaking, the source of a rumor's value is that it claims to depict a reality about which the public should not have known, a secret or bit of information that should have been kept hidden, undiffused or that was hitherto unknown. But information loses value with time. Therefore, like any other depreciating commodity, its value must be exploited while it still exists. That is why people feel compelled to exchange it or to pass it on. They want to maximize the return they expect from this exchange behavior [107].

The typical traits of rumors are consequences of this quasi-economic behavior. A rumor's diffusion speed always catches observers' attention. In a rumor process, a receiver seems to feel an urge to pass on the information, thus rapidly assuming the sender's role. This behavior is normal when one remembers that information's value, unlike that of gold, often decreases with time. Knowing something way in advance is a source of competitive edge, whether in the economic or social spheres, or in day-to-day life. The immediate rediffusion of a rumor by someone who just heard it can be compared to consumer behavior in countries where the local currency depreciates rapidly: people spend their money as soon as they receive it in order to capitalize on its momentary value.

As more and more people hear the information in time, its scarcity and value decrease. Its residual value must be exploited at once, before it is too late: hence the speed of the information's diffusion.

The Media and Rumors

Nowadays it is impossible to dissociate speed of propagation (and a rumor's change over time) from the attitude of the media, whether local or national. Everything can fluctuate if they remain silent about a rumor or devote columns and air time to it.

When the mass media began to develop, it was thought that they would put an end to rumors. The press and the radio were expected to toll the death bell of this ancient form of media. This view was based on a conception of rumors functioning as a media because there was nothing else. Now mass media have not at all snuffed out rumors—far from it. That view of rumors was thus mistaken; they do not exist because there is nothing else, constituting instead a media in their own right, with a particular function: accounting for what is left unsaid. Even in a democratic, pluralistic society, the unsaid has not disappeared: every journalist knows the limits of what he has the right to say, write or announce publicly, without risking being sued for slander. Journalists always claim to know a great many things they cannot publish. In Western society, realms of secrecy have by no means disappeared: there are political, military, governmental, and economic secrets, discretion about one's private life, and so on. The mass media, moreover, are engaged in a competitive struggle for scoops. To check one's sources, following them back to their origins, takes time; it can be tempting to make information public without waiting for official confirmation. As an editor-in-chief once put it, publishing a rumor credits one's paper with two scoops: being the first to have heard the rumor, and perhaps also being the first to publish a formal denial of it.

Even if they don't all adopt such an extreme attitude, no mass media is perfect. For example, two weeks after the terrible earthquake in Armenia in 1989, every television station in France was talking about the miraculous discovery of thirty survivors who had been trapped underground. The information was attributed to a nurse or a doctor of the World Doctors' Humanitarian Organization. Unfortunately, nothing of the sort had taken place. But the expectation of a miracle was so strong that the information went around, though it was but a rumor at that point in time.

In an entirely different realm: a French magazine has a section entitled, "Everything Is True: No Trial Possible." In 1987, the magazine published the rumor about Procter & Gamble's relations with Satan, declaring it to be true! The magazine based its allegations essentially upon the reading of the American leaflet translated into French, which began circulating within conservative circles (which the magazine targets).

Considering the media's clout in spreading rumors, what is their attitude towards rumors? Paradoxically enough, rumors give the media a fairly free hand. All media are equal when faced with an event: if a train goes off the tracks in Washington, all the media must cover the event—they have no choice in the matter. The event forces itself upon them. When presented with rumors, however, they have a great deal of room in which to maneuver. "Will we bring it up or not?" "Will we do a study to see what's behind the rumor, be it true or false?" The range of possible decisions is wide; it goes from the pure and simple creation of a rumor right up to an anti-rumor crusade, englobing censorship and total silence. The former attitude involves making a big deal of a localized rumor phenomenon. Previously existing simply in the form of talk limited to a particular group or neighborhood, a rumor explodes, thanks to the media: they literally sign its official birth certificate. For a rumor to jump from the local to the national level, it must converge with the interests of a lobby or pressure group: the push given a rumor is never fortuitous. For example, it was the leftist press—hardly suspected of harboring pro-military feelings— that widely circulated rumors explaining the mysterious disappearances of soldiers from the Mourmelon military base. Similarly, the French satirical paper *Le Canard Enchaîné* specializes in the disclosure of political leaks (whose sources are always kept anonymous); it has been behind a number of important political rumors such as that of the diamonds offered to former French President Giscard d'Estaing by the Emperor Bokassa, and former Prime Minister Chaban Delmas' tax returns; according to leaked information, Delmas paid no taxes whatsoever.

Le Canard Enchaîné is reputed to check its sources—hence its longevity and considerable credibility. The two above-cited examples were, notwithstanding, simple rumors when published, and the people incriminated generally denied the information, saying "no comment."

The media can also create false information from scratch. In show business, it happens all the time [10]. One must feed the insatiable desire of fans, their thirst to know above all the latest ups and downs of those they admire. In 1986, two TV announcers admitted to having themselves sparked off the rumor about a love affair between Catherine Deneuve and Pierre Beregovoy, minister of finance. A specialized press lives off of such rumors [187].

A retrospective analysis of the media coverage of the Chernobyl accident [161] on April 26, 1986, at 1:23 a.m. (Soviet time), shows that the media themselves started the false rumor of two thousand deaths at Chernobyl. On April 29, out of thirteen Parisian and regional daily papers, eleven spoke of an "accident"—the same term used by the official Soviet press service in their first dispatch dated April 28—only two using the word "catastrophe," found in none of the Chernobyl dispatches of the French Press Agency (AFP) dated April 28 and 29. It wasn't until April 29 and from its Washington (not its Moscow) office, that the AFP announced "deaths." According to the AFP, then citing a figure of two thousand deaths, the number was said to be accredited by a declaration "on NBC television of a high-ranking Pentagon official who preferred to remain anonymous" and who supposedly added that the information seemed to him to be "exact." The number "two thousand" came from a dispatch sent by an American press agency from Moscow on

April 29 declaring that "One unconfirmed report from the area said the death toll may have reached two thousand. Eighty people died immediately and some two thousand people died on the way to the hospitals." Now according to the official Soviet source, there had been two deaths at Chernobyl that day—period. At the end of 1986, the official figures concerning Chernobyl's consequences stood at thirty-one deaths. The media had thus created the rumor of 1,969 additional deaths.

The result, revealed by European and American public opinion polls, was that the public believed the Chernobyl nuclear accident to be an unprecedented catastrophe, leaving two thousand initial victims in its wake—the press had invented similar stories about what happened in Bhopal, India (at the Union Carbide plant) and in Seveso (an accident in Italy due to a dioxyne leak in a chemical plant, which in reality led to no human deaths whatsoever).

On the political level, the invention of explosive information is part and parcel of destabilization campaigns. When a journalist publishes such information without taking precautions, he exposes himself to a considerable legal risk (unless a law suit is precisely what he is after). His preferred tactic thus consists in speaking obliquely, i.e., indirectly—as if he was but doing his duty, objectively relating what others said—or in repeating what was said while refusing to align himself with the allegations. Having recourse to insinuation and innuendo, one can thus "rumorize the information" [158] and keep risk at bay—"I didn't assert anything." As Jean Cocteau said, "there is such a thing as signed anonymous letters."

Research has been conducted to investigate the effect that incriminating innuendo by the media has on the public's impressions of those targeted [261]. A first experiment showed that people's impressions of a target got worse after they were exposed to prototypically insinuating headlines: incriminating questions like, "Is Bob Talbert Linked with Mafia?" A similar but weaker effect was observed in the case of incriminating denials like, "Bob Talbert Not Linked with Mafia." A second experiment somewhat unexpectedly showed that, although variations in source credibility (high or low) affected the persuasiveness of directly incriminating assertions (e.g., "Bob Talbert Linked with Mafia"), they had appreciably less impact on the persuasiveness of innuendos.

In order to say things without really saying them, but saying them all the same, it is helpful to be able to refer to a few other media. Thus the rumor about the military origin of AIDS had its source in information published for the first time by the Indian newspaper *The Patriot* during the summer of 1985. It was quickly repeated by Soviet papers as it accused American army personnel of having created the AIDS virus. But it seems that the rumor fanned by the Soviets concerning the military origin of AIDS was a rejoinder to another rumor that had been started by the Americans in spring 1984: the *Wall Street Journal* had accused the Soviet Union, without any proof whatsoever, of having prepared new deadly microbes through genetic engineering (*La Recherche,* April 1987, p. 486).

The creation of rumors can work in two directions: one involves circulating them to the whole public right from the start. The mass media public allows for instantaneous transmission of news to tremendous numbers of people. Those targeted by a rumor can thus be pressured. This is what happened at the beginning of the Watergate and Irangate scandals, as well as in the Greenpeace affair in France (involving sabotage of a Greenpeace boat in New Zealand by the French secret service). But if a rumor is potentially unfounded, printing it can be risky. Another tactic consists in letting the social mechanisms of transmission go their natural course: the rumor travels by stages, from known public figures to the first-line adherents, from the latter to second-line adherents, and so on. Each stratum takes on the task of convincing the next. That is the role allotted to the innumerable confidential newsletters, circulated within very tight circles of important people, that are supposed to provide them information and scoops every morning. Every sector of economic and political life has its confidential newsletters. Interestingly enough, these latter even have a special rumor column, leaving the reader free to believe or disbelieve. A public relations director for an important municipality explained how he started up false rumors in a trial form: "it suffices to slip a slightly sibylline sentence or an ambiguous allusion into the confidential newsletter received only by the town notables."

Without having created them, the media sometimes act as powerful transmission relays and accelerators. Thus the "letters to the editor" column is where many rumors first show up, in the guise of simple requests for information. "Dear Ann Landers: Please tell your millions of readers the real truth about Procter & Gamble's tie-in with the Moonies and the Unification Church. A friend of mine told me that her cousin ... " (*New Orleans Times,* September 6, 1982). Another possibility is that of word-for-word repetition of the rumor by journalists. During the last study on the Villejuif leaflet, investigators asked where and how those interviewed had obtained it. Newspapers and magazines were cited first, way ahead of leaflets slipped into mailboxes or posted in schools, workplaces, and hospitals. Many papers and journals had, in fact, simply reproduced it in alarmist articles. Most often it was seen in "local" press—county, city, professional, and union papers. The editors of these innumerable papers are well aware of what interests their readership but, having no real team of journalists at their beck and call, rarely check their information before publishing it.

Thus during their lifetimes, rumors are sometimes relayed by the media.

The verb "relay" is rather weak—rumors are accelerated and accredited. The acceleration effect is physical. In one fell swoop rumors penetrate into thousands of homes. The accreditation effect is psychological. The medium is the message: every time a rumor is transmitted by the media it gains tremendously in credibility. The media "informationalize" rumors. The latter thereby acquire the status of truth and definitively become a part of popular knowledge.

A third possible stance on the part of the media consists in encouraging the rumor by taking facts that up until then had gone unnoticed and making them ambiguous. That is what part of the Brazilian press did during President Tancredo Neves' illness; having fallen ill on the eve of taking power, his investiture would have put an end to twenty-one years of military regime. This striking coincidence sparked off rumors. The press orchestrated what might be called the "presidential serial," adding "information" to the fire everyday, and feeding the rumors that something was being hidden behind the future president's sudden illness.

After his first operation, which took place during the night of March 14–15, at a hospital in Brasília, the president had to be taken to another hospital in São Paulo by plane. A picture appeared on the front page of every newspaper: there was the stretcher being carried off the plane at the top of the gangway. *Fatos* magazine—the local equivalent of *Newsweek*—examined the photograph and concluded that it was a fake: it was not the president! The argumentation ran as follows:

• Nothing proves that the plane in the picture had come from Brasília nor that the picture was taken in São Paulo.
• The man holding the serum is not wearing a hospital uniform: that is suspicious.
• The person carrying the bottom end of the stretcher doesn't seem to be exerting any effort whatsoever: is the stretcher empty?
• Someone (seen from behind) is looking at one of the engines. He resembles a well-known politician, who, in that case, should be looking at nothing other than the stretcher, if it really was the president, etc.

Rumors are also encouraged when the media put forth exactly the same hypotheses the frightened public legitimately could have made itself. In the small town of Mattoon, Illinois, a woman, fooled by her imagination, declared to the police that she had been anesthetized by an individual who had surreptitiously entered her home [132]. The individual was claimed to have sprayed a gas, which paralyzed her and made her sick. By the very next day, one of the town's papers had already jumped to the conclusion: "Crazy

Anesthetist on the Loose: Mrs. X. the first Victim." And if there is a "first" victim, there will inevitably be others.

The fourth stance the media can adopt is that of critique or combat. This attitude is frequent in political editorials: the most recent fashionable political rumor provides a subject for reflection and skepticism. The attitude can also be frankly militant, the media actively participating in the counteroffensive. In each of these cases, a question is often asked: what happens to a rumor that is denied? We shall come back to this thorny problem further on (see chapter 18).

"Narrow-casting" and "Xeroxlore"

On the border between mass media and word-of-mouth there are leaflets and flyers that are generally anonymous or, when they are signed, apocryphal. In the past few years, many rumors have circulated in France and Europe through such leaflets:

- A French translation of the American leaflet about Procter & Gamble.
- A French translation of the American leaflet warning against certain tattoo stamps for children (e.g., with Mickey Mouse picture) supposedly containing LSD instead of glue.
- The "Villejuif" flyer warning against alleged carcinogenic food additives and brands.
- A flyer warning against the hidden meaning of certain drawings found near the doors of houses—coded signs indicating which houses to burglarize.
- A flyer in the form of an altogether official interdepartmental memorandum on the dangers of wearing contact lenses when welding with electrical arcs.

Leaflets are necessary whenever a rumor conveys a lot of information. One cannot trust one's memory to remember, for example, the great many supposedly dangerous food additives. Word-of-mouth would focus on one of them and on one or two well-known foods. Similarly, a leaflet must be used to inform consumers of all Procter & Gamble product lines so that they can all be boycotted. Such leaflets have proven to be very persuasive: when things are written down they seem more authoritative. Moreover, as they circulate they often acquire *Good Housekeeping* seals from influential people who believe them and decide to collaborate. A professor of dentistry in Montpellier (in the south of France) put his stamp of approval on the flyer about Mickey Mouse tattoo stamps for children that contained LSD, endowing it thereby with an insignia of authenticity. From its status as a mere, anonymous flyer, it practically became an official in-house memorandum.

The use of flyers also endows rumors with an appearance of credibility, like that enjoyed by the flyers distributed during World War II in occupied zones. Flyers constitute an underground media: they are the voice of the resistance. They are a part of what G. Fine has called the Goliath effect [102]: the media of the weak and oppressed, i.e., those whose only weapon in the struggle against the official, structured and organized media is their solidarity.

The simple Xeroxing of flyers has given birth to the term "Xeroxlore" to designate this kind of rumor. In photocopying a flyer and slipping one or two hundred, for example, into people's mailboxes or onto employees' desks, one changes the usual rumor-transmission process [244].

Rumor Conduit

What is the pattern of rumor transmission? We haven't raised the question until now, for its answer largely depends on the transmission medium used: word-of-mouth, leaflets, or mass media.

The classical model that molds people's perception of rumor transmission is the well-known telephone experiment carried out by Allport and Postman. After having looked at a picture, an eyewitness tells someone else what he saw; this relay repeats what he heard and so on. This is a typical serial reproduction experiment, as was shown in figure 1.1.

FIGURE 3.2
Allport and Postman's Rumor Simulation

A → B → C → D → E → F → G →

Many features are worth highlighting in this simulation, though it departs rather dramatically from rumor behavior in real life. Many theorists have pointed out that the relays are uninvolved; their mere purpose is to pass on, as reliably as possible, what they heard from the former relay, concerning some non-ego-involving message [157]. The flow of information is unidirectional and noninteractive. *A* speaks to *B* who speaks to *C* and so on. In real life, there are loops in the process. *D* may call *A* to warn him about a rumor. In addition, rumor transmitting is not a simple flow: *B* does not simply pass on a message to *C*. The communication is truly interactive. In real life, *C* asks *B* questions and both elaborate on the message itself. Each may add his own details to the rumor, a process which leads to a snowball effect, rather than the leveling process described by Allport and Postman [6].

Degh and Vazsonyi have emphasized two other essential features of rumor transmission: receivers are selected and each receiver is free to re-emit or not [71]. Re-emitters are self-selected. The observation of information flows within lines in prison camps during World War II led them to detect the transmission process depicted in figure 3.3.

FIGURE 3.3
Degh and Vazsonyi's Experiment

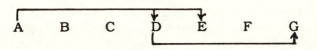

Unlike the armchair-telephone experiment, their experiment showed that, despite the boredom which made everybody eager to receive any and every kind of information, *A* selected his receivers (*D* and *E, not B* or *C*). Furthermore, not all receivers did re-emit (*D* but not *E*). Degh and Vazsonyi coined the term rumor "conduit." By this term they understood the contact established between individuals who qualify as receivers or transmitters. In a specific group, a rumor is transmitted by members of the rumor (or legend) conduit. These authors assume that "jokes are dispensed through the joke conduit by a sequence of witty people; riddles pass through the riddle conduit made up of riddle fans" [71, p. 212]. These people are not the same: "people who like to tell ghost stories, for example, are not the same as those who enjoy cracking jokes" [71, p. 213]. Storytellers learn their stories from similar personality types and likewise pass them on to selected peers.

It is not possible to analyze how the media, by broadcasting or "narrow-casting" (leaflet), alter the natural flow of rumors. In word-of-mouth circulation, one doesn't hear a rumor by chance: emitters often select those to whom they will speak. They avoid those likely to refute the rumor. This selection process is particularly important when it comes to gossiping [101]. Since gossip aims at other people of the same community (village, office, sports club, etc.), it is vital to gossip about someone only with one's allies. In crisis situations, however, social barriers drop away and everyone speaks with everyone else. It is well known that in the minutes that followed the announcement of President Kennedy's assassination, people spoke to each other in the streets [17]. In general, a narrator has a tendency to select his receivers, i.e., his audience. In real life, unlike chain experiments and lines, a person may well transmit a rumor to more than one receiver: this is why retailers, hairdressers, and idle people have a reputation of being real media sources. They are at the crossroads of many communication networks. Lastly, in natural rumor flow, oral communication is interactive: *A* and *B* discuss the rumor told by *A*. The latter uses *B*'s feedback to adjust or modify the story itself and his own opinion or stance. In word-of-mouth, performance is voluntary and one has a free choice of material.

This natural conduit is impeded by leaflet transmission. Once a leaflet is photocopied and slipped into a hundred mailboxes, there is far less selection of receivers and communication is no longer interactive. Receivers are still free, however, to re-emit or not. As a result of the lack of interaction, leaflets actually freeze rumor content. This is *a fortiori* true as well for mass media: they act as standardizers of folklore by diffusing to a very large audience one single version of a rumor.

Diffusion Networks

A rumor's diffusion is, naturally, affected by the network of social relationships, roles and statuses within the group in which it circulates. Although informal and unofficial, these relationships are the paths by which rumors are selectively communicated. An interesting case history is provided by rumors in socialist Romania, under N. Ceausescu's reign.

Under the despotic rule of Nicolae Ceausescu and his family, Romanians were subjected to a total information blackout, state mobilization, and constant economic hardship. This generated discontent, cynicism, anxiety, and frustration. At that time in Romania, "the public sphere constantly imposes itself on the private, while intimate social relations of family and friendship close ranks and resist. This is done by intensifying interpersonal exchanges of information. By means of idle chatter, informal oral communication becomes a means to combat state control over information, to find out "secrets," to go around the censors, to neutralize the bureaucratic forces of society, and to locate or procure scarce resources" [228, p. 144].

Because Romanians in the higher levels of society are granted access to more reliable and extensive information, rumors flow down the vertical hierarchy. But in the Eastern European countries, one also finds horizontal circles and informal groups. These horizontal segments thrive on the exchange of information. Horizontal relationships thus guarantee rumors' wide circulation. Whereas in the West, rumors are a *supplemental* media, in Romania they constitute an *alternative* media in direct competition with the official media.

How does information trickle down from the upper classes? The people most likely to play a bridging role are those who are allowed to move in different strata: maids, repairmen, waiters, chauffeurs for high-ranking officials, and so on [228, p. 147]. There are also individuals whose occupation brings them into contact with a variety of social categories: taxi drivers, hairdressers, and doctors. In the spreading of rumors, those who are allowed to travel within the country play a key role: salesmen, truck-drivers [23], local officials, people having family abroad or in Bucharest, etc.

This trickle-down model of diffusion is not an exception to the rule: it runs parallel to the now classic findings of rural and urban sociologists on the diffusion of innovations [209].

4

Why Do We Believe Rumors?

Introduction

At some time or another, we all discover—to our surprise—that a particular rumor we believe is in fact altogether false. Whenever that happens, we are confused by our mistake, and wonder how our critical sense could be so deficient. The question thus arises: why are rumors so convincing? Why do we so easily believe stories we are told? A rumor's credibility is related to the very specific characteristics of the person from whom we hear it and of the message he or she transmits to us.

From a Believable Source

Hundreds of experiments done on the persuasive efficiency of messages highlight the primordial role of the source, i.e., of the person who tells us the facts [113]. We pay attention only to those we want to listen to, and we especially scrutinize our source to decide what to think of the message that is to follow [57]. Several factors lead us to lend credence to a source: our feeling about his expertise, reliability, unbiasedness, disinterestedness, dynamism, and personality.

I Heard It from a Well-Informed Source

Oral messages do not randomly circulate in groups or the public at large. Thus even while we all find out from the media that Stanley Kubrick's latest movie has just come out, we often wait before formulating an opinion until we have heard that of opinion makers: film critics writing for the press or radio, or friends we find competent in cinematographic matters—more competent, in any case, than ourselves.

Rumors originate from unofficial media: they circulate through personal affinity networks and by proximity. They often reach our ears from an expert on the subject, or from someone better informed than we are. Mothers in the cities of Laval, Dinan, and Orléans, for example, heard from their daughters that something suspicious was going on in certain very chic shops. The adolescent girls in those towns who sometimes did their shopping in those very "fashion-oriented" boutiques acquired instant competence in the matter. Rumors and political gossip come to us from those who are more interested than we are in the life of the town or in municipal affairs. Generally speaking, we take advantage of others' specialized expertise about micro-subjects so as to stay abreast of things and know what to think.

Moreover, if our informer senses that his story is not having the desired convincing effect, he immediately refers to someone, closer to the source, if not the presumed original source himself, i.e., someone with greater expertise: "I heard it from a girlfriend whose brother works at hospital X. He personally saw the president go in for an oncological examination." This is an essential point: the person who repeats important information (and if it weren't important, why would he bother to repeat it?) often intends to convince and persuade. The informer is thus not neutral: he does not confine his attention to indifferently announcing news. He is totally wrapped up in the event; he has become one with it. If we refuse to believe it, we reject him. That is why the circulation of rumors involves a series of persuasive acts.

Thus when he realizes that his audience is becoming incredulous or wants to avoid such an eventuality, a rumor-monger invokes the argument of ultimate authority. He claims to have heard the information from a super-duper expert whose competence is above suspicion: an eye-witness of the event or the sender himself—the original source. There are in effect two different languages of rumors. Rumors present themselves either in the forms of "hearsay" or as follows: "according to a well-informed source...." Hearsay refers to the group or collectivity: it is the others who are speaking about it, i.e., the community to which we belong, as does the person relaying the rumor. Hearsay is like discrete elbowing—it is a request for one to rally around the consensus currently being formed. As the absence of reference to experts or original sources shows, hearsay does not count on rational acceptance; it plays, rather, on one's desire to belong, to join in with the group, to participate in and melt in to the larger "they"—nascent unanimity. Hearsay is an appeal to the social community [222].

The other language of rumors calls upon someone the group considers to be worthy of trust: his competence and honesty are irreproachable. Thus rumors about presidential illnesses are supposed to emanate from the directors of hospitals where operations took place, nurses who saw, interns who palpated, ambulance drivers who drove, and delivery men who personally brought the CAT scan equipment to the White House. Rumors about misdemeanors obviously come from the police officer on duty that day, the secretary who typed up the report, the police commissioner or a relative of the examining magistrate. As for the libertine escapades of a candidate for mayor, the informer is necessarily a close friend of the candidate's chauffeur, maid, gardener, or one of his many sexual partners.

During World War II as well [68], studies showed that the people living in regions where leaflets had been dropped by plane later attributed the information contained in the leaflets to radio programs or newspapers. The tendency to attribute what one believes to some sort of believable source was displayed more recently during the coup d'état leading to the fall of President Salvador Allende in Santiago, Chili, on September 11, 1973.

In working-class neighborhoods and occupied factories, a rumor began to spread: General Carlos Prats, who had remained loyal to Allende, was said to be coming up from the south with his troops. The news had supposedly been picked up by short-wave radio from Argentina. The immediate effect of the rumor was that everyone began expecting Prats—just as at Waterloo, everyone was expecting Grouchy. In reality, Carlos Prats was in Santiago, under house arrest. But, as it was attributed to a foreign—and thus credible— radio station, the rumor lasted three full days. In such situations, that is more than enough to overturn a revolution.

The quest for a likely, reassuring paternity and linguistic shortcuts, coupled with a desire to convince, or simply repeat what the last relay said, leads the rumor-monger to present himself as very close to the rumor's origin. He naturally did not personally meet the original source—the fundamental expert who saw and knows. But he knows someone who did.

In every case, the chain is short: the initial witness is just a stone's throw away—but one middleman separates us from him. The middleman constitutes a sort of leap or point of discontinuity that is always present in rumors. It corresponds to reality in that the person who speaks to us did not hear it from the fundamental source. It also corresponds to a function, discouraging one as it does from going to check. The initial witness is both dramatically close by, but nevertheless beyond one's reach. It is always a question of believing, not of verifying.

The fundamental expert's eternal proximity renders the relay considerably more persuasive, and increases the value of his information: it becomes hot "news"; just barely out, it is still virtually a secret.

Selective Relays

The second factor determining the credence we lend a source is its reliability: has the person who warns us usually provided accurate or inaccurate news? The words "accurate" and "inaccurate" are misleading here. They perpetrate the idea that there is such a thing as objective information, a "standard" of truth, and a physical reality observable by everyone. Was the previous information furnished by this person invalidated or not? The news, for example, that the corner grocer has a heavy hand on the scale when he weighs fruit and vegetables acquires the status of truth, not because of an in-depth investigation, but simply because nothing argues against the hypothesis, and because the day comes when, alerted to the fact, we notice that he "seems" to have added a few ounces to our tomato purchase.

People bearing news don't come to us at random. They know who lends them credence and who does not: it is because we take them to be reliable that rumor-mongers address us. In a certain sense, we hear rumors from our doubles.

Moreover, reliability is like off-track betting. Having won a few times by following the advice of a particular tipster, we underestimate the number of bad steers he gave us and continue to consider him a good source of "hot tips." Psychological research [133] has shown that once we've formed an opinion of someone, our perception of facts which could confirm or invalidate the opinion becomes skewed. We underestimate the facts that invalidate our initial opinion.

Similarly, we believe certain people because now and then what they tell us turns out to be true. Selective forgetting, i.e., skewed attribution of correctness, puts the other cases out of our minds.

Unbiased Information

We believe many rumors because we cannot imagine who could possibly benefit from such assertions *if they were false*. In general, when we cannot evaluate a rumor on the basis of its content, we proceed to causal attribution by elimination. If we cannot determine who would benefit from the diffusion of such false claims, they must be true. Our intimate knowledge of the group allows us to imagine, in the case of gossip, to whose advantage it might be to circulate unfounded allegations about someone: thus we are on our guard. The same is true of political rumors, for we know that misinformation is one of the zones of electoral struggle. On the other hand, when faced with a leaflet announcing that certain Mickey Mouse stickers contain "acid" (LSD) instead of glue, parents are unable to imagine why anyone would distribute such a leaflet if the information were false. Failing to find a malignant motive behind it, they conclude that there isn't any: the leaflet must thus be true.

Our questioning also bears on the relay who simply communicates the rumor to us. Does he have some personal interest in having his listener believe it? Does he seem to be pursuing some personal objective? The suspicion of private motives kills one factor of credibility, as it does in the case of salesmen. That is also what hinders a great deal of gossip from circulating in businesses, villages and groups: people would too easily detect the ulterior motives. To gossip in such a context is to no longer be simply a relay, but a full-fledged accomplice.

In the case of rumors, the relay would like to seem motivated by altruistic considerations alone. Should suspicion arise, he hides behind his function as pure relay, thus enjoying total transparency: hearsay is the voice of others, that of the community or group of which he is but an emissary. Thus, while putting himself on the line in his attempt to convince, our interlocutor has two important trump cards at his disposal: he can invoke some super-duper expert or the consensus of the group to which we all belong, i.e., the group that addresses us through him.

Moreover, the vocabulary he uses is in and of itself a message [223]. Depending on the words he uses, he can confine himself to descriptive neutrality ("people have been saying that . . ."), reserving himself the right to disapprove of the rumor in the course of the discussion. He can thus take his distance by announcing the rumor as an hypothesis he doesn't believe ("people have been claiming that. . ."). He can strengthen the rumor's credibility by using a vocabulary of certainty showing that he is whole-heartedly convinced ("it has been shown that . . ."). Lastly, he can yield ground concerning certain details of the story while defending the central message: if it's not altogether true, it's at least true in part.

Thus whether he appeals to expertise, reliability, unbiasedness, or plau-sibility, our informant enjoys a considerable confidence potential. It is thus understandable that we are susceptible to rumors. But the nature of the source doesn't explain everything. A rumor's content must itself satisfy two conditions of belief: one must be *able* to and *want* to believe it.

Plausible Information

However great our desire to believe something may be, it must at least seem plausible to us. Comments made about unfounded rumors never fail to point a moralizing finger at those who believed the unbelievable. In reality, rumors spread because they are viewed as plausible. Every rumor is necessarily taken to be realistic in the group in which it circulates.

A Convincing Proximity

One often witnesses an outburst of rumors: an alleged event is said to have taken place in a score of towns. The reported event generally happened very recently, close by, and to some known person or somebody with whom one can readily identify (a mother, a college girl, etc.). Each telling of the story tends to be adapted to its specific environment.

Rumors undergo a continual process of temporal updating, social narrowing and local implanting. This process is quite normal from an "economic" vantage point. It is a value-adding device: people get more involved in news concerning their own geographical locality than some unidentified or distant place. Similarly, even the oldest stories are always presented as fresh news, i.e., as virtual scoops. This should come as no surprise; indeed it could not be otherwise. Information cannot circulate unless it has "recency" value. Who's interested in yesteryear? In order to communicate, people have to constantly update what they hear to make it an ever fresh release that must be rapidly circulated.

Stretching the Limits of What Is Plausible

During a radio program devoted to rumors, an announcer admitted his surprise on the air: "certain rumors are really far too improbable!" The study of rumors shows that, on the contrary, what is plausible keeps getting broader and broader. What could possibly be considered to be improbable nowadays?

The announcer's surprise concerned a rumor running rife in the Périgord, Lot, and Vaucluse regions in France. Pro-ecology groups were said to be dropping venomous snakes by plane into certain counties in order to preserve these virtually extinct species as well as (depending on which version one heard) to feed hawks and other birds of prey or destroy rats and field mice. Such a rumor has nothing improbable about it to most people:

1. The motives mentioned seem praiseworthy and plausible for the majority of the population. Who in effect would think it more rational to feed birds of prey with garter snakes (which are longer than venomous ones) or to mobilize owls to eliminate rodents? No one compares what it costs to rent a simple truck with what it costs to rent a plane for as little as an hour.
2. It wouldn't be the first case of reintroducing animal populations in the backwoods of France. The media widely covered the painstaking re-population of lynxes in the Vosges mountains in eastern France.
3. Most people, having but an abstract knowledge of venomous snake physiology, do not imagine that, like any animal dropped from a great height, snakes die on impact. They probably think they bounce. After all, aren't their bodies flexible and springlike in nature? Unless, being very light (who has ever weighed a snake?), they fall very slowly!

Given this kind of information, nothing immediately arouses suspicion. Some detail must seriously run up against our elementary critical faculties for us to more carefully examine a message's content. It is not clear what that detail could be in the above-cited case.

The stretching of the limits of what is plausible can also be exemplarily illustrated by the regular spreading in France of the rumor about how contact lenses can make you blind.

In August of 1984, the highly respected Regional Federation of Public Works in the Ile-de-France region sent a memorandum to more than six hundred businesses concerning a mishap suffered by two employees of an unspecified company. A worker and an arc welder were working on a main circuit breaker "when a grave and hitherto unheard of phenomenon occurred. In order to do the meticulous part, they took off their protective shields, but inadvertently lit their electrical arc at that very same moment. Both men were wearing contact lenses. When they got home that evening and took their lenses out, the cornea stuck to them and they went blind." According to the rumor, such arcs produce microwaves that can almost instantaneously evaporate the liquid film on which the lenses rest, leaving them directly glued to the cornea. This unheralded kind of accident can be utterly painless, the victim not realizing that it has happened at the time.

Because of this incident, the memorandum advised people not to wear contact lenses in the workplace. All six hundred companies that received the memo immediately took measures to forbid their employees from wearing contact lenses at work. What's more, moved by concern for their employees' well-being, they transmitted the memorandum to all of their subcontractors. The Regional Federation of Public Works is not an isolated case. In hundreds of companies, the social and occupational-health departments have published identical memoranda; the same took place in many city government departments. Thus was born the conviction that in certain cases contact lenses blind people. The rumor was, nonetheless, utterly unfounded.

It came to France through subsidiaries of foreign companies, defectively reverberating something that happened to a metal worker at the Baltimore arsenal on July 26, 1967. That day, it was found that he had serious cornea lesions on both eyes; he claimed to be suffering from the effects of an "explosion" that occurred when he turned on his welding equipment. An in-depth examination showed, however, that he had worn his contact lenses for seventeen to eighteen hours after the accident: his lesions were due to the fact that he had kept his lenses in too long, and disappeared after a few days (*Contactologia,* 1984, vol. 6, no. 1, pp. 44–45). In the meantime, before the final diagnosis could be made, the ambiguous phenomenon had given rise to other interpretations. The rumor was launched: several months after the fact, the welder's mishap was mentioned in newspapers in countries as far off as Australia and New Zealand. Since that time, the same story has been periodically retold in North America, and first spread to Europe in 1975. (*Libération,* October 18, 1984). The rumor has blinded French industry.

The event described is not only historically false but above all physically impossible. But despite the numerous articles published in scientific journals—read thus only by specialists—the rumor continues to mislead people.

Here, once again, the rumor is plausible: any nonprofessional agrees that contact lenses "focus" light rays. Why not imagine an incredible magnifying glass effect, which would nevertheless be painless and perhaps even imperceptible? This imaginary scenario seemed plausible to all the doctors in the thousands of occupational-health departments the world over that posted this memorandum, thereby endowing it with absolute authenticity for all employees and executives: the rumor was certified by the legitimate agencies of knowledge. Its plausible appearance and the expertise of its source (another company's health department) gave it carte blanche in every government office and business.

Why did such a stretching of the limits of the plausible take place among the wider public, and among doctors and ophthalmologists? There were two contributing factors: the specialization of knowledge and the growing abstraction of our relation to the physical world [79]. The era of Renaissance men such as Pic de la Mirandole and Montaigne has long since ended. Nowadays, even within a single field, the division of knowledge is extensive: many doctors find it normal that, under certain conditions, contact lenses can make you go blind. Nowadays we generally have abstract relations with our environment: how many Frenchmen today have ever seen a venomous snake, or any other kind of snake for that matter, close up? Who knows where, how and at what distance from the coast a Canadair fire-fighting plane fills up on water? We have learned (have we really?) in physics class the laws governing the speed of free-falling bodies, but this knowledge remains unreal, without any real anchoring in personal experience; thus we are not shocked by the idea of dropping crates of snakes out of airplanes.

On the whole, words have lost their physical referent: they no longer relate to anything more than images and ideas. Words have become autonomous. We now react to sentences as if they were combinations of abstract signs: the only thing that now counts are words' magical qualities and their positions in grammatically correct propositions. "It's been said that, near where you live, Jewish shopkeepers have been drugging girls to sell them to a white-slave-trade network." In Orléans, the first people who didn't believe the rumor were those who knew the shopkeepers personally; in their minds, it was impossible. Their relations to the incriminated parties were not abstract. For everyone else, the above sentence was but a series of symbols: shops, Jews, drugs, girls, white-slave trade. When one has no empirical experience of words' referents, doubt is easily sown. The result largely depends on one's mental frame of reference at the time.

Which Frames of Reference?

Accepting information as true depends on the frame of reference each individual uses to evaluate it. If the information is coherent with the frame of reference used, it acquires a high degree of probability of being held true. The fact that the rumor linking Procter & Gamble with Satan was able to spread in the United States is not surprising considering the Gallup poll published in 1989 by the magazine *Psychology Today:* in the United States, 66 percent of the adults interviewed said they believed in the devil. The figure fell to 30 percent in Great Britain, 18 percent in West Germany, 17 percent in France and as low as 12 percent in Sweden. Given these figures, the rumor obviously had to evolve in order to spread in Europe; references to Satan were abandoned and the Moonies became the central focus. The famous case of the Martian invasion also dramatically illustrates the importance of context and frame of reference to a rumor's reception.

On the evening of October 30, 1938, on a nationwide radio show, Orson Welles broadcasted a play: a simulation of what would happen if a flying saucer landed in New York as a prelude to an invasion by Martians [52]. The play was in the form of live coverage, with teams of reporters trying to get close to the landing area, specialists in astronomy and astrophysics arriving out of breath or giving their views live over the phone, comments by the generals of the mobilized army corps and Red Cross officials, etc. The play was duly written up as a "play" in all the radio program schedules printed in the newspapers and magazines.

That evening, thousands of Americans turning on their radio sets during the program were literally panic struck. Throughout the United States, people began praying, crying, and fleeing by car with just a few hastily packed bags. Others rushed to the homes of their loved ones to find and warn them, allowing them, thereby, to escape from danger. People contacted their neighbors, called to warn or say goodbye to their dear ones, and rang up the police and media for details. Of the six million people who heard the radio broadcast, one million claimed to have been deeply moved. In their minds it was far more than a realistic play: it was outright information—reality in the making.

The unexpected and unintended consequences of the broadcast encouraged researchers to question those who had the most completely believed, to the point of not even seeking to check whether it was real information or simply a successful simulation. The majority of them had frames of thought that allowed the information to seem normal, i.e., to fit quite naturally in with the order of normal and foreseeable things. They were:

1. Very devout people, above all members of fundamentalist religious communities who expected the world to end at any minute.
2. People very sensitized to the increasing risk of war who believed in the imminence of an attack by a foreign power. An invasion, whether Japanese, Nazi, or Martian, seemed not unlikely.
3. People who believed in the extraordinary powers of science and who implicitly expected some sort of impending catastrophe along the lines of the "sorcerer's apprentice" scenario.

A great many Americans who had truly believed in an invasion by Martians owed their belief to an absence of frames of reference needed to evaluate such information, either because they had had very little schooling, or because of the prevailing conditions at that time. Many families had suffered through the decline of economic conditions and the Great Depression in the 1930s. Unemployment was high and life was tough all over. No one seemed to be able to find the cure, neither the politicians nor the economists. The Martian invasion fit in with the context of unexplainable and uncontrollable events that were shaking America.

This absence of frames of reference has in no sense disappeared in our era. The popularization of science has spread the idea that all theories are tentative. Who, in 1910, would have believed that people would walk on the moon in July 1969? The hypothesis was totally farfetched. The speed of scientific and technical changes makes all knowledge doubtful and certainty impossible when it comes to the order of the world around us. Believing nothing any more, the public can now believe anything.

Sensitivity of the Moment

The emergence of a rumor is thus linked to momentary circumstances: what is plausible today wasn't plausible yesterday, and will no longer be plausible tomorrow.

Between April 14 and 15, 1954, in Seattle, Washington [180], the police received more than two hundred phone calls announcing that automobiles had been damaged. In all, close to three thousand cars had been affected. The damage involved windshields: they were potted with small lacelike marks. The mayor, faced with such a sudden and unexplainable phenomenon, declared that the damage exceeded the police's competence. He called upon the governor of the state of Washington, who himself called upon President Eisenhower. In Seattle, many drivers protected their windshields with newspapers and doormats, other left their cars in the garage altogether. The local press discussed the sudden aggression against windshields in great detail. The problem was taken seriously, and a well-reputed research institute—the Environmental Research Laboratory at the University of Washington—was assigned to carry out an in-depth study. The report made by the expert chemists was published on June 10, 1954; the marks on the windshields were due, quite simply, to the constant but natural bouncing of small particles of blacktop from roads onto windshields. In addition, the number of marks was directly related to the age of the vehicle: old cars had more marks than new ones.

How can we explain what happened in Seattle in mid-April? A clue can be found in the content of the rumors going around the city: the small lace-like marks were being attributed to fallout from A-bomb testing that had recently been in the public eye. In November 1952, one of the islands in the Eniwetok atoll had disappeared from the face of the map during the first explosion. Sixteen months later, on March 1, 1954, the Bikini explosion had taken place, leaving a crater almost a mile in diameter, and sending tons of coral and radioactive debris into the stratosphere [116]. Situated on the Pacific coast, Seattle's inhabitants were anxiously awaiting some form of fallout.

Their fears came true when, instead of looking as usual *through* a windshield, someone looked *at* it. He spoke of his "discovery" with his neighbors, and they too looked at their windshields; finding the same marks, they in turn passed on the news. Soon the whole town was scrutinizing their windshields, paying attention to details to which they'd never paid attention before. It goes without saying that they found the detail astonishing and even disturbing. In Seattle, the expectation of some aftermath of the nuclear tests had created an epidemic, not of potted windshields but of examined windshields.

No French president has been assassinated in a long time (not since 1931). Attempts were made to kill General de Gaulle, but he miraculously escaped harm. The current probability of an assassination seems very slight to the French public and to the journalists who inform them (on the other hand, premature death after a long illness kept secret is on the French hit-parade of ready-to-use mental scenarios). Thus the rumor that President Mitterrand had been attacked on July 23, 1982 was short-lived: no one could believe it (*Le Matin,* July 24, 1982).

According to that particular rumor, circulating in editorial committees and press rooms, President Mitterrand had just been attacked in front of his home at 22, rue de Bièvre in Paris by a man who had knifed him in the stomach. When the facts were made known, something had indeed happened in that street: a man had gone into the building at 23, rue de Bièvre, not 22, and had knifed a third-floor resident. A few minutes later, the victim made his way down the stairs and collapsed in front of the policemen guarding the president's home; the police officers immediately called an ambulance. These important and ambiguous facts sparked off speculation and thus the rough outline of a rumor.

All Purpose Proofs

We rarely hear a rumor all by itself: it is always accompanied by a whole slew of proofs that endow it with undeniable credibility. In a certain sense, its power comes from its ability to structure our perception: it gives meaning to a large number of facts that we either would never have noticed or whose meaning hadn't seemed obvious to us. It thus supplies a coherent explanatory system for a great many scattered facts; in that sense it satisfies our need to find order in the world around us. Let us examine each of these statements.

In Seattle, the rumor had drawn attention to formerly neglected details concerning car windshields. Rumors also attract attention to facts we have already noticed, without having drawn any conclusions from them. For most facts are silent: they are meaningless in and of themselves; we give them meaning, and that meaning varies from one individual to another, and from one era to another. Rumors make events that had hitherto been viewed as insignificant, significant. The rumor about Paul McCartney's death constituted a seductive interpretation for all the odd details on the covers of the two Beatle albums that had most recently come out. Interviews with Americans who had been affected by the radio program simulating an invasion of New York by the Martians were also very enlightening. Some of those who heard Welles' program didn't know what to think and decided to seek further information. Certain people called the local police and, finding that all the lines were busy, concluded that the police were overwhelmed. When they did manage to get through to the police, the latter said they knew nothing about it—hardly a reassuring response for the worried callers. One person interviewed said he had looked out the window: the street was crammed with cars. He concluded that the exodus had begun. Another, surprised by the lack of traffic in the streets nearby, concluded that the cars were blocked on the already destroyed streets. Having no one around to suggest to them that the facts could just as well have the opposite meaning, their conviction grew little by little: all signs converged to validate their hypotheses. That is the way rumors work—they structure our environment. They organize our perception to validate themselves.

This construction of "proofs" is not particular to rumors alone: it attests to the general effect of communication on the interpretation of subsequently arising facts. If we are told that a child is "nervous," each and every one of his brutal physical outbursts will be labelled a "nervous outburst." If we are told that he is full of energy and vitality, the same physical outbursts will be labelled "outbursts of vitality." It is the structural ambiguity of most events which makes of them a screen upon which we can project previously existing images, hypotheses and opinions: *the perception of events is self-validating.*

A Chinese parable from the third century B.C. beautifully illustrates this process: "A man couldn't find his axe anywhere. He suspected his neighbor's son of having taken it and began to watch him carefully. He looked like a typical axe thief; what he said could only be construed as the words of an axe thief; all his attitudes and behavior were characteristic of a man who has stolen an axe. But quite unexpectedly, in spading the ground in his garden one day, the man suddenly found his axe. The next day, when he saw his neighbor's son again, he saw nothing—neither in his looks nor his behavior—suggesting an axe thief" [77].

The Pleasure of Grand Explanations

Rumors win us over because they provide an occasion to better understand the world; they considerably simplify it and allow us to detect therein a framed order. Their ability to assemble in one single explanatory scenario a large number of facts, is one of the essential factors in their appeal. The human mind seems to constantly seek balanced explanatory schemas allowing it to link up events which seem scattered and unrelated. We don't like disorder, uncertainty or randomness. Superstitious behavior, incantations, and magic also attest to our need to imagine that *a hidden order* exists behind the apparent randomness and disorder.

In the course of the eighteenth century, the French were subjected to six long periods of famine during which wheat supplies ran short and prices sky-rocketed. Rumors systematically announced a gigantic plot to starve the people concocted by the king's ministers, bankers, local bureaucrats, superin-tendents, and bakers [146]. Certain historians have taken the haunting fear of a plot as a product of a sort of collective paranoia or chronic hallucinatory psychosis, indicative of some kind of mental underdevelopment. In such explanations, one sees a tendency towards the "psychiatrization" of rumors.

But as a matter of fact, as Kaplan too points out, the plot theory was highly convincing as "it alone seemed to account for the nature of the crises. When they looked around them, men of the eighteenth century discovered things . . . that seemed to fit together like pieces of a puzzle" [146]. Many facts anchored their suspicions in reality: companies and speculation certainly existed, as did hoarding, monopolies, and intervention by high-ranking individuals. For a variety of pretexts, grain was even thrown into rivers; life under the Ancient Regime was indeed chock full of intrigues within the king's court and feudalities. There were many separate elements that could carry some explanatory weight, but only the plot theory allowed them to be connected.

The attraction of the rumor also derived from a characteristic human trait: between a simple explanation and a complicated one, human beings prefer the latter. Between two competing theories supposed to explain the same facts, philosophers of science have pronounced the rule of Ockham's razor: the simplest must be chosen. Let us examine a revealing experiment [259] that uses the well-known principle of false feedback. Two individuals, A and B, are asked to carry out the same task: examining a series of slides, they are required to distinguish the healthy cells from the unhealthy ones. Whenever they give an answer, a flash of light (the feedback) tells them whether their answer was right or wrong. A and B do not see each other during the experiment, being separated by a screen.

A's flash is honest: it lights up as "true" when A provides a correct answer, and "false" otherwise. Thanks to the feedback, A progressively learns to identify the features of healthy cells and those of unhealthy cells. *B*'s flash has been tinkered with: unbeknownst to *B*, there is no relation whatsoever between his answers and what the flash indicates. He believes that the flashes effectively indicate whether his answers are correct or not. He thus looks for a way of distinguishing healthy from unhealthy cells on the basis of random signals.

Halfway through the experiment, *A* and *B* are asked to discuss the signs that signal healthy and unhealthy cells. *A* gives a simple explanation based on a few criteria. *B*'s explanation is very complicated, based on many different criteria, details and conditions: indeed he has sought order where there wasn't any. He has purely and simply invented it.

Now *A*, far from rejecting *B*'s explanations as overly complicated or elaborate, rather admires their sophistication. When the experiment begins anew, B's performance remains the same while *A*'s worsens, *A* having adopted some of the complex, invented ideas *B* laid out to him, which by the very nature of the experiment cannot possibly work.

The same is true for rumors. A rumor is an explanatory system, i.e., a hypothesis that gives order to observations. In general, when a rumor is farfetched or sophisticated, people like it. Should someone be so foolhardy as to offer a simpler and more rational explanation, he can more or less count on being treated condescendingly. There is a certain pressure at work: not believing the sophisticated, imaginative explanation proves that one is naive and not at all in the swing of things. Believing the more complex version, on the contrary, shows that one is with it and clear headed. The more complicated the explanation, the more the Sherlock Holmes dormant within ourselves awakens and springs to action. There is prestige involved in revealing an extraordinary affair, i.e., a brilliant, imaginative scenario in which all the concrete facts fit together perfectly.

The search for hidden order accounts for rumors' geometrical leanings. We like to think that the details fit into some sort of hidden figure whose meaning is ineluctable. This is why numerology and astrology are so appealing, and why we encounter the "accursed triangle" in many mysterious cases. In Reims, not far from the Mourmelon military camp, the newspaper *l'Union* (from August 3, 1987) spoke of the "accursed Mourmelon triangle" and of the locations where soldiers had disappeared as forming an "axis" comprising three towns: Mourmelon, Châlon sur Marne, and Mailly. Lacking a methodical and minute field investigation, the rumor had recourse to abstraction and theoretical conceptualization: it looked to scientific geometry, as other rumors look to symbolism, to provide one of the keys to the mystery. The famous "Bermuda Triangle" in part owed its popularity and appeal to the fact that it tickled our geometrical fancies.

Power and Repetition

As a rumor spreads it becomes more convincing. Repeated at the outset just for fun, it becomes a certainty. Indeed, one's conviction grows when one hears the same information from several different people: if they all say the same thing, then it must be true. Asch's experiment [12] remarkably proves how unanimity can shake our deepest convictions.

In a room, eight people participate in the following exercise: they are shown, on the left of a screen, a line of variable length, and on the right of the screen, three other lines. One of the three lines is of the same length as the line to the left of the screen, while the other two are, beyond a shadow of a doubt, much longer or shorter. The group's task is to indicate which of the three lines is identical to the one on the left. The exercise is repeated in showing slides with different lines. Each of the eight people must say out loud, and without talking about it with the others, what he perceives.

What one of the people doesn't know—call him *S*—is that the seven others have received instructions to unanimously give an answer that is patently false. The line they designate is unquestionably much longer or shorter than the one with which the three lines are compared. What is the effect of their unanimous error? A significant number of *S*'s rally around the answer of the unanimous majority. While objectively speaking, there can be absolutely no room for doubt, they prefer to conform to collective sentiment. Comments made after the experiment are revealing. One *S* who stuck to his own view of things declared: "I preferred to say what I saw, but reason was telling me that I myself could have been completely in the wrong." Another said, "I won't deny that at a few different moments, I told myself: 'Come on, that's enough! Do like them'." The comments made by someone who had gone along with the group's opinion were crystal clear: "If I'd been the first person to speak, I certainly would have answered differently. But they seemed so sure of what they were saying." Certainly (and fortunately), some of the *S*'s in the experiment stuck to their own views. The group's influence was not total. But this is not a reflection of everyday life:

1. In the experiment, the right answer was objectively obvious, reassuring those who were "resistant" to conformistic pressure. In the case of rumors, the situation is altogether ambiguous: "it seems that East German women swimmers are more male than female." What is the right answer?

2. In the experiment, the group was a simple collection of eight individuals who didn't know each other at all. In everyday life, our reference group consists of people with whom we speak precisely because their opinions count in our minds. One can thus imagine that consensus is even more influential in such cases.

Conversational Rules

Rumors are communicated in informal conversation in social settings. Foreseeing the likely reaction of some members of the audience, the story can be related in one of many narrative forms [22,42]:

1. It can be told as an anecdote or memorate, directly involving the narrator himself or herself.
2. It can be semi-incorporated by starring a relative, some named friend, or locally known character.
3. Lastly, it can be distanced from the performer by giving no source ("I heard . . . ").

The narrator adapts his approach to the audience, reserving himself the possibility of backing up and distancing the story (it did not happen to me, nor to my sister's boyfriend but to a friend of his . . .), without denying the story itself.

During the narrative performance, and because of that very performance, there is a suspension of disbelief. A vast number of rumors possess a crucial flaw. But since the audience is not in a critical set but in a participatory set (as when one goes to the movies), the story need not actually recount possible events but events which seem possible while we are listening to the story [263, p. 219]. In the Solid Cement Cadillac rumor, a cement-truck driver, coming home early one day, hears voices in his kitchen and sees his wife talking to a well-dressed man he doesn't recognize. Seeing a shiny new Cadillac in his driveway, he empties an entire load of cement inside it, filling the car completely. When he comes home later, his tearful wife informs him that the new Cadillac was for him—bought with her hard-earned savings—and that the stranger was the local car dealer. Although many have heard this story, hardly anyone ever asks: how do you fill a car with cement without making any noise?

In addition, in social settings politeness limits the ways in which nonacceptance of the "facts" can be expressed. When unconvinced, one generally remains silent: the story generates quiescence if not acquiescence. Therefore, even if the audience is unconvinced, a lack of counter arguments and challenges may reinforce the performer's belief in the truth of the story and part of the audience's belief as well.

Desirable Information

Up until now we have examined why we *can* easily believe information related by friends, neighbors, and relatives. But the most important reason has not yet been presented: rumors convey information we want to believe. Our desire to believe is sometimes so strong that it overturns our usual criteria of realism and plausibility, the latter in fact being governed by our desire to believe, not the other way around.

The Desire to Believe

Regardless of the efforts made by informative sources and of their prestige, if the information they convey does not satisfy a desire, answer to a latent preoccupation, or provide an outlet for a psychological conflict, no rumor will arise from it. Harmless words and innocent confidentialities may, on the contrary, be snapped up and turned into rumors because there is interest in their consumption.

One could go so far as to say that rumors do not convince or persuade people: rather they seduce them. It is as if we seize upon them through a sort of revelation that we then hurry to share with our friends. This phenomenon is not due to rumors' evil, hypnotic power that transfixes us: quite simply, rumors express and justify out loud what we think to ourselves or do not dare to hope. Thus a rumor, unlike any other message, enjoys a unique characteristic: it justifies public opinion while revealing it, i.e. it rationalizes at the same time that it satisfies. Before hearing a particular rumor, we perhaps *thought* that such and such a politician was a shady character; after hearing it, we *know* that he is. In every case, a fact justifies the public's deepest feelings: the fact thus validates its feelings and authorizes their free and communicative expression. For in speaking and inveighing against the traitor, aggressiveness born of frustration dissipates. *To speak is to unburden oneself.* Moreover, when we learn of facts that justify what we already more or less consciously believe, our views are confirmed, and hence we want to share them by talking about them.

An infinite number of examples could be provided. For one, I might mention the above-cited case of the rumor about venomous snakes being dropped out of planes into the French countryside. Analyzing the rumor, one finds that it justifies, expresses, and confirms four beliefs that are widely held in the countryside. Ecologists who get mixed up in defending nature are dangerous: though well-meaning, their plans backfire. This is the theme of the sorcerer's apprentice. Ecologists have no real contact with the land: they build castles in the sky (thus they stay far from the ground in their airplanes). Ecologists are incompetent; they should know that in order to feed birds of prey, longer snakes are better, ie., garter snakes—not to mention the fact that they are less dangerous. Generally speaking, administrative decisions made in Paris come from "out of the blue," are extremely expensive (involving planes and helicopters), and are harmful. The rumor's content was no accident.

The political arena offers other illustrations of the satisfying and liberatory nature of rumors. To say that the socialist electoral victory in France on May 10, 1981, upset part of France would be an understatement. Already by that very evening, many people were contemplating how to reconquer the political ground lost. They weren't about to wait for seven full years (the usual presidential term in France); something had to be done to annul the election. To begin with it had been predicted that the socialists would be forced out of power by the economic catastrophe that would take place if they took power: but in the course of the following months, nothing of the sort happened. A hope remained for the antisocialists that was made plausible by the recollection that Georges Pompidou had died before the end of his term—an illness could put an end to the man who symbolized the regime.

It was because it expressed and at the same time satisfied this wish that the rumor about the president having cancer spread rapidly starting in fall of 1981 (it in fact began on May 10). Moreover, questions had already been raised about François Mitterrand's health starting on August 24, 1973, when he did not attend the plenary session of the Socialist International in Stockholm. The rumor struck again in 1975, and once again in 1977 after his poor performance during the televised face-off with Raymond Barre on May 12. In 1981, the rumor was thus both plausible and highly desirable to many people. Taking into account the frustration that rumors are supposed to resolve, the rumor could but have involved cancer. Rumors of consultations at the Val-de-Grâce Hospital marked the end of Mitterrand's state of grace.

Once again in France, but in another realm, margarine remained for quite some time in consumer purgatory. It directly opposed the very symbol of France's cultural patrimony and untainted "natural goodness": butter. There were, nevertheless, plenty of arguments in its favor: it was supposed to have the same culinary virtues as butter, but to cost only half as much [78]. This situation was a source of conflict for homemakers. How were they to reconcile the two dissonant thoughts: "I am a good homemaker" and "I refuse to buy a product that is just as good and only half as expensive"? Astra brand margarine aimed one of its advertising campaigns at exacerbating this cognitive dissonance: "Now you're rid of a bias that was costing you a lot of money."

To dispel this uncomfortable situation [95], homemakers seized upon the slightest negative rumors going around about margarine: it was supposed to contain the worst of ingredients, be made with tallow and bone waste-products collected in butcher shops, and be produced in unhealthy factories, etc. By believing these rumors and actively spreading them, homemakers recreated a more comfortable situation for themselves; they provided the facts justifying their cultural obligation to use butter.

Rumors' ability to express our feelings explains in part the "snowballing" effect, i.e. the addition of details often seen in the evolution of rumors. Indeed, far from remaining passive in relation to information, we seek within ourselves—i.e., in our memories—elements and details that support such comforting rumors. As rumors express our opinions, we seek to improve them to make them more persuasive to others.

Echoing Ourselves

As has already been seen, it is no accident that rumors we hear often find an echo within us. This is due to our belonging to a social group whose opinions, values and attitudes we share.

The fact that rumors vindicate our intuitions, feelings, and opinions explains why barely believable rumors are able to spread with some degree of success. The psychological benefits reaped in adopting and participating in rumors clearly justifies our not being too punctilious about their plausibility: hearing a rumor that comforts a deeply rooted feeling naturally makes us less critical. Yet, rumors are not dreams. Dreams need not worry about staying close to reality. Rumors, however, must include a certain dose of realism. thus the success of a rumor that seems "unbelievable" to certain people, cannot be chalked up to blindness caused by a fanatical desire to believe the rumor: it attests to the fact that, given the current state of the public's knowledge, the rumor was not improbable.

Between 1978 and 1982, in the United States, a rumor accused the famous restaurant chain, McDonald's, of mixing earthworms into its hamburger meat. This rumor has often been taken as a typical example of a rumor that was unbelievable but nevertheless believed. In my opinion, this view is mistaken: the rumor is quite understandable. It metaphorically expresses certain Americans' increasing anxiety about their eating habits. To warn the population of the risks involved in such habits, the concept of "junkfood" was forged. The hamburger is one of the symbols of American food that is now on the firing line. In the United States, many people are very concerned by Americans' fundamentally unhealthy eating habits. The earthworm hypothesis gave concrete and palpable form to people's phobia of the rotting on the inside brought about by constant ingurgitation of soft drinks and hamburgers. Worms symbolize, on the one hand, trash or garbage, and, on the other, the inner destruction that follows its absorption.

Can we reasonably imagine McDonald's adding earthworms to its hamburger meat? Certainly not literally, but perhaps symbolically. The rumor expressed the resentment certain people feel towards the giant company whose identity seems to be founded on a product which is now recognized to be unbalanced and thus unbalancing. In trying to sell as many hamburgers as possible to Americans, the company affirms its status as a producer of poison. The rumor just barely symbolically expressed the idea that every hamburger is poisonous and that McDonald's knows it, though it nevertheless pursues its thorough food-poisoning program. Thus, far from being an aberrant idea dreamt up by fools, the rumor was a warning signal.

5

Rumors: Their Public and Their Functions

Introduction

When we speak to someone, that someone is not chosen at random. Every rumor has its particular public. But the term "public" should not make us forget that each individual plays a precise role in a rumor's circulation. Further on in this book, we will examine the parts played by each of a rumor's actors.

The Rumor Market

Every rumor has a market of its own. For convenience's sake, people generally say that a rumor has spread everywhere and that the whole town is talking about it. In reality, only a part of the town hears of it, and a still smaller part believes it. Freely circulating in France since 1976, the "Villejuif" flyer lends itself to a study on rumor penetration: who in the French population read or had the flyer in hand? In the ten years following its first appearance, the flyer had affected one out of three French households. An examination of its penetration into different strata of the population reveals considerable disparities [144]. In families where working husbands were professionals or high-level executives, two out of three housewives had read it; where the husbands were white collar employees or middle-level executives, one out of two; and where they are blue-collar workers, one out of three. Naturally, the more children there were in the household, the more likely it was to have been read. Fifty percent of all households with children had been affected by it, 30 percent of the households with no children, and only 17 percent of people living alone. Lastly, the younger the housewife, the more likely she was to have read it.

The fact that every rumor has its own public can be rather surprising at times. We abusively speak of "the public at large" as if there were some sort of homogeneous whole, ready to react as one man to the slightest rumor. In reality, every rumor speaks of a particular event. A rumor's public consists in those who feel concerned by this event's consequences. From one rumor to another, the consequences change, as do their publics. What factors make someone part of one public and not another?

The Effect of Experience

In the twenty French towns in which the rumor that a white slave trade was going on in clothing stores has run rife since 1965, men generally did not believe it. Of course one could argue that as they are not targeted by white slave trading, they did not feel concerned: but that would be to neglect the fact that men are also fathers, brothers, husbands, and/or lovers. The explanation lies elsewhere: men have greater experience of life in the city and are more aware of what is realistic and what is not. By contrast, such rumors often arise in girls' boarding schools, i.e., in closed environments that cut off their adolescent populations, with very little experience of city life, from social reality. Such rumors very easily circulate among senior citizens as well: they ignore or misunderstand the conditions of modern life, and live with fixed schemas in mind. It is a significant finding that the girls most affected by this rumor often declared that they had been warned of such things since childhood by their great-aunts and grandmothers [186].

But experience does not work uniquely against rumors. The effect of experience explains why, in countries where a form of censorship exists, the intelligentsia attributes a great deal of credibility to rumors. In a study carried out in the USSR [23], those people interviewed were asked if, according to them, rumors were *more* reliable than the official media: 95 percent of those in high-ranking positions said yes, as did 85 percent of the white-collar workers, 72 percent of the blue-collar workers and 56 percent of the farmers. These results are understandable: closer to the dens of power, those in high places can easily see the gaps between official versions handed out by the media and reality. They are experienced in dealing with official media.

Thus the effect of experience, rightly or wrongly, excludes part of the public. These people cannot believe the rumor to be plausible: it runs counter to their frames of reference and cannot stand up to examination. I will insist upon the reservation "rightly or wrongly." Indeed, one might wonder why rumors about the existence of concentration camps did not circulate more widely during World War II [60]. Aside from the fact that silence was deliberately imposed by the United States government (so as not to give the impression that it was engaging in a "Jewish" war and run the risk of awakening opposition to the war because of part of the population's anti-Semitism), the effect of experience had a negative influence on certain people. French resisters refused to publish information about the camps in the underground press: their experience of propaganda and counterpropaganda made them take such rumors for a brilliantly planned scare tactic. According to their frames of reference, considering the Nazis' already atrocious cruelty, gas chambers seemed totally improbable.

A Clientele for Every Content

In addition to the grand sociological, political, and sociocultural splits that trace out a rumor's potential empire, individual psychology can accentuate sensitivity to rumors. Having studied a rumor about white slave trading, for example, Paillard observed that the women the most anxious about the rumor were "rather old (when compared with the youthful clientele) and ugly" [186]. Belief in the rumor had a narcissistic basis for them: fearing they would be kidnapped, they felt that they were worth kidnapping. The youngest and prettiest of the women were more inclined to just have fun with the rumor, repeating it because of the excitement its tale of forbidden fruit aroused (and for narcissistic reasons as well?).

An interesting experiment illustrates the above paradox in an altogether different context. Researchers set out to discover whether one could start up a rumor about anything whatsoever, e.g., a rumor claiming that coffee was very harmful. In a business office, two employees were chosen to stand near a coffee machine and relate that they had heard that coffee was "bad for the nervous system and involved carcinogenic risks" [78]. Theoretically speaking, the rumor should have most concerned high "risk" takers: heavy consumers. The opposite turned out to be the case: the less people drank, the more they believed the rumor might possibly be true. Heavy consumers couldn't accept it; aside from the fact that there was hardly any logical link between coffee absorption and cancer, the rumor was also refused as it would have led to an uncomfortable and unacceptable situation of cognitive dissonance.

During World War II, the frequency of rumors, and their possible negative effect on the troops' morale, inspired many studies. These latter illustrate how a rumor's public takes shape: people who have certain psychological reasons to believe literally seize hold of it. As the French proverb has it, "No one is less deaf than he who wants to hear."

During the war, the population was subjected to serious deprivation.

Everything was in short supply: butter, meat, sugar, gasoline, wood, and so on. Rumors continually arose according to which, while some people had to "tighten their belts, others were living high on the hog." It was claimed that the scarce goods were all stocked up somewhere in order to force prices up, or that they had all gone bad in storage. Two investigators decided to precisely analyze the kind of people who believed such rumors [4]. They selected twelve rumors among all those then circulating. Their selection criteria were simple: the rumors could not correspond to any factual situation, however far off and deformed it might be. The rumors thus could not be believed on the basis of some personal experience or some recollection of a related fact.

To exemplify their approach, here are a few of the rumors they selected:

- There is plenty of coffee, but the companies are holding onto it waiting for prices to go up.
- The military bases have so much butter in their stockpiles that it goes rancid before they use it.
- There is so much gasoline stored in the petroleum companies' tanks that oil tankers are dumping part of their cargo into the ocean.
- At the last dinner at the nearby military base, there were loads of cooked turkeys for only eight officers.
- The company contracted to build the nearby military base is wasting all the wood. Acres upon acres of trees have been uselessly cut down and burned; which is understandable in that the company is paid by the acre: the more land they clear, the more money they make.

On the average, these rumors were heard by 23 percent of the Americans interviewed, confirming the notion that rumors are not "everywhere" as people often like to think. Twenty-seven percent of the people were inclined to believe the rumors, and in any case claimed that they were certainly not impossible.

The analysis done of the people who said they believed the rumors showed which segments of the population were particularly open to them. It illustrated the role rumors played for these people, and elucidated the reasons for their belief.

These rumors were more often believed by those who found rationing unjust or useless than by those who found it equitable and necessary. Hostile to the rationing program, they seized upon any argument lending credence to their hostility. At the same time, the rumors allowed them to express their resentment out loud: they could thus quite legitimately attack the object they were criticizing.

To Each His Own Scapegoat

Every collectivity and social group has its preferred, virtually institutionalized scapegoats. One can thus guess a rumor's market by examining who it proposes as whipping boy, and asking: whose traditional whipping boy is he? During World War II, for example, anti-Semitic rumors ran rife more particularly in the eastern United States (a white Christian environment); rumors accusing blacks of the worst kind of evil-doings spread mostly in the South; and rumors condemning the Roosevelt administration flourished mainly in the Midwest (America's breadbasket).

In the eastern provinces in Canada, a rumor sprang up in 1984 accusing the La Batt's company, makers of La Batt's beer (highly popular in Canada), of in reality being owned by Pakistanis. The latter are the current scapegoats: their recent presence in large numbers in eastern Canada—which has suffered a high unemployment rate—makes them the target of Vancouver's working classes, and thus the subject of rumors.

The ultimate scapegoat, guilty of all evils and accused of all sins, is the Devil or Antichrist. The anxiety-producing era of economic crisis, of questioning of values, of American hostages being hijacked in a TWA plane, and forced to land in Beirut, was seen by many Americans as a sign of the predicted return of the fallen angel. Indeed, according to a pessimistic reading of the texts on the Apocalypse, dramatic events are to precede the Last Judgment: they will be the signs that Satan is furiously waging his last battle. In fundamentalist religious communities in the central and southern United States, the time had clearly come: the abnormal signs all pointed to the Devil's active presence. The concrete problem was to localize him, as well as the accomplices he was necessarily using to extend his dominion. Thus were born the rumors about the biggest American companies (e.g., Procter & Gamble, McDonalds, and so on). The famous rock groups, Led Zeppelin, Black Sabbath, and even the Rolling Stones, were also suspected of being the Devil's active agents [185].

All of these rumors arose in the Bible Belt, the most religious of the American states. It was there that satanic rumors found their natural public. But they spread far beyond those states. In a recent poll carried out in the United States using a representative nationwide sample, 34 percent of the people interviewed said that the Devil is *a real live being*, 36 percent that it is more a concept than a being, and the remaining 30 percent that there is no Devil [176]. It is thus normal that the rumor could spread beyond the Bible Belt: wherever you look there are people who believe in the Devil.

In France, it was normal that fashion shops became scapegoats in rumors about the white slave trade. First and foremost, such shops are highly eroticized: people undress there to please and seduce. But we cannot limit ourselves to this generic psychological cause. Such stores also have a social function: they create change. They constitute an institutional support for changing standards of behavior: they introduce new styles, primarily aimed at young people, allowing them to forge new identities that break with those handed down by their parents. Such fashion shops activate girls' identification with reference figures who are quite foreign to their hometowns, i.e., celebrities from Paris, London, and New York. Clothes thus visibly demonstrate decreasing parental control and city control over teenagers who have been won over by trends from the big city or abroad.

This situation is a source of frustration: it quite naturally leads to resentment towards those who sew seeds of change in adolescents, especially when they are Jewish shopkeepers (still considered in the provinces to be prototypical outsiders). The townspeople's previously repressed irritation found an ideal justification to let loose. Having become scapegoats, the shops paid for the fall of the towns' young people. The same is often true for other sites of emancipation: discotheques and community centers.

Motives and the Public

Groups generate their own folklore and rumors. There are, for example, specific rumors in the surfer subculture [250]: as this sport is individualistic, ego-building, competitive, and dangerous, these rumors show a marked respect for daredevil surfers, strength and skill, heroism, and feats of all kinds. They depict heroes who are not remote, superhuman forebears, but rather individuals known through personal acquaintance or recent observation. These rumors promote and reinforce models to imitate and respect: they have a socialization function. Football clubs have also produced their own folklore; locker rumors focus on famous coaches, team jokers and rules governing players' behavior. These rules are informally taught to newcomers through rumors, stories, and jokes [26].

Rumors are not told at random. As stated by Degh [69, p. 63], the opportunity of story-telling in itself is related to situations in which momentary danger, frustration, fear, and excitement are very enjoyable. For instance, certain stories "alleged to have happened recently" are used by teenagers to keep their younger brothers and sisters away from a hidden clearing in the woods. Many rumors concern alleged events involving parking lots and "lovers' lanes." Such lovers' lane narratives are generally circulated by college boys who tell them to their dates while the couple is sitting in a car at that very spot. The rumor telling is purposive: the girl gets scared and draws closer to her "fearless male." Other stories are told by college girls to their girlfriends while they are engaged in common activities. They concern sex maniacs or similarly dangerous guys (e.g., the "hatchet man" or the "man with a hook").

For each rumor, it is possible to identify a selective "conduit": those who act as receivers and re-emitters. As we shall see in the chapter on the interpretation of rumors, the precise identification of a particular rumor's market provides a major clue to understanding the rumor's deeper meaning. Often people are not even aware of the reasons for its specific appeal: many themes are camouflaged within a rumor. If we know that a rumor appeals to males, females, high school girls, or young mothers, we have at hand an indicator of its hidden symbolic message.

Rumor Settings and Context

Beyond the socioeconomic and personality factors that delineate a rumor's specific "market," there are objective conditions which at times create a market for all kinds of rumors: a demand for information.

One of these conditions is secrecy. We already discussed the case of rumors generated by censorship in Romania. More generally speaking, when a group, company, or profession is dominated by secrecy or censorship, a frustrated demand for information which encourages contraband and an informational black market is inevitably created. Doctors, for example, must strictly conform to the rules of secrecy: hence medical rumors abound. In 1986, the movie star Isabelle Adjani was said to be "very ill." The rumor spread throughout medical circles. Every physician interviewed claimed to have a colleague who had a friend who had examined her, and could name the hospital where she was undergoing treatment, and even her room number!

Medical rumors (relating concealed illnesses of famous public figures) are rendered possible by leaks, indiscretions, and the fact that, in hospital settings, a large number of employees have access to files, rooms and so on. Furthermore, while each doctor recognizes his responsibility to maintain professional discretion concerning his own patients, he generally does not feel bound to secrecy when it comes to a colleague's patients.

Uncertainty about the future is another factor that breeds rumors. In times of economic upheaval, political turmoil, and sociological change, anxiety and latent fears need to crystallize around an external object, i.e., something to be afraid of [166, 213]. Prolonged states of boredom also create a market for any and every bit of information. Studies of life in prisons during both world wars showed that no collective distraction was possible: no group singing, social games, or playing was allowed. Men were eager to hear anything that could relieve the boredom, and hurriedly passed information on to others [71].

6

Actors

To Each His Own Role

A rumor is a collective product resulting from the participation of many individuals. Particular roles in this dynamic process are, nevertheless, carefully distributed. An example will illustrate the division of labor presiding over the creation and extension of a rumor. Investigators have indeed been able to witness the spontaneous emergence of a rumor in a limited group setting and study its evolution [96]. Such cases of continuous observation of a rumor from its genesis on are sufficiently rare to merit our attention here.

The scene takes place in a low-rent housing project in the United States, without much of a social life. Though a tenants' union was created a few years before the action begins, there were no childcare facilities nor student activities. The most the tenants' union had been able to accomplish was to organize a party for children and Saturday night dances from time to time. Their lack of success in getting group activities going was due to the cold social relations among the housing project inhabitants: each inhabitant was a bit ashamed of living there and thought the others must be from a lower class background than he. A regional management representative decided at some point to send a community worker to the housing project; the latter met with the tenants' union and proposed a series of concrete projects that could be managed by the union's members. An attempt was thus made to mobilize the troops for a new beginning. With the help of the community worker and his assistants, they managed to get forty women and three men to attend a first meeting at which the work was to be divided up. Special committees were formed, allowing new people to acquire some status in the project. The members of the former tenants' union, on the contrary, lost their leadership roles, the general secretary being particularly affected.

A few weeks later, all of the projects that had been started stopped dead in

95

their tracks: a rumor spreading that one of the most active of the new leaders was in fact a communist, and that the projects all had unavowed goals that could nonetheless be guessed.

The rumor's origin was determinable: the secretary of the former tenants' union spoke with a neighbor about his ruminations. What were the reasons for the sudden arrival at the housing project of this community worker and his assistants? Even if it were only part-time work, he could not believe that their work was motivated uniquely by academic concerns. The secretary's neighbor, a specialist in communist witch-hunting, declared that one of the most active people in the housing project was, in his opinion, a communist. His hypothesis explained everything perfectly, and they recounted it to a number of women neighbors. The latter asked the regional management representative for more information about the community worker. He refused to give any, but suggested they stay on guard. That was enough to give the go-ahead to the rumor. In no time, people in the housing project were convinced that the activities were of communist inspiration, and put an immediate halt to them.

This mini-rumor illustrates a few of the possible roles in rumor processes:

1. The "instigator," in this case someone whose leadership was threatened by the change that had taken place in the housing project.
2. The "interpreter" who answers the questions raised by the instigator, proposing a coherent, convincing explanation.
3. The "opinion leader" whose view determines the group's opinion. Kurt Lewin calls him the "gate-keeper," as the group's openness to the rumor depends upon his judgment.
4. The "apostles" who, having become one with the rumor, try to convince others.

In the rumor-spreading process within a social group, other roles exist as well:

1. The "profiteers," i.e., people who take an interest in having the rumor spread, without necessarily believing it themselves. Throughout the French Revolution, there was a clear separation between the "little people"—who spontaneously reacted to rumors which often expressed but their own worries or magic dreams of the much-desired arrival of the Golden Age (tomorrow we'll dine gratis)—and the bourgeoisie who pursued political aims and a precise strategy, taking advantage of the crowd's irrational movements and rumors. When it comes to political rumors, recuperators are rampant.
2. The "opportunists" are smaller scale profiteers. In the case, for example,

of rumors about the white slave trade, mothers and teachers used them to approach "certain subjects" with adolescent girls or to assert their moral authority.

3. The "flirters" who do not believe the rumors, but find them delectable. They play with them in relating them to those around them, enjoying ruffling their public's feathers [126].

4. The "passive relays," i.e., those who claim that they are not convinced by the rumor. A slight doubt has, nevertheless, crept into their minds. They do not mobilize against the rumor, nor do they confine themselves to neutral silence: they are suspicious and question those around them.

5. The "resisters" lead the counter-attack as anti-rumor protagonists.

Are There Types?

Attempts to paint a portrait of people who systematically play the same role have hardly given convincing results. Rumor-mongers have, for example, been taxed with exhibitionistic, solicitous, chronically gullible, and anxious tendencies. Despite the supposedly scientific appearance, the moralizing aim is clear: rumor-mongers are said to necessarily have personal problems. Moreover, the desire to reduce rumor-telling to individual psychiatry is evident, even though we now know that rumors are products of precise situations in particular groups at particular moments. In the rumor going around the low-rent housing project, the parts played depended on each person's role and status in the structure of the housing project. Rather than seek out invariant psychological types, it seems more fruitful to carry out a contextual analysis of the rumor setting to understand why person X takes on a specific role in the rumor process.

Fine reports on such an analysis done in southern Minnesota, concerning the diffusion of the Pop Rocks rumor among prepubescent children [98]. According to the rumor, Pop Rocks candy explodes in people's stomachs. Fine carried out an analysis of group membership structure using the sociometric technique developed by Moreno. One essentially asks members of a group (e.g., school classes, athletic teams, etc.) to indicate who they would prefer to work with or choose as a roommate. The choice patterns reveal who is the most popular and influential within the group, and what relationship patterns exist. Fine discovered that those most likely to initiate the circulation of a sensational piece of news such as rumors were "loners" in the network, i.e., the least popular members of the group under scrutiny. For them, rumor telling was a way of getting attention, communicating, and gaining status by being the person who tells sensational stories.

Corroborating Fine's findings, Koenig [157, p. 114] found that, in the transmission of Satanic rumors, "there seemed to be a tendency for the lower-status-ministers to be the ones to initiate rumors within the religious network." In fundamentalist circles, these ministers are called "weak brothers" as opposed to "strong brothers." This is somewhat similar to findings on the adoption of innovations: research has shown that early adopters within a community are not necessarily those considered to be opinion leaders. They actually use innovations to build their own identity in relation to other group members.

The Role of Women

One must now take up two widespread ideas: women are thought to be particularly prone to rumor-mongering, and the intelligentsia is always assumed to put up resistance to rumors.

To speak of women in connection with rumors is to expose oneself to being accused of trotting out crude, old-fashioned antifeminist stereotypes. It is nevertheless a fact that an association exists between women and rumors in popular culture [31]. We will try here to examine its origins, if not its motives.

History lies perhaps behind this association. Historian J. Delumeau, in his retrospective history of the great fears that shook the Western world between the fourteenth and eighteenth centuries, noted that in all the sedition to which rumors gave rise, women were found to have front-row seats. Whether it was a question of the riots due to the high cost and scarcity of grain, the kidnapping of children in Paris in 1750, taxes or the French Revolution, women played a determining role: "They were the first people to perceive the threat, welcome and diffuse rumors, spread anxiety to those around them, and thereby push people to extreme decisions" [77].

This was due to the fact that they became frightened before men did, not because of some psychological predisposition, but for objective reasons: they were directly concerned by the absence of foodstuffs and the insecurity of their children's future; with husbands far from their hometowns, wives and children found themselves defenseless, their lives endangered. They were thus the first people touched by the potential consequences of rumors at that time. This is also the case of twentieth century rumors: in France, aside from the classic rumor about the white slave trade, one cannot but be struck by the number of rumors announcing threats to children. Whatever their meaning may be, these rumors naturally concern women. But the question must also be turned around: aren't many rumors about missing children and girls set going by women themselves, by feminine fantasies reflecting a high level of anxiety? Responsible for life and its renewal, do they perhaps feel more exposed to the risks of our era than men?

Etymology provides a second possible way of understanding the association between women and rumors. *Commérage* ("gossip" in French) comes from *commater* (godmother). Replaced by the word *"marraine"* ("godmother"), the former term has kept the meaning "gossip": discussion about the private lives of townspeople. The English word "gossip" has the very same roots: "god-sib", i.e., godmother [225]. The drift that has taken place in meaning perhaps derives from the fact that the close affective bond with one's children's godmother authorized a certain openness with her about one's own feelings about the life of the village or group. English etymologists explain this drift by the discussions amongst women assembled at a relative's house where a baby was about to be born. Even if this etymological explanation were correct, it would not explain the pejorative connotation that the word has acquired. Must one read therein a bothered reaction on the part of men? Indeed, gossip among women was the visible sign of their solidarity: to speak is to speak with others. Were patriarchal societies perhaps irritated by this solidarity? They had, in fact, carefully excluded women from all public activities: they had no formal right to discuss their town's business. Through gossip they appropriated the rights men refused to grant them, talking not only about the town's business, but about its seamier side as well. Deprived of public life, they made private life public. A lasting habit may have stemmed therefrom, due historically to their exclusion from public life by men [183]. The exclusion also gave them less experience of town affairs. Noticing, for example, that in Orléans in 1969, men were unconvinced by the white slave trade rumor, E. Morin attributed their disbelief to the effect of experience mentioned earlier in this book: "Men's tendency to verify stems less from more critical spirit than from their ease in operating in the town (e.g., going to the police commissioner to verify things)" [186].

The Role of the Intelligentsia

Studies done on the extraordinary circulation of the "Villejuif" flyer revealed that out of one hundred general practitioners who read the flyer, eighty did nothing to verify the information contained therein [144]. As for the others, they essentially contacted colleagues or consulted articles in journals. Of the same hundred doctors, half of them believed that the information was authentic while the other half had "reservations" about it. It is thus not surprising that it was posted in certain doctors' waiting rooms, hospitals, and social medicine centers, or that it was actively distributed by nurses, medical interns, and pharmacy students. In a book on "everything you need to know about cancer" for a general reading public, the doctor-author even reproduced the list without taking any precautions whatsoever!

In Orléans, investigators were struck by the fact that teachers either did nothing about the rumor or in fact helped spread it. The teachers' union (the FEN) published a simple statement. Most teachers did nothing, professors at the nearby university stayed out of the picture, and the teachers in boarding schools contributed to the rumor by their repeated warnings.

Thus we have here two cases of "false" rumors, and two cases in which intellectuals did nothing. The same is generally true of notables: important towns' figures. When an Orléans-type rumor sprang up in November 1974 in Chalon-sur-Saône, the notables remained silent. As long as the rumor only accused a clothing store, or later a number of such stores, run exclusively by Jews, the notables didn't budge (*L'Express Rhône-Alps*, January 1975). Neither the mayor nor his deputy took a stand. The police commissioner hid behind the hierarchy, refusing to make any kind of official declaration. This strange neutrality on the part of the town's officials fed the rumor. The judicial system confined itself to stating that a file had been opened because of an official complaint registered by Mrs. X.

Retrospectively, a question always comes up: how could cultured, reasonable people believe such rumors? The editor-in-chief of the very serious newspaper, *Le Monde,* Pierre Vianson-Ponté described his astonishment on one occasion: "One would be tempted to believe that the crudely false rumor and mysterious explanation ... were given no credence by people who are supposedly aware of the mechanisms and processes of national life, and who keep more or less abreast of public debate. But that was not at all the case." (*Le Monde,* September 28, 1987). The paradox does not, in reality, lie in the intelligentsia's inadequate behavior, but rather in the question itself and its presuppositions. The question is based on two tenacious myths: that there are beings endowed with pure intelligence, and that a "false" rumor can be detected as such by the naked eye: "Its absolutely absurd nature should have tipped people off," as Morin says.

Every rumor proves that individual coherence is a myth: we expect people to always have the same attitudes, regardless of circumstances. But every rumor creates a specific situation defined by its content, implications, the time at which it arises, and the relays that spread it. Every situation calls forth a different facet of ourselves.

A member of the intelligentsia does not belong to that group alone; he may also be part of a sports club, or of an ecological or political group; he may be a parent; his experience varies according to the field in question. In Orléans, the rumor's anti-Semitic facet should have tipped off the intelligentsia, but it also played on its political leanings. The teachers could only find normal a rumor that confirmed what they already thought, i.e., that the town's notables—

accomplices in the trade (this being attested to by their silence)—were rotten to the core, as was the political regime in general at the time. In the case of the "Villejuif" flyer, teachers had no reason to be shocked by the ideas underlying the rumor: big businesses and monopolistic trusts place profits ahead of the health of the French in their priorities. Similarly, general practitioners, before counting as people endowed with the faculties of reason and all-purpose skepticism, are first and foremost conformists. They belong to an extremely coherent and united reference group. They are not isolated beings, but rather members of an order. Why would they throw into question a sheet of paper on which the name of a well-reputed hospital appears?

In addition, the absurd character of a rumor is often no more obvious to the intelligentsia than to the wider public. The intelligentsia has an increasingly abstract knowledge of the world around us, and a partial vision of it. The Enlightenment era characterized by lucidity and skepticism has long since ended: education now consists in the transmission of knowledge and certainties. Now, as Morin says [186, p. 86], "education itself becomes an undercultivated element in and about the modern world. . . . The white slave trade is a phenomenon that is as mysterious and mythological to teachers as it is to their students." The same could be said about the reality of the leaflet on food additives. And of general practitioners. Though they are expected to know everything, they clearly cannot. Surveys show that their views on most subjects are the same as those of the public at large.

Lastly, and paradoxically, one can sustain that it is of the very nature of the intelligentsia to believe certain rumors. In every country, the closer one is to power, the more one knows that reality as announced to the public can differ from the truth. In order not to die stupid, one must listen to rumors, those that tell us what truths lie hidden behind appearances, official statements, or silence. In the classic study done on the credibility of rumors in the USSR [23], 95 percent of the intelligentsia, as compared to but 56 percent of the peasants questioned, said that rumors were more reliable than the information transmitted by the official media.

It is worth noting that people's opinions about the reliability of rumors did not depend on their attitudes towards the Soviet regime. People's answers were analyzed according to whether they were for or against the current regime in the USSR. As the following table shows, similar figures were found in both cases.

The study also revealed that the use of rumors varied in accordance with socioprofessional categories. Peasants were the least inclined to consider rumors reliable, but they used them the most. In their minds, rumors are a substitute for official media as the latter are inaccessible to them. On the contrary, the intelligentsia relies a great deal on official media, but needs rumors to counterbalance them. In their minds, rumors are a corrective: they allow one to intelligently read and listen to official information transmitted by *Pravda* and television. What's more, to prove that one belongs to the class nearest power, one must show that one has information before others do. Spreading rumors shows our public that we know things before it does. The conclusions of this study can also be applied to India, France as a whole, Paris, or any small city. *The intelligentsia needs rumors to keep its distance from the mass media, thereby proving that it is not the public at large.*

TABLE 6.1
The Credibility of Rumors in Russia

Percentage of people interviewed who agreed with the following statement, "To my mind, rumors are more reliable than the official media," broken down into social group and their position concerning the political regime.

Opinion Group	Generally against the regime	Generally in favor of the regime
Intelligentsia	94%	96%
White-collar workers	87%	83%
Blue-collar workers	69%	74%
Farmers	58%	54%

(From R. Bauer, D. Gleicher, *The Public Opinion Quarterly* [23])

Why No One Verifies

The problem raised by the intelligentsia's attitude towards certain rumors is part and parcel of a more all-encompassing problem. Generally speaking, very few people verify the stories they hear from others. Of all the roles adopted during a rumor's lifetime, the role the least in demand is that of the verifier. We believe or reject rumors at people's word.

Journalists are always flabbergasted and shocked by the lack of interest people display in verifying rumors, whatever their social stratum. In a journalist's profession, the least one can ask is that the authenticity of what will be transmitted to thousands of people be checked. As Lacouture rightly reminds us [158], a journalist's job consists less in relating the birth and death of kings than in mediatizing, rejecting, or authentifying rumors that precipitate, surround, deform, or follow their births and deaths.

The very fact that it is necessary to inculcate in future reporters the immediate reflex of checking their sources shows that it is not in the least automatic. Why is it thus so normal for no one—or almost no one—to verify rumors?

An explanatory lead is suggested by the cases in which rumors are always verified: *when one must act* on the basis of hearsay and *there is a risk that one might be mistaken.* When military, stock market or OTB decision making is at issue, rumors must be checked: the stakes are too high. A businessman who hears by rumor that one of his suppliers is having problems will carefully seek information before signing any further supply contracts with him. When one can act without taking risks, the need to check disappears: e.g., race riots are sparked off when one community hears rumors of atrocities that have supposedly been committed by the other community. The fact of being in a crowd gives one a feeling of invincibility, i.e., the sense that all risks have fallen away. Moreover, a crowd assembles in order to act, awaiting a sign of any kind to begin hostilities [171 and 190].

Many rumors do not call for immediate action on our part. As we do not have to make a decision, the motor force needed for a verificatory inquiry is lacking. Only professional skeptics (e.g., journalists) or those who would potentially be hurt by the rumors make some personal effort to verify them.

To say that the public at large does not check would be erroneous. Individuals certainly do not personally verify, proceeding instead by intermediaries. Indeed, rumors come to their ears with the best proof they could possibly ask for: that of irrefutable direct testimony ("according to the head of the hospital where he was operated on" or "according to an office worker at the city hall where the investigation was carried out ... ").

While rumors may not have precise sources, referring instead to hearsay, the group is delegated the task of verification. In effect, one finds that the more a rumor is transmitted, the more convincing it becomes. So many people cannot be wrong: rumors acquire their credibility from our confidence in a mechanism of information-related *natural selection.* Were the rumor false, it wouldn't have gotten beyond the innumerable other people—like us but who came before us—who heard it. Individuals base the attitudes they adopt towards rumors and their truth-value on other people's behavior.

The group is thus assumed to have filtered the rumor *before* it reaches us. Moreover, telling rumors to those around us also amounts to verifying them: we rely on those who hear them *after* us to corroborate or question them. On the whole, it is normal for us not to check the narratives we hear; a set of natural processes is supposed to separate the wheat from the chaff for us. Furthermore, to check them oneself would require two conditions that are often absent in the case of rumors: the *ability* and *desire to do so.*

Hearsay is unofficial information that is often bothersome when publicly made known: hence its surreptitious circulation. In the case of slander, for example, it would be indiscreet to address the person at stake, especially if he or she enjoys a certain amount of prestige. Mentioning the rumor gives others a negative image of oneself. Instead of treating the rumor with disdain, speaking seriously of the rumor suggests that one is unsure about it. In his recent book [174], the former minister of the interior, R. Marcellin, shows that—due to such considerations and the delicate nature of the process— President Georges Pompidou was unaware for eight full days of the "slanderous declarations made by a convict at the Fresnes prison, while they were known to the Prime Minister, the Minister of the Interior and the prefect of police."

All questions related to nonverification are based upon the assumption that those who hear rumors have a natural desire to verify them. Nothing could be more open to doubt. A rumor's power often resides in the fact that it conveys information that justifies one's intuition or fulfills a barely formulated wish. Its information sounds sweet to our ears. To set out to verify would be masochistic: it could in effect lead to dissonant information. Anxiousness to believe precludes verification.

On the other hand, a rumor is repeated in its early stages less because people believe it than for the fun of it, i.e., for the surprise and excitement that accompany it. It is entertaining and provides an opportunity for several people to share a juicy bit of information. Why put an end to such pleasure? Let it be said in passing that, while related at the outset without much conviction, the rumor surreptitiously acquires credibility by the very effect of numbers. Once it reaches that stage, one is no more inclined to check it than at the outset, but for different reasons.

The frequent absence of a desire to verify is not entirely due to the psychological factors mentioned above, but also to rumors' contribution to social cohesion. Indeed rumors are a collective phenomenon that does not involve thousands of isolated individuals, but rather the group. *To believe a rumor is to manifest one's allegiance to the group's voice,* i.e., to collective opinion. Rumors provide a group with the opportunity to stand up and be counted, and to express itself; in general that takes place at the expense of another group which is taken as a scapegoat. Group identity is more easily built up through the unanimous designation of a common enemy. In the example of the low-rent housing project, discussed earlier in this chapter, the cohesion of the tenants came about at the expense of one individual who was suspected to be a dangerous, subversive agent. In such a context, it was out of the question to suggest that the accusation be verified; that might have troubled the social order which had finally come into being. That is why, in the life of businesses, political groups, unions, villages and collectivities of all types, the people who try to check a rumor's source are few and far between. In small groups, such an attempt would be tantamount to throwing into question one's partners' views and thus to disrupt unity: skeptics are dissidents.

7

The End of Rumors
and the Meaning of Silence

Introduction

Every rumor is destined to die out some day. The common terms used to talk about the end of rumors are very revealing: one speaks of the "death" of a rumor, of "killing" it, "snuffing it out," and "hushing it up." These expressions manifest a will, that we have already come across in the course of this book, to make rumors into living things with a life of their own: wild beasts that are most often taken to be dangerous. In doing so, the public dissociates itself from rumors, making an external thing of them, allowing it, after the fact, to present oneself as the victim of a force that has come from outside. This explains why the questions usually raised about rumors are generally of the magical sort: how does this mysterious, ungraspable being disappear?

Necessarily Ephemeral

In reality there is nothing magic about a rumor's end. It is structural and thus necessitated right from the outset: rumors exhaust themselves in their life cycle. They create the mainsprings of their own disappearance.

A Fleeting Interest

Most rumors are first and foremost entertaining: they keep the conversation rolling, obliterate boredom and vacuousness. When a rumor's content doesn't strike very close to home, its lifetime is no longer than that of odd news items one finds in the papers. In that sense, rumors enjoy the same interest cycle as any other daily newspaper news. After having made the front page for a few

107

days, it soon slips onto the inside pages, eventually fading into the anonymity of the news in brief columns in the back pages.

Rumors, like giant pieces of collective chewing gum, inevitably lose their flavor and must be replaced by other rumors that are just as pleasing, keep people's mouths just as busy, and are thus just as ephemeral. They are swept away by the news that rains down everyday in the media, or by fresher, livelier, concurrent rumors.

The public's loss of interest does not mean that they no longer believe a rumor; people have simply stopped talking about it, moving on to other news. This explains why denials are often unnoticed. When people are questioned later, having had the feeling that a rumor was never denied, they deduce that it must have been founded!

Self-dissipating Exaggeration

Exaggeration is common when it comes to rumors. It is not some kind of pathological or aberrant phenomenon, but rather a logical consequence of communication. Rumors can be viewed as a process of commodity exchange. In the rumor process, once information is shared among too many people, its value seriously diminishes, and the rumor thus stops short. *The end of a rumor* does not mean disbelief: it means silence. People have ceased their exchange behavior as concerns this particular information commodity. Shared by all members of the group to whom the information is relevant, the information has no residual value to sustain its exchange. The sudden death of a rumor is a logical consequence of its speed and of its becoming public, i.e., less and less scarce.

Snowballing is the only way for a rumor to last. It is a necessary condition of rumor persistence. Indeed, identical repetition kills the news value of all information. Were a rumor to be repeated word for word, without any modification whatsoever, throughout its diffusion process, its death would be thereby accelerated. If everyone's friends have already heard it, or everyone imagines that they have, nobody would then dare speak of it again: for there would be a high risk of receiving no reward, or worse, of receiving negative reinforcement (e.g., others believing one to be in one's dotage).

On the contrary, the permanent addition of new details, systematic inflation of figures (at the outset, one dead man; then five, then one hundred, etc.), amplification and exaggeration are value-boosting devices. They make possible the continuation of communication within a group. Snowballing is not some innate or odd trait rumors have: a rumor, i.e., a contagious process of information exchange, would not last long without this value-adding process.

Exaggeration is just as likely to be found in news-in-brief columns in the papers and in the growing number of films about catastrophes. To hold readers' interest in a subject, every editor-in-chief knows that he must always pepper it with something new and gratifying. Once the effect of surprise has been taken as far as it can go, declining interest requires a shot of excitement.

When a rumor defends a particular hypothesis, it reorganizes the world: the least little fact becomes a clue, and the slightest clue turns into proof. In its attempt to account for all the facts, including the denials, the construction scaffolded by the group becomes exaggerated and as fragile as a house of cards. Thus in the example of the rumor about Paul McCartney's death, the explanatory inflation necessarily came to a dead end and lost credibility. Similarly, in Orléans the rumor tried to incorporate the counter-rumor: the press, authorities, police, bishop, and political parties were all said to have been bribed! This all-encompassing conspiracy theory became unbelievable.

The notion of exaggeration is, nevertheless, terribly subjective. No rumor is exaggerated for he who fears the worst. After the explosion of the atom bomb in Hiroshima on August 6, 1945, as Japan was subjected to censorship, the most outrageous rumors began going around about what was to be expected from American bombers: Japan was probably going to be sunk into the Pacific Ocean. In highly tense emotional situations, exaggeration is not a fortuitous event: it is the very product of tense climates.

Until the threat ceases to be a motive, rumors which articulate and validate the threat will be believed and communicated without question. There is a necessary balance between the amount of anxiety and threat, and the sensational character of a rumor.

Many rumors—said to be unbelievable—are believed precisely because the receivers are very tense. The time is thus not propitious for Platonic reflection about the reality of reality. When the tension drops off, certain of our critical faculties return and we perceive the rumor's fragile nature. Crowds provide an illustration of this point. Crowd situations are highly rumor-prone: people's proximity facilitates the circulation of rumors, and excitement makes us accept without objection the most astonishing of rumors that have no chance of seeming plausible the next day, once tension has subsided.

The Context Changes

A rumor constitutes testimony concerning a certain context; if the latter changes, the rumor loses its *raison d'être* and immediately ceases. It no longer has any relevance. In 1982, for example, a whole slew of rumors was set off by hidden barrels of chemicals from Seveso, Italy. When it was learned that barrels containing a terribly toxic gas made by the Hoffman-Laroche plant were hidden somewhere in France, a whole wave of local mini-rumors rolled in: every vaguely suspicious warehouse gave rise to the worst fears on the part of those living in peaceful nearby villages. Then when the barrels were relocated, the rumors' content changed: liberated opinion sought a scapegoat. Rumor thus suspected the minister of the environment of having been long since forewarned by a German colleague. One thing was certain: when the barrels left France, the imagined threat was expulsed and the rumors stopped short.

The French were very concerned about what they were eating in the 1970s: the country reacted to the slightest mention of carcinogens contained in consumer goods. Since that time the French public has changed; whether due to fatalism or realism, people now realize that the time when there were real goats in real meadows has long since past, incompatible, as it was, with low-cost mass production. Now there are less new rumors about carcinogenic products.

In the United States, racial rumors going around big cities ceased after the assassination of Dr. Martin Luther King, Jr., the renowned black pacifist. In the new climate of sadness and sympathy, the time for animosity had drawn to a close. In every country, on the contrary, the closer elections draw, the more the prevailing climate becomes tense and the rumors grow hostile. When the vote is over, hostility loses its *raison d'être*. Having become inappropriate, the rumors disappear.

When Rumors Persist

Certain rumors seem, however, to defy time's corrosive action. This can be explained by the fact that these rumors keep finding new publics who discover them for their first time, thinking that they've put their finger on ultra-recent, certified news.

The persistence of a rumor about a French female pop singer, Sheila (suggesting that she is a man), is based on the same dynamic: every year, there is a new freshman class in medical schools. The new students learn from the upperclassmen the exemplary stories that found the group's identity. To believe this rumor is to become part of the group. Moreover, besides for the fact that it is presented by "those in the know" (the upperclassmen), the rumor is also supposed to come straight from a big boss—a specialist in sexual operations—who spoke about it in private with someone. Unlike the "Ville-juif" leaflet, where the first people affected are no longer afraid of finding poisons everywhere, the rumor about Sheila is believed to be true by the upperclassmen. Thus the freshmen receive positive reinforcement when they seek information from their elders. The rumor should nevertheless eventually die out, as the pop star from the sixties is no longer a star or an exemplary figure for new medical students: in order to remain "exemplary," this exemplary story has found other more contemporary stars, with more up-to-date problems (e.g., AIDS).

Clumsy reactions to rumors can also make them longer lasting. In October 1979, a newspaper, *Le Canard enchaîné,* disclosed information that sparked off many rumors about President Bokassa's diamonds. The attack was earnest, cutting, and precise—just the kind of rumors that could trouble public opinion. President Giscard d'Estaing, said by the rumor to have received these diamonds, made the situation ambiguous by not reacting right away, whereas people's still hesitant, not yet formed doubts would have dissipated with a few precise, well-timed words. An ambiguous situation is a trampoline for rumors—the very vitamins of their persistence.

The mayor of the small city of Lorient, France, also transformed what was mere talk into a veritable rumor. When in September 1984, talk was going around of a massive influx of immigrants (a thousand according to certain people) to be housed in the town, the mayor remained silent or reacted ironically. Thus at the city council meeting on October 4, he answered allegations of immigrants coming in the following terms: "Immigrants will arrive from all the big cities, and why not from Senegal as well?" (*Liberté du Morbihan,* November 17, 1984). Given such a touchy subject, no more was required to provide the rumor's impetus, whose persistence led the mayor to organize an extraordinary press conference on November 16 to try to deal the rumor a knockout blow.

At some point the public loses interest and the rumor gives way to silence. But let it be pointed out—to avoid falling into error—that the end of the explicit excitement seen in collective discussions does not mean that the subject has been forgotten, or that the underlying tension has disappeared.

After the Rumor

What happens after a rumor passes holds little interest for people. Everything seems to return to normal; life goes on as before. A storm has passed through, but with the return of clear skies, all is forgotten, nothing happened. The rumor? What rumor? This is true for the majority of rumors, as they are ephemeral bursts in the group or mere distractions in everyday life. On the other hand, in cases where tension is high and passions are at the breaking point, it seems illusory to think that no trace or residue will remain. The silence that settles back in after such a rumor has passed through can be misleading. On the face of things, after an earthquake, each person returns to his former position; further below, considerable masses have been displaced, and a new, provisional balance has been established. As long as underground tensions are present, on some unforeseeable day a further upheaval will take place. Similarly, when the retort silences the rumor, it wins a battle against speaking, but does that make it master of the ground?

Generally speaking, what happens after a rumor passes raises the question of the meaning of silence. Are people no longer speaking because they no longer believe the rumor to be true, or rather because they believe it, but it is no longer kindly taken to speak about it, or lastly because, as they believe it, there is no longer any reason to talk about it? Each of these hypotheses traces out an entirely different after-rumor ground. As the manager of one of the brands attacked by the "Villejuif" leaflet remarked: "When the volume of upset letterwriters decreases, is that a good sign? Does that mean that the rumor has slacked off or merely that questions have died down because they have been replaced by the conviction that the rumor is founded?"

The following dialogue concerning the rumor of white slave trade is exemplary in this respect:

1. If the story of the white slave trade was trumped up, then why all the noise about it?
2. The papers have to try to sell, and business has got to go forward.
3. It was in fact the Jews who created it, to focus media attention on them.

Thus stereotypes are always reinforced by rumors. Whatever the rumor's outcome, the old stereotype of the "merchant who'll do anything to make money" walks triumphant out of the smoke.

This phenomenon is not characteristic of rumors alone, but they perhaps show the bare bones of this structure with the greatest acuity. As mentioned above, human beings have within themselves a fantastic psychological mechanism for stabilizing their environments. Once our first impressions of a person, group, or country are formed, they exert a structuring and selective effect on our evaluation of subsequent facts. In short, the facts that are coherent with these impressions are considered accurate, while those which seem to contradict them are taken as anomalous. When Talleyrand said "Beware of your first impressions: there is truth in them," he was speaking, unbeknownst to him, of their structuring effects.

Thanks to selective perception, we manage to make a stable environment of one which is in no way stable. Once we have labelled a person or group, we are struck by the accuracy of our first evaluation; in reality we are victims of our own psychological mechanisms. It is in this sense that, regardless of the number of races he won, the bicyclist Raymond Poulidor eternally remained number two in people's minds. Stereotypes always find grist for their mills.

8

The Eternal Return?

Introduction

In March 1985, the main town in the Vendée region in France, La Roche-sur-Yon, was topsy-turvy. Everyone was talking about a rumor, the prefect of police was worried, the public prosecutor was investigating, and the police were overwhelmed by telephone calls: a store, "la Boutique mauve" located on the outskirts of the downtown area, was under attack. The basic version was simple. The reader will recall the scenario published sixteen years earlier by the magazine, *Noir et Blanc*, in their May 6–14, 1969, issue, upon which the Orléans rumor had already been modeled.

The socialist mayor of La Roche-sur-Yon, Jacques Auxiette, accused the opposition party of having created this rumor from scratch in order to stir up trouble for the socialists, playing on people's extreme sensitivity about insecurity and immigration. (*Le Matin*, March 29, 1985). That may have been the case, but one should realize that this exemplary story went around Toulouse, Arras, Lille, Valenciennes, Strasbourg, Chalon-sur-Saône, Dinan, Laval, and other cities as well. In Paris, talk went around concerning the garment districts (rue de la Chaussée-d'Antin, rue Tronchet, and the boulevard Saint-Michel) and the very symbol of popular clothing stores: Tati. Moreover, Orléans was in no way the point of departure for this rumor. The scenario took place in 1966 in Rouen, according to the very terms of the narrative published by *Noir et Blanc* three years earlier, as well as in the city of Mans in 1968.

If we look back in time we find that the sexual symbolism of the needle prick that changes these ready-to-wear shops into ready-to-exploit shops is not recent. In December 1922, an epidemic of such pricks suddenly broke out in Paris: "In the Printemps department store, women—customers, salesgirls, etc.—felt they had been pricked by mysterious maniacs. The number of people pricked, almost all of whom were women, immediately took on considerable proportions in tramways, city buses, the subway, and so on" [117]. The author of this narrative recalls, moreover, that a similar pricking epidemic made quite a stir in Paris in 1820.

Such facts suggest that a good rumor never dies. It temporarily quiets down and, like a volcano, reawakens at some later date. But in addition, certain rumors have the ability to move around: no one knows where they will turn up next in an identical or similar guise. How can this phenomenon be explained?

How We Remember Rumors

In April 1984, in the town of Loyettes in the Ain region in France, a rumor accused one of the town's inhabitants of having assassinated a high school girl who had been missing for a few days. Interviewed on this subject, the woman proprietor of a coffee and stationary shop said, "So it's like the Orléans rumor. But over there it *was true*. The girls were chloroformed. It was all over the papers." In August 1986, I interviewed a young couple from Laval. One of their statements is worth repeating here: "Oh yeah, the Orléans rumor. Come to think of it, no one ever found out if it was true or false, that story about the girls who were kidnapped. Do you know?"

These two statements are exemplary. They shed light on the role of memory [122]. The judgments made about a rumor sixteen years later depend on information still available in people's memories when they think about it. In itself, the coffee shop owner's statement can stem from one of the following processes:

1. At the time (1969), she had interpreted the media's action as attesting to the rumor's truth. In 1984, she still remembered her interpretation (that the rumor was true), faithfully stored in her long-term memory.
2. At the time, she had noticed the media campaign and heard that the rumor was doubtful. But over time, the latter bit of information was forgotten, the only thing remaining being the narrative (the chloroformed girls) and its effects (that it had been in the papers). Naturally, the woman interviewed imputed these real effects to the sole logical explanation that could come to mind today: it was true—they had been chloroformed!

The second statement illustrates the long-term effect of not coming across denials. For those interviewed, having no more information in mind, doubt was possible. This clearly demonstrates that the label "rumor" does not overturn a proposition. As the concept "rumor" has a variable and more or less extensive or definite meaning, it leaves the way open to all kinds of interpretations. Now the great "false" rumors are passed on to posterity in the form of a *neutral* telex: the Villejuif leaflet, the Orléans rumor, the Marie Besnard affair, and so on. The labels, stored in our memories, say nothing explicit about the rumors' groundlessness. One should not be surprised if, related a few years later in another place, these stories provide a plausible scenario for a fresh local explosion.

The Reproduction of Symptoms

Rumors, let us recall, are not magical events. We often unconsciously consider them like subjects, exogeneous beings mysteriously arising here or there like a goblin or some kind of comet. In reality, rumors are objects, results, or mental productions: a group's members "rumor" at a certain moment, in a certain place, and generate a content, narrative or hypothesis.

The typology of rumors led to the distinction of several typical situations that are propitious to the production of rumors: (1) when signs whose meaning is well known are uncovered by front-runners or insiders who hurriedly speak about it in private; (2) when ambiguous events create an unsatisfied demand for answers; (3) when a highly sensitive social body spontaneously speaks up to express itself in isolation from any particular event.

The first case is that, for example, of rumors about currency exchange rates. Certain indexes have, over time, been found to be reliable indicators of probable change in relative currency values. Thus we witness the cyclical reappearance of rumors about the devaluation of the French franc, more or less encouraged, moreover, by those who see in the rumors irrefutable evidence of the current government's useless attempts to manage the economy. The return of rumors of this first type is essentially due to exogenous factors: indexes waiver, and everyone knows what that means, even if officially nothing has been announced. Same symptoms, same diagnosis.

The second case is that of ambiguous situations leading the group to raise questions. Lacking a precise knowledge of facts, reality and truth will be defined by unanimity. Throughout the eighteenth century, for example, the French people had to deal with serious famines: in 1725–26, 1738–41, 1747, 1751–52, 1765–70 and 1771–75 [146]. Few items were in as scarce supply as bread: grain supplies practically founded the tacit contract between the people and their king. In their eyes, the king was the last-resort baker, committed to ensuring the people's subsistence. In October 1789, when the women of Paris marched to the Versailles palace, it was to seek out the baker (the king), the woman baker (the queen), and the baker's boy (the dauphin).

Beginning with the 1725–26 crisis, the people began wondering about the reality of the famine: the conviction arose that dark machinations were behind the shortages. There was a plot to starve the population, not involving the king himself—whose inexhaustible beneficence was never questioned—but, unbeknownst to him, his ministers, their local agents, bakers, and secret allies of the conspiracy. This explanatory scenario was identically reproduced during the six great famines that ravaged France. During each subsistence crisis, rumors pointed the finger at some frightful conspiracy [162].

The reappearance of the same rumors, when public opinion is confronted with the same ambiguous and life-threatening circumstances, can be explained in two different ways:

1. On the one hand, memories of explanations recalled from the preceding crisis are fertile ground for rumors seeking to account for the current one. Memory is a temporal bridge that provides hypotheses and scenarios to a public opinion in search of explanations.
2. The preceding explanation does not account for the first rumor, which served as a model for the following rumors thanks to memory. Should one want to include this first rumor in the explanation of the eternal return of the "famine conspiracy," one must observe that people seemed "constrained to understand the order of things in these terms. The repetition of the same model of perception and evaluation of concrete crises, each of which had its own peculiarities, allows ones to assume that belief in a famine conspiracy pre-exists in collective mental structures" [146]. Nothing here would be left to chance. According to public opinion, nothing happens that does not stem from a duly mediated and controlled will [110].

A rumor's eternal return thus attests to the realization, on the basis of propitious events, of an explanatory system deeply embedded in collective consciousness. The theme of the famine conspiracy has not, moreover, altogether disappeared from our mentality: it has simply shifted from wheat, of which the West produces a surplus, to raw materials. Thus more recently, when gas ran short in Europe and the United States, many people felt sure that the shortage was trumped up, and considered OPEC to be a simple alibi used by the oil companies.

The Permanence of the Problem

One type of rumor does not derive from ambiguous facts: it creates and shapes them. By careful, circular reasoning, a rumor thus presents itself as the ideal explanation for the clues it has itself imagined. Like all urban legends, the story of being pricked in clothing store dressing rooms is of this type. Its reproduction from one city to another, and from one time to another, cannot be explained by the reappearance of a suspicious *objective* situation (as in the first two types of rumors). It thus attests to the reappearance of an identical *subjective* situation: the social groups share to a high degree the same profound problems, anxieties, or uncertainties. These latter will be expressed through a floating myth: hypnotic seduction in eroticized places (e.g., dressing rooms, but also in gymnasiums, saunas, etc.). The return of a myth thus reflects the lasting and even ubiquitous existence of the fear it expresses.

The very word "return" is misleading when it comes to rumors: rumors don't come back like Halley's Comet, which is foreign to our planet that observes it like a spectator. In reality, fears, diffuse anxiety and frustration have never left the social body: it is simply that their expression has been repressed, channeled and legitimated. These latter are embodied in rampant talk that, under favorable conditions, can become rumors. Talk targets the places, sites or people who can propitiously incarnate the myth: the prototype being a store that promotes new lifestyles and is run by a "foreigner."

The repeated appearance of rumors is due to fortuitous conjunctural factors that release the usual control, repression and channeling mechanisms. What is latent is no longer inhibited: it expresses itself. The return of the rumor is an indicator of the permanence of the city, social group, or country's problem. It is like the episodic resurgence of an underground water supply where fissures allow it to spurt up to the surface.

The Reproduction of Situations

Certain rumors are modern forms of legends. In November 1938, for example, before World War II but after Munich (September 1938, where British and French prime ministers met Hitler and believed there would be no war) the following story was often told [39]:

> In November 1938, a man was driving his car. He was stopped on the road by a guy looking like a poet or vagabond who he took for a hitchhiker. The guy said, "Hitler will die on December 8th, 1938." He added, 'I'll prove to you that what I have said is true. Something will happen to you: on the road to Blois, you will give someone a lift and he will be dead when you get to . . . .' And in fact, the driver came upon a car accident. Someone had been wounded and had to be immediately taken to the hospital. At the precise spot predicted, the driver turned around and saw that the wounded man was dead.

This story goes by the name of "The Cadaver in the Car." It has a variant in which the poet-vagabond predicts exactly how much change the driver has in his change-purse and receives money from him. Now, curiously enough, these narratives were circulating in France, Great Britain, the Benelux countries, South Africa, the United States, and in Germany as well (though Hitler was replaced there by an allied leader). One might think that its ubiquity was due to communication and the efficiency of the postal system. According to Bonaparte, the fact that the tale of the cadaver in the car reproduces the tale of the cadaver in the carriage, going around in 1914, authorizes us to think that the legend was spontaneously refabricated.

In effect, these two tales present, in the innocent guise of a news item, the very structure of magical rituals in archaic societies. In both cases, an ardently wished for death is brought about, in one case by means of a human sacrifice, in the other by the offering of a substitute. For the archaic myth to resurface, there must be stressful conditions akin to those of wartime. These conditions engender processes of regression, thus liberating the eternal themes that thousands of years of Christianity and civilization have not managed to suppress. These conditions were present in 1914 and 1938, in France and Pretoria, London and Düsseldorf. Thus "myths fade like flowers, only to be born elsewhere under the same seasonal and climatic conditions" [40].

Universal Themes

One could find plenty of other cases of the return of the same myths, incarnated in the form of rumors. The bromide myth, for example, runs through all barracks, high schools and boarding schools. Adolescents thereby express their anxiety and uncertainty about their confined sexuality and project onto outside forces—authorities and their bromide power—all responsibility in the event of a fiasco when they have permission to leave the premises.

Since 1982 in France, many people have set about frantically cutting out the electronically read bar codes that are now printed on the packages of all foods. Rumor had it that collecting five thousand such codes starting with the number three would win one a free wheelchair. In different versions, the number of labels varies as well as the number with which the codes have to begin. The rumor in fact stems from the lightening-fast generalization in the whole of France of a lottery that was never intended to concern any more than a certain parish in Corsica. Thus collectors on the French mainland tried in vain to find out to whom they had to send their mountains of bar codes.

The rumor's success was not surprising. Back in 1963, an identical rumor had gone around: one had to collect empty Gitanes cigarette packs in order to win a wheelchair for a handicapped person. The bar codes in reality only extended the paradigmatic class of currencies: capsules, cigar bands, and Gitanes packs. What they have in common seems to be the idea that a fraction of a company's indirect taxes could be diverted to 4haritable works (M.-L. Rouquette, personal communication, June 14, 1985). It is true that certain indirect taxes (among them from the sale of car stickers) had been created in France to finance certain specific foundations (e.g., aid for the elderly). People soon realized that it is was nothing of the sort, as the moneys collected were not specifically slated for precise uses. This eternal rumor perhaps reduced the cognitive dissonance generated by people's disappointment when they see that indirect taxes do not go where they are supposed to go.

But rumors leading people to patiently collect objects surely have some more deeply rooted source. If not, how is one to explain that children themselves adore such collections? A few years ago, for example, General Foods Corporation, producers of the famous Malabar (giant chewing gum), had a true surprise. Envelopes full of Malabar stickers were sent to them. A rumor had made its way around children's playgrounds that one had to save these stickers. Beyond a certain number, one could write to the company and request a gift in exchange.

Certain children had erected veritable winning formulas. Each Malabar sticker was labelled one to fifty-six, a number of kids had collected one sticker numbered one, two stickers numbered two, right on up to fifty-six stickers numbered fifty-six. One can imagine the safari necessary to make that kind of collection! Such children went so far as to ask General Foods for a bicycle.

Naturally the use of collections is frequent in the marketing of candy for children, but that does not explain spontaneous collecting in the absence of an official announcement by Malabar. Given children's attachment to Malabar, is it a question of a gift ritual calling for reciprocity—a counter-gift—i.e., the spontaneous reproduction of the potlatch ritual?

Another nice rumor enjoys eternal youth. In 1968, the author, then a student, had desperately sought nine other people with whom to buy the new four-horsepower Renault car on sale for about $100. They had not been sold in the United States, and Renault—a well-meaning friend had told me—was obliged to ship them back to France. The cars were thus in Le Havre harbor, but had to be purchased by groups of ten. Later the rumor concerned bulk orders of Dauphines. In 1985, a Renault executive to whom we mentioned the anecdote said he had recently received a phone call from someone who wanted to know where he had to go to buy a brand-new Renault 16 for $800 (they have not been manufactured since 1980). Such rumors are perhaps kept alive by Renault workers themselves: indeed, a rumor regularly and strangely circulates in Billancourt (site of a major Renault plant) that the famous and yet mythical four-horsepower vehicle is still being sold by the state-owned company, though it has not appeared in the catalogue since the late 1950s.

It is clearly a universal theme, that of the rare gem that has miraculously escaped the wear and tear of time. In the United States in 1968 [44], it was said that one could buy old prestigious Harley-Davidson motorbikes in new condition for but twenty-five dollars, as long as one bought a lot of fifty. In a variant of the rumor, one could buy old Ford Model-A's.

One could find many other examples of rumors springing up here and there in countries spread far and wide. This is true for all rumors about poison in new forms of food or restaurants (e.g., hamburger joints serving rats). The exemplary story about the dog (or cat) forgotten in a microwave oven is also a classic. This modern version of the "hot dog" seems to spring up everywhere one finds modern ovens. It is as though whenever new technology becomes available, someone sets about imagining the funniest or most dramatic aftermath. This oral extrapolation can very well come about identically at different moments and in different places, though in a totally spontaneous way. The common element is the new technology. In France in 1984, for example, a rumor was going around about microwave ovens. One day, while reaching into the oven to remove a dish, a homemaker saw her hand drop from her arm—cleanly cut—right before her very eyes. According to the rumor, repeatedly putting her hand in the oven to put dishes in or take them out, the homemaker had let the waves cut it off imperceptibly. This example is quite similar to that concerning contact lenses that blind.

From the White Slave Trade to the Snake in the Bananas

At times a rumor's form evolves and one might believe that it is a new, independent rumor when in fact it is still the same old thing. Thus in France in the past few years, strange animals have shown up in big department stores. In late spring of 1981, the public rose up in the Languedoc region: a child playing on a coin-operated horsey ride near the cash registers in a department store was said to have been bitten by a snake hidden in the machine (*L'Alsace*, August 1, 1982). In July 1982, the Cora supermarket near Mulhouse was, according to the rumor, the site of an atrocious accident: a child had been bitten by a snake hidden in a bunch of bananas (from Africa, obviously). In December 1983, at the Auchan supermarket in Aubagne, a little girl was said to be dead, having been bitten by a snake hidden in a teddy bear that she was touching, imported from the Far East. In Nice, it was not a snake but rather a scorpion, and elsewhere a large venomous spider. In each case, the public literally deserts the store targeted for several weeks. In Paris, in January of

1986, a young woman was said to have barely escaped death. The yucca tree she had been given seemed to come alive, every time she watered it. She called the florist and then the Museum of Natural History. A team of experts from the Museum discovered the horrible truth: in opening the tree trunk, they found a nest of mygales (*Le Journal du dimanche*, February 16, 1986).

Upon analysis, the "snake in the department store" rumor is in fact a metaphorical development of the Orléans rumor. In reality, the two tales are the expression of the same basic, latent myth that is always ready to make itself current, as the table 8.1 shows:

TABLE 8.1
The Rumor's Eternal Return

The myth's basic structure	Orléans-type variant	Typical variant: child bitten by a snake
Strangers in the group	Jews, shopkeepers	Third world immigrants, entertainers
Sexual violence	Biting, Hypodermic needles	Snakes, scorpions, spiders
Deporting	White slave trade	Death
Victims	Girls, young women	Little girls, children
The site of inescapable temptation	Fashionable clothes stores	Supermarkets, fairs
Sites of the myth's return	Dinan, Laval, Rouen (1966), Le Mans (1968), Poitiers (1969), Châtellerault (1969), Orléans (1969), Amiens (1970), Strasbourg (1971), Chalon-sur-Saône (1974), Toulouse, Tours, Limoges, Douai, Lille, Valenciennes, Paris ... Dijon (1985), La Roche-sur-Yon (1985)	Montpellier (1981), Dordogne (1981), Haute-Garonne (1981), Landes (1981), Saint-Etienne (1981), Chambéry (1982), Mulhouse (1982), Liège (1982), Nice (1983), Aubagne (1983), Avignon (1984) ... Paris (1986)

The emergence of this new variant confirms that the appearance of a Jew in the preceding version was not necessary. In fact, in several towns, the boutiques targeted were not run by Jewish shopkeepers. It seems that its appearance depends on the extent of latent anti-Semitism from one town to another. Its emergence in Orléans was not a total accident. Orléans is the major town in the Loiret region; now the Loiret is not just any region as far as

Jews are concerned. Two concentration camps, Pithiviers and Beaune-la-Rolande, had been set up there, and many of their prisoners had first been held at the prison in Orléans [38].

The Permanence of the Scapegoat

To give a complete picture, we must speak of another kind of return of rumors. The preceding examples concerned the reproduction of the same tale in different places at different times. One must also take as the return of a rumor the multiplication of different rumors bearing on one and the same object, person, or group.

The eternal return of rumors is tied to the fate of scapegoats. All societies experience their serious crises as punishment: one must thus seek out whipping boys who are unconsciously taken to be responsible for the community's sins. On the other hand, to designate a guilty party when one is confronted with an unexplainable crisis is to point to the cause of the problem, and thus take a first step towards its resolution. The potentially guilty parties are always the same: foreigners, those who are not well integrated into the collectivity, and those who do not share the latter's beliefs. In the Western world, Jews have thus been ideal scapegoats and automatic targets of rumors, from the supposed contamination of wells during the plague epidemics spreading from 1348 to 1720, right down to the underlying ritual murder in the theme of the Orléans rumor, not to mention the so-called "conspiracy of the Sages of Zion" [49,59].

Recurring rumors also deal with substances whose symbolic value makes them into automatic projective surfaces and ready-made scapegoats. Thus, well before studies began of cavities and obesity, sugar was not an ordinary foodstuff. As a symbol of oral and solitary pleasure, of a certain infantile regression and of the sin of gluttony, over the past 150 years, sugar has always been the target of rumors in medical circles. It seems that as soon as one scientific inquiry was closed due to lack of evidence, a new one was opened. Such persistence seems characteristic of a belief that one absolutely wants to validate, as if sugar upset people or stirred up some unconscious discomfort. As soon as a great fear was born, it was normal for one to view sugar as the guilty party. The contraceptive pill is another product that systematically inspires rumors. The latter arise from opinions taken up and amplified by the press, and from reports by more or less well-informed experts concerning whom it is not yet clear if it is the scientist in them that is speaking or the man who wants to teach women a lesson.

Modern Legend or Latest Version?

In the late 1960s, a number of folklorists coined the term "modern legend" to refer to recently collected stories; their sources were not a tribe's elders or peasants, but rather teenagers and college students in city bars, clubs, and so on. This sparked off intense debate over the validity of calling such stories "modern legends" or modern "urban legends" [46]. These stories are now considered [29] to be neither urban (as they also circulate in rural communities) nor modern (in most cases, one can find a historical prototype, i.e., an earlier version which has undergone cultural updating). Furthermore, due to the popular meaning of the word "legend" (something that is not to be taken as though it were true), labeling them in that way blurred their study. We prefer to call them "exemplary stories," since, like fables, their function is to set forth examples from which moral implications can be drawn. We prefer "stories" to "fables" for, in their narrative mode, they are told as stories about vicarious personal experience—something that just happened to people who are like those hearing the story.

Examining exemplary stories from a historical vantage point reveals different degrees of historical resurgence. The first case is when older narratives are simply adapted. Though taking place on modern highways and in cars, the phantom hitchhiker, for instance, already existed more than a century ago: he was not called a hitchhiker at that time, as the story took place in carriages [24,25,28,44]. The second case is that of rationalized motifs, as seen in the case of the spider boil. In this story, a girl has been vacationing in some southern land (e.g., Africa or the West Indies), and when she comes back she has a boil on her cheek. The boil swells ever larger and finally bursts one night; a lot of small spiders crawl out of the boil, covering her whole cheek. Interestingly enough, Klintberg [152] found a Gothic short story from the nineteenth century, Jeremias Gotthelf's *Die schwarze Spinne* (1842), that is set in medieval feudal community where villagers make a pact with the Devil, and a woman receives the Devil's kiss to seal the pact; when the villagers try to cheat the Devil out of his payment, a black boil starts growing on the woman's cheek. It eventually bursts, and poisonous spiders crawl out. Although the modern story is not identical to the Gothic one, the meaning of the black boil is similar. In the modern story, the girl has typically come back from vacationing in some southern land: she has met a dark southern man with whom she has had a fling. This story typically targets women traveling south on vacation who have sexual relationships with black men (the equivalent of having commerce with Satan in the feudal plot).

Klintberg mentions that the story may have cropped up around 1975 in Sweden because of real news reports about two Swedish tourists who had taken a trip to Africa [p. 280]. While sunbathing on a sandy beach, a "tumbu" fly had deposited her eggs in their skin, and boils filled with pus had soon appeared. Once back in Sweden, the boils had burst and maggots had reportedly crawled out. This event may have revived the legend, but is definitely not the original source of spider boil stories.

There are many others examples of modern stories that contain rationalized motifs from age-old supernatural tales [157]. Simpson [240] points out a parallelism between certain superstitions about witches and modern stories. In the story of the "severed fingers," a man is driving his car home at night. While waiting for a light to change, he is attacked by a gang of youths who try to flip his car over. He drives off as quickly as possible. The next day he discovers four fingers that have been amputated by the fan in the air-cooling system. Simpson reminds us that some generations ago, there was a widespread belief in rural areas that witches had the power to immobilize carts, and that "the correct counter-measure was to flog the wheels, cut notches in them, or scrape them with a knife. . . . The witch was imagined to be actually gripping the wheel invisibly and that it was her fingers that were injured" [240, p. 206].

Since it is usually possible to detect in rumor stories the updating of an age-old motif, is there really anything modern in so-called "modern legends"? It would, in fact, be overly simplistic to consider all modern stories as resurgences, disguised only by modern surface details and life-styles. Some facets of these stories have been recently created.

Exemplary stories are not created once and for all. New problems generate their own folklore. Technology, for example, is definitely the mark of our century. We live in a world of technology, though we do not really understand it. How many people really know how an engine or a telephone works? Hence the popularity of rumors depicting accidents due to modern technology: the pet in the microwave oven, the dangerous food additives, etc.

In examining rumors that have sprung up in France over the past twenty years, one can but be struck by the public's sensitivity to innovation, and in particular to technological innovation. As soon as an innovation begins to spread and be publicized, a rumor often appears that rejects this innovation. Insofar as the public always feels concerned by what truly affects it, the world of mass consumption products provides a typical example of rumor-fertile ground.

In 1984, a massive advertising campaign began promoting the first liquid clothes detergent in France, called "Vizir." A few months later it was said, "by several people who did not know each other, that the liquid detergent ate away at washing machine drums, leaving gaping holes in them. According to one person, it happened to a friend of his mother. Another said he heard it from his cousins in the provinces who were friendly with a household appliance repairman." The same rumor appeared when "Omo" detergent came out on the market many years ago: Omo was supposed to destroy fabrics and eat away at washing machines. Of the many other innovations that have been targeted by rumors, let us mention: fluoride in toothpaste, "Tefal" (Teflon) pans that don't stick, margarine, "Baranne" brand creams to polish leather, and contact lenses (which, as the rumor had it, could lead to blindness). More recently, sacrilegious products such as pastis without alcohol met the same fate: rumor held that the most famous of them, "Pacific," was carcinogenic.

Even before knowing the exact answers, rumors try to reject innovation— the intruder, foreigner, or symbol of changing habits. Rumors are one of the defense mechanisms by which certain citizens try to preserve their old habits. They proffer up "facts" that justify resistance to change and, more generally speaking, to our society governed by science and technology.

Our times are also the first to have lost control over the food creation process. In peasant societies, people knew what they were eating: they could observe the process from seed to harvest, and did their own cooking. In the age of industrialized food, there is total delegation of food creation to anonymous others. This rather new situation has spurred on a great many fast-spreading exemplary stories that are symptomatic of the latent anxiety they reveal. Furthermore, the rules governing social life have themselves evolved: it is illegal, for instance, to take the law into one's own hands, or to take revenge on someone who has committed a crime. This is a source of frustration and bottled-up aggression: hence the surge in rumor stories where the thief mutilates himself (as in the "hook" and "severed fingers" stories), or where the criminal is mutilated by an animal. Our desire for revenge is guiltlessly fulfilled therein. It is worth noticing that, in these stories, the narrative does not say that the criminal was put in jail. In the "choking Doberman" story, the narrative ends when one realizes that the dog swallowed the burglar's fingers. The inflicted pain seems to be cathartic in and of itself. Similarly, in the story of the "severed fingers," nothing is said about the street gang being imprisoned. The fantasy of revenge is sufficiently fulfilled by the rumor story [151].

These rumors are thus highly characteristic of our times, our anxieties, and our wishes. But rumor stories can be modern in yet another way: in the behavior of their actors. Ghostlore has by no means disappeared: teenage boys all know of some haunted house, lane, or cemetery [200]. These stories fulfill the role of initiation rituals, challenging, as they do, boys to dare set foot in such places. In modern stories, however, ghosts are not what they used to be. In the sixteenth century, ghosts exhibited exemplary behavior: they came back to earth to fulfill a mission or accomplish a duty. Later they confined themselves to aimlessly terrifying people during churchyard appearances. In recent stories such as the phantom hitchhiker, the ghost remains mute and unresponsive. What is really "modern" in the phantom hitchhiker story is not the story itself (there are hundreds of historical antecedents of supernatural encounters on the open road), but rather the way the main character behaves. In this specific form, the story cannot be more than a hundred years old [28].

PART II
The Interpretation of Rumors

9

The Message: Accidents and Necessities

Introduction

A classic temptation consists in making an inventory or classification of rumors' contents. Thus black rumors have been distinguished from pink ones. One of the first analysts of this phenomenon discerned three types of rumors [154]: those that mistake desires for reality (pipe-dream or wish rumors); those that express fear or anxiety (a catastrophe is about to take place—bogie rumors); and those that sow dissension by attacking certain people within a group (the wedge-driving or aggression rumors). One can also detect permanent rumor themes across the centuries. Whether it be the Middles Ages or 1990, there are nine kinds of rumors: the return of Satan; the hidden poison; the underground conspiracy to take or retake power; artificial scarcity (stockpiled wheat in the Middles Ages, and today the trumped-up oil crisis and the secret discovery of a water-powered engine); fear of strangers (e.g., anti-Semitism); kidnappings; the illnesses of princes, their love-lives, and their financial or villainous deals. We will not pursue this kind of classificatory approach here, as it is based on rumors' apparent content and not on the meaning they have for the groups in which they circulate. Let us take an example. While soldiers are returning home from combat, a rumor starts going around a division: all the soldiers from another division are said to have been killed by the enemy! At first sight, it seems to be a dramatic, pessimistic rumor. Its real function, notwithstanding, is perhaps just the opposite: in believing that another division has been annihilated, the first division considers itself lucky to have gotten off with serious casualties. Similarly, rumors that sow dissension in a group are sometimes based on fear and anxiety that find an outlet in aggression directed at a scapegoat. Can one thus truly assert that they constitute two different types? More interesting are analyses in accordance with the forms of rumors.

Three other questions arise: Why are most rumors black? Why do they often concern the best-known people? And how are rumors' messages distorted?

Forms of Rumors

Rumors reach our ears in many different forms. Some of them are very short, while others constitute veritable scenarios; some of them are very sparsely furnished while others present a true wealth of details. Regardless of their diversity, rumors, insofar as they constitute "news," always concern the very recent past and people who are still alive, and present themselves as factual. In that sense they differ from "traditional legends" that are explicitly situated in the far-off past or at some indefinite time, and stage fantastic characters who are accepted as fictional. (The term "modern legend" refers to stories told as if they were true. Because of the fabulatory connotation of the word "legend," this term is a misnomer.) They also differ from myths—as sacred history about origins—that most often concern nonhuman characters.

It is nevertheless possible to distinguish different types of rumors on the basis of a classification related to their narrative form and the extent of their characters' specificity. Certain rumors deal with a very precise person (or business), who is generally quite well known to the group in which the rumors circulate: the town mayor, a movie star, a factory owner, the local K-Mart or hairdresser, etc. Others involve an anonymous person who is, notwithstanding, generally socially and geographically situated: a high school girl, a mother with young children, a retired couple from the next town over, or an American traveling in Italy. While rather different, both of these extreme kinds of focal actors have a public: the former are the object of focal attention in their factories, streets, buildings, towns, states, or countries. People talk about them; they naturally mobilize speech. They are sources of interest, and word of mouth thus has no trouble setting rumors going: their market already exists. Anonymous characters also create the kind of audience involvement that is indispensable to a rumor's success. By their anonymity and concrete references to their age, profession, status or role, they allow for identification. The telling of what happened to them arouses vicarious participation and involvement. When something horrible has happened, the audience itself feels as though it were the victim.

Rumors can also be classified by their narrative form. On the one hand, one finds simple propositions of the following type: person (P) did something (F). A rumor is a short sentence or direct assertion: Ronald Reagan has a tumor; there are rat bones in Kentucky Fried Chicken; a young woman found a mygale in a yucca tree; girls have been disappearing in the basement of such and such a store; a sadist with a hook is running loose in the surrounding areas; an actress slept her way to the top, etc. At the other extreme, even if structurally speaking—i.e., examined with X-rays—a rumor maintains an "A did B" or "B happened to A" form, it presents itself here as a complete story endowed with a veritable scenario. Such stories are called "modern legends" by folklorists, but considering the connotations and already acquired meanings of the term "legend" (that of being a fictional narrative), we prefer to designate them with the descriptive term "exemplary story."

The structure of such exemplary stories is stable, following, as they do, a fixed sequence: introduction, setting (the everyday world), normal event sequence (ordinary people doing ordinary things: eating fried chicken, shopping, dating, traveling, driving, etc.), unusual or mysterious event (the narrative climax), and consequences of the event (the people end up in police stations, hospitals, or whatever). Told as personal experience, stories that happened to someone close to us—a FOAF (friend of a friend)—these rumors resemble fables in their ability to focus warnings and threats. They are like fables of "exemplary stories": the narrative is often concluded by a moralistic comment—"so you see, even in nice apartments you never know; even your own neighbors can turn out to be criminals"—just as in each of Aesop's fables. But whereas Aesop's fables are not told as if they were true, but rather as conveying a truth, rumor stories are told both as if they were real and exemplary.

Although classificatory schemes divide rumors into static, separate types, one should not forget that a rumor is a dynamic process: a rumor may shift over time from a structural form (a simple assertion such as "a man with a hook just escaped from a nearby prison") to a classical migratory form known as "the hook story" (see further on, p. 151). Similarly, a rumor targeting a well-known public figure may later be dissociated from him and float anonymously, only later to be reattached to someone whose public image corresponds to the plot.

Is there a link between form and rumor etiology? In chapter 2, a typology was presented that was based on the rumor process and source. Certain rumors, on the one hand, are prompted by an event whose meaning is unclear. Their public typically engages collectively in a causal attribution process: why did this happen? This generally leads to direct, incriminating assertions or innuendos concerning public figures or at least stereotypes: *A* did *B*. Over time and thanks to snowballing, the assertion becomes embedded in a plot, largely drawing on fantasy and collective unconscious schemas. After the mysterious and still unexplained disappearance of young recruits at the

Mourmelon military base in France [143], for example, rumor designated a "crazy legionnaire" who was either hiding in the nearby forest or still living on the military base. The rumor increasingly resembled the theme of horrific encounters with ogres in initiatory forests (as in *Little Red Riding Hood*).

At the other extreme, certain rumors literally create an event from scratch. Thus many stories pop up without the slightest factual basis. "Exemplary stories" are of this kind: an unnamed person is said to have found a worm in a hamburger or a mygale in a yucca tree. Since they do not need a real event or person to exist, these stories become real events by virtue of the abundance of details and the full narrative scenarios they develop. Over time, however, the "events" they describe may be causally attributed and localized. Hence a rumor will target such and such a local store where "it happened." This embedding in reality and in a specific vicinity maximizes local public involvement, persuasion, and the urgent need to pass the information on.

Why Are Rumors Black?

Most rumors announce a mishap, catastrophe, peril, or treason: rumors' dominant color is black. There are, nevertheless, pink rumors: in 1945, during World War II, rumors of the much-expected capitulation of Germany sprang up everyday; in businesses there are rumors of promotions and raises; at the stock exchange, rumors announce that stocks and bonds are on the way up. As for stars, there are plenty of rumors about marriages, engagements, and births. While any kind of accurate count would be difficult, pink rumors nonetheless seem to be in the minority. Why is that so?

A quick and practical answer would be to think of rumors exclusively as slander [112] or to postulate that the public prefers black, i.e., that it has a leaning for misfortune, catastrophe, and death. Making reference to Thanatos or the death drive is a convenient way to get out of a tight spot. In our mind, rumors' blackness is a necessity: for there to be news, there must generally be a negative element. On the other hand, blackness doesn't always mean bad news: certain accidents are wished for. Lastly, rumors' negativity is useful for the group in which they circulate. Blackness has a cathartic effect.

The Informative Value of Black

Every bit of news (i.e., every rumor) is a declaration: someone (call him P) has done, is doing or will do something (call it F). Structurally speaking, it is a proposition of the P-F kind (someone is doing something). This person can be either negative or positive: for the South Africans, "a black" is negative; for George Bush's supporters, Michael Dukakis was negative; office girls have a favorable opinion of Caroline of Monaco and Mickey Rourke. Similarly, the act (F) may be negative (dying, killing, stealing, white slave trading) or positive (helping, rescuing, marrying, etc.). Thus all information may take one of the four following forms [222, p. 58]:

TABLE 9.1
The Four Types of Information

Type	A person	Does something	Probable reactions
1	liked (+)	positive (+)	So what?
2	liked (+)	negative (-)	Is that right?
3	disliked (-)	positive (+)	Sounds fishy...
4	disliked (-)	negative (-)	I told you so!

The first type of information is not often found in conversations. This is perfectly normal as it contributes little supplementary information when compared with what one expected of the person in question. This type of information goes no further than stating that a good person did something good. It is almost a tautology, not news. It has almost no "value," and hardly risks being spread by rumors.

The second type of information is totally surprising or incongruous. It announces a break in the established order of things, shaking one's view of the world: "Our dearly loved president is secretly receiving diamonds from a bloodthirsty African emperor"; "our favorite female vocalist is not what she's cut out to be"; "a thoroughly normal college co-ed, like your own daughter, has been kidnapped"; "in a nice little yucca tree mygales were found." Such propositions are unbalanced: they combine negative and positive elements. Now unbalanced statements are the easiest to remember [202]: they surprise and mark readers and listeners. We can understand why the rumor about the real circumstances surrounding Cardinal Daniélou's death so indelibly etched itself in people's minds: it brought together the Devil and God. Contrary to what the official version sustained, the academic Cardinal Jean Daniélou did not die from a heart attack on the sidewalk of rue Dulong (in Paris), but rather in the bedroom of a young call-girl known by the name of Miss Mimi, who lived at number 56 of that same street on the fourth floor. (*Le Canard Enchaîné*, May 29, 1974). Rumor had it that his body had been found, in his "birthday suit," on the lady's bed.

Since we prefer balanced propositions, this kind of information can have two consequences when the person is very well liked: either rejection ("that's impossible—it couldn't have been him!"), or a marring of the person in question's image, which thus becomes negative. Nevertheless, the incongruity is such that the information has, at the outset, every chance of being transmitted, if nothing else to persuade people collectively that it is impossible or, on the contrary, not impossible.

The third type of information is also an unbalanced proposition: a negatively valued person did something positive. It could be, for example, "A criminal came to the rescue of someone injured in a car accident and saved his life." This type of unbalance gives rise to suspicious information. The facts are not contested, but one minimizes their importance. In effect, it throws back into question the negativity of the category "criminal", i.e., a whole stereotype. This information generates cognitive dissonance and painful disequilibrium: making people ill at ease, it has little chance of being spread as is. In the end, the cognitive disequilibrium must cease: this comes about either through the mechanism of exception ("yes, but he wasn't a criminal like the others"), or by making his act seem less positive ("his true motive was to steal the man's wallet, but he couldn't do so"). Thus, when it is not simply passed over in silence, such information has a good chance of being transformed in the "negative-negative" direction, veering away from its initial "negative-positive" configuration. The event will be interpreted in such a way as to comfort the stereotypes in force.

The fourth type of information involves propositions containing negative people and negative acts: "The gypsies are drawing symbols near our doors to tip off burglars." This type of information constitutes news: of course we expect negative people to commit negative acts. But it is vital to know about such acts that endanger the collectivity. On the other hand, a rumor of this type feeds stereotypes: it justifies prejudices about foreigners, those who are not yet integrated into the community, and gypsies. It authorizes the open expression of aggressiveness, thanks to a presupposed fact (the geometrically shaped graffiti described by the rumor). Information of the negative-negative type has thus not only an alerting function, but also one of expressing and strengthening prejudices.

As can be seen, the introduction of a negative element into the proposition necessarily increases the message's informative value, and thus its likelihood of being rediffused. Moreover, in the course of its circulation, unbalanced information (positive-negative and negative-positive) necessarily evolves. If rumors tend towards positive-positive, they lose their interest and die out insofar as they are rumors; if they become negative-negative propositions, their usefulness for the collectivity is what will spur on their propagation. Thus in the majority of cases, only negative propositions survive as rumors.

The Gratifying Value of Black

Shortly after the terrible earthquake that leveled San Francisco on April 18, 1906, the worst rumors went around what remained of the city: "A tidal wave has swallowed up New York"; "Chicago was engulfed in Lake Michigan," etc. Such rumors are certainly black, but they have a positive function: they temporarily relieve the anxiety and frustration of the inhabitants who survived the cataclysm. If other capitals have been hit as well, misery has found company and thus decreases. Similarly, as we saw above, spreading the rumor that the 113th division was entirely annihilated by the enemy relativizes the seriousness of the losses sustained by one's own division.

Generally speaking, we constantly seek to measure our performance or capacities against those in other reference groups. If their situation is worse, we are satisfied. If theirs is better, rumors function to reduce the painful frustration that is generated: one must save face by attributing the others' greater success not to talent, but to roguishness, villainy, or trickery. Thus during wartime, one finds rumors claiming that a certain social group "is rarely seen on the front" or "enjoying exorbitant, unjustifiable privileges." In both cases, blackness plays a cathartic role.

Black Creates Unanimity

A rumor is a collective act. Unanimity is created more easily when directed *against* something than *for* something. When they sense that unanimity is declining, political regimes do not hesitate to create a new crusade from scratch, a new war against the enemy. Denouncing foreigners is one of the tried and true recipes for refound national unity.

The negativity of rumors provides a similar benefit. By accusing foreigners in one's town, one creates solidarity against them. The group becomes aware of its own existence and power as the rumor spreads farther and wider. A negative rumor is a powerful lever with which to reconstitute threatened social cohesion.

Rumor Targets

Analyzing corporate rumors, Fine [102] noted that, over time, they tend to switch from small corporations or unimportant products to more important ones. The worm in the hamburger rumor, for instance, started at Wendy's on the West coast and later latched on to McDonald's, number one in the burger market. Similarly, many leading corporations have been incriminated by rumors of evil doings and deception. Fine provides a motivational explanation for this empirical regularity: market leaders become the inheritors of all rumors because they mobilize people's fears and mistrust. Running counter to the popular adage, "What's good for General Motors is good for America," Americans now fear "bigness," associating it with suspicion, negligence, and at times malevolence. In other words, people's relationship to these huge corporations is akin to the myth of David and Goliath. Size would thus, in Fine's mind, have surplus meaning that would go well beyond its mere market share: it would announce danger, hostility, and even outright evil. Rumors would then be both the voice and the weapon of the defenseless.

There is another explanation for the gradual switch made by rumors from less-known to frontline figures. This explanation is structural and is linked to our view of rumors as commodity exchange processes. To ask why rumors target the largest corporations is to mistake cause for effect. The gradual shift is what, in fact, makes rumors possible: it is a necessary condition for rumor extension. If it did not occur, communication would cease.

Two people can communicate only if they share a common field of experience. Let us imagine a worm in the hamburger rumor starting in San Diego, concerning some locally known burger chain, call it X. Talking about X on the phone to a friend living in New York City, proper communication about this chain requires reference to some common language; just as "Coke" has almost become a generic term for carbonated beverages, the communication leader symbolizes the product category: it is a common reference vocabulary from the West coast to the East. Its name thus becomes a necessary bridge for communication to continue from one coast to the other: "You don't know X-burger? It's like McDonald's." The brand that enjoys mass recognition is the largest common reference in the country: rumors cannot achieve wide diffusion if they do not move upwards. This is only logical.

Furthermore, public names not only have a larger public, but they also maximize the surprise effect created by the storyteller: "How can this famous X do that?!" The "news value" is higher for names that represent real social institutions.

The Evolution of the Message

One Sunday in July of 1945, Jiang Junchen, a Chinese professor in the United States, decided to take a drive in the very beautiful Maine countryside.

He stopped in the small village R.——— to shyly and courteously ask for directions. He wanted to drive up a mountain, indicated in all the tourist guidebooks that was near by, and from which one could admire a splendid view. An hour later, the whole village was in an uproar. Everyone was talking about the Japanese spy who had come to scale the mountain in order to take pictures of the region [6].

The rapid evolution of the content of rumors, as well as the shift from real to imaginary, have struck observers for quite some time. Certain analysts have even made of these distortions one of the defining characteristics of the rumor phenomenon [222]. This is an error: just as not all rumors are black, not all rumors give rise to distortion. In the above example, a doubt persists: is the final version the product of progressive distortions made in going from one relay to the next, or in fact a faithful replica of what the first witness declared, the one to whom the honorable Chinese professor spoke? What one must explain are the circumstances leading to the absence or presence of distortion during a rumor's diffusion. Moreover, when distortion takes place, it does not operate randomly: it obeys a logic that can be identified.

Degradation or Construction?

Allport and Postman's experiment [6], of which we have already spoken above, is interesting in this respect: an individual looks at a photograph or a drawing presenting a scene from everyday life. Then he tells what he has seen to a second individual who in turn tells what he heard to a third individual, and so on. The chains comprise seven or eight people. The results are striking: there is but a distant relationship between the initial photograph and the version given by the eighth person. The authors identify three processes involved all along the communication chain: reduction, accentuation and assimilation.

1. Right from the very first relays, most of the details are omitted, the message being seriously reduced in length. Then it becomes stable in length and form, changing little in subsequent relays.
2. The counterpart of this reducing effect is the accentuating of certain details. As particular details survive the original massacre, they acquire considerable visibility and importance in the reduced message. Moreover, when there is action involved, or numbers and sizes, the details about them are magnified: ten turns into a hundred, fast becomes very fast, and a gunshot becomes cannon fire.
3. As a message evolves, it tends to acquire a "good form," that of a well-constructed narrative respecting the stereotypes that are prevalent in the

group in which the rumor circulates. All the details are incorporated into a scenario: the latter assimilates, integrates, and transforms the facts related in the direction of increasing coherency. In a photograph, for example, a white Caucasian man, holding a razor in his hand, is standing near a black man in a subway car. After a few relays, it turns into a black man attacking a white man, threatening him with a razor blade: that is a classic scenario that gives meaning to scattered details. Rumors thus take the form of dominant stereotypes.

Allport and Postman used the laws of forgetting and Gestalt theory to explain these three effects: reduction, accentuation, and assimilation. The reference to forgetting is due to the similarity between curves representing the number of details remembered by each relay, and the serious falloff characteristic of forgetting curves: in both cases, people remember many details to begin with, but omit more and more of them over time, up to the point at which memory stabilizes. Their reference to Gestalt theory stems from the fact that the details that are remembered or created help build "good form," i.e., a coherent and satisfactory scenario. Thus through the effect of forgetting and assimilation, rumors seem to acquire an economical form that is able to resist forgetting, and that perfectly corresponds to attitudes, prejudices, and stereotypes of the group in which the rumor circulates. Let it be observed that while the gap between the first and final versions is large, the shift from one version to the next hardly exceeds the limits of plausibility.

Carried out in 1945 and reproduced since that time in all sociology and communications classes, these experiments contributed to discrediting the rumor phenomenon. Rumors were to be condemned by virtue of every technological society's ideal of transmitting very carefully controlled information.

Apart from the critiques that have been made of the underlying ideological component of these experiments, many facts challenge the relevance of such experiments to the natural phenomenon of rumor circulation. Several studies have revealed that rumors show remarkable fidelity to their initial messages [53, 233]. Others have observed the opposite of the reduction process: on the contrary they have found an increase in details or "snowballing" effect [201]. Thus, far from being representative of reality, these simulations of chain transmission create a particular and atypical situation that cannot be generalized. In what sense do these simulations differ from natural situations?

Allport and Postman envision rumors as degradation processes: in the beginning there was truth, and in the end everything is false. Their experiments are, in fact, a theory about the formation of rumors: the content of a rumor results from the destruction of the original truth.

That amounts to forgetting *that often, there is no original truth:* rumors result from a constructive process. Faced with an ambiguous event, the members of a group put their intellectual resources together to arrive at a satisfying definition of reality. After the event, many interpretations arise: at the outset they coexist and feed off each other. Certain interpretations are abandoned while others continue to spread. The common trunk of all the different versions is what one usually calls the rumor's content, i.e., that which is passed on to posterity, transmitted by articles or books. In the field, however, one finds a swarm of interpretations, each trying to account as well as possible for "reality," i.e., to construct its own truth.

At the outset, each version is constructed by the accretion of further details leading to a coherent and credible scenario: we see here once again a snowballing process. Once the scenario has been created, it can undergo forgetting, as in Allport and Postman's experiments. It is a possibility, not a certainty. The degradation process, if it supervenes, only comes about at a second stage, after the constructive phase. Moreover, it only concerns the future of isolated versions. The synthesis process comes about by agglomeration of details emanating from different versions (snowballing), but also by substitution of one interpretation for another. This is also true when rumors are born right after an event that is taken to be important but ambiguous. One can thus see how far chain simulations are from this kind of grand collective deliberation often involved in rumor formation.

There are two crucial differences between the laboratory and the natural environment: noninvolvement of the relays and absence of discussion. In a natural situation, each relay *decides* to be a relay. No one obliges him to relay the rumor: he does it of his own accord, because he is moved by the message and wants to share his feelings. In this case, he does not simply repeat what the preceding relay told him: he tries to convince his interlocutor. Moreover, the diffusion of a rumor involves exchange: at each transmission point, two people converse. The receiver does not remain silent, passively recording what he hears (as in laboratory simulation): he reacts, elaborates, responds, and asks questions. After engrossing discussion, the relay himself may have modified his own initial version of the rumor.

Here we are light years from the mechanistic, technological, one-directional scheme of laboratory-simulated chains. The latter are only representative of a rumor's terminal phase. The initial event has lost some of its interest, the relays and receivers are less involved and communication thus more closely resembles transmission, undergoing the effects of forgetting alone.

How Messages Are Constituted

The founding fathers of the study of rumors were guided by the notion of distortion. This notion is revealing: it refers to some ideal reality that has undergone degradation. In our minds, the well-known alterations that often take place in rumor phenomena should be approached positively: they reflect how messages are constituted. What governs them is not forgetting but rather the desire to communicate, to share one's feelings and to convince.

Simplification is the golden rule of any and all communication. A rumor goes right to the heart of the matter. Things are or are not—there is no middle ground. Whatever is not essential to the tale is eliminated.

To make this point even more clear, without using images, rumors must strike people's minds by *amplifying* details: e.g., if, at the beginning, there were three people, by the end there are a thousand; a simple gift turns into a river of diamonds; an assassin becomes a sex maniac; the candy that makes bubbles turns into an explosive. This "extremization" of content is like caricatures. In accentuating a person's features, all ambiguity is dispensed with, all hesitation and doubt: the person is no longer anything but the accentuated feature. This intensification of signifiers reinforces the Manichean view of rumors. To go from a few diamonds to several rivers makes the message more convincing, but it is also the result of persuasion: the more one is convinced of someone's guilt, the guiltier the behavior one attributes to him. Now rumors acquire their persuasive power little by little as they reach a growing number of people: it is thus normal that accusations and details intensify, even bordering on exaggeration.

The addition of details is also the result of persuasion. In hearing a rumor from a friend, the listener subscribes to it in his own way by furnishing other arguments that corroborate the thesis. This is the basis of "snowballing": each individual makes his own contribution to the rumor's thesis. It is in this way that, though taking off from a single argument, a rumor inherits others in the course of its transmission. "The French businessman Bernard Tapie is said to be recycling Russian money by buying up businesses for the Russians. Isn't he, after all, a worker's son? Moreover, he always makes agreements with the CGT (a leftist trade union) before buying a business. And haven't his purchases always involved companies that have been pushed into a tight spot by serious strikes organized by the CGT, as was the case of Motobécane (a well-known bicycle manufacturer)? Isn't his bank the Banque de l'Europe du Nord—known to be a Russian bank?"

The addition of details, like exaggeration in relation to the extended version, is due to the fact that we are much more involved when we are transmitters than receivers. *One chooses to be a transmitter:* it is an act of free choice that is the sign of considerable involvement in the rumor; one makes it one's own, projecting thereon one's own imagination and fantasies or remembrances.

How can we reconcile the tendency to suppress details that are inessential to the demonstration with snowballing that leads to an increase in the number of arguments? In fact, they are not antithetical: the logic of simplification leads to the evacuation of whatever is useless. The only facts that remain are those that are relevant to the rumor's main thesis. But these facts may be insufficient: e.g., if the rumor throws into question someone who, up until then, has been highly credible, a whole battalion of incisive facts may be necessary. It is as if a rumor sought to attain a balance between its volume of information and its emotional potential. When the latter is weak, a few validating facts suffice. When emotion increases, on the other hand, further facts are called upon to come to the rescue, and the message consequently grows in volume.

Attribution to a credible source also constitutes a characteristic feature of a rumor's evolution. The persuasive intention is evident here. Rather than remaining anonymous, uncertain hearsay, rumors often bestow upon themselves incontrovertible references: direct witnesses of the event, a "high ranking" friend, a hospital director who personally examined the president or operated on the well-known star, the "Villejuif" seal, and so on.

The "Villejuif" leaflet owes its name to the fact that, like any other rumor, it sought an indisputable original source, altogether above suspicion. As naïve people (but were they really?) typed and retyped it on their typewriters, the statement "according to an article in *Sciences et Vie*" (a popular scientific magazine)—the real though distorted source—disappeared, giving way to references to a "hospital in Paris" or "a hospital specializing in cancer" before finally setting on the symbol known to all French people as the mainstay of French oncological research "the Villejuif Hospital." (In fact it is the Gustave-Roussy Institute in the town of Villejuif).

Rumors bring everything *up to date:* the event took place today. This is quite normal: people are more interested in new, current, or upcoming events than in atemporal facts, events which have taken place elsewhere or at some earlier date. The tendency to constantly update events give rumors *eternal youth.*

This constant rejuvenating process is logical. Like all information, rumors lose value as one gets further in time from the event narrated. For rumors to circulate, one must constantly recreate value for them.

Rumors *condense past time:* events attributed to one person are transferred to another—a contemporary. This is not particular to rumors alone: legends submit historical facts to the same fate. Thus in the United States, one finds virtually the same ''Satanic'' components in the rumor about Procter and Gamble in 1981 as in that about McDonald's in 1979.

In the course of its evolution, rumors *reverse* certain statements to make them acceptable to the collectivity. The razor moves from the Caucasian's hand, for example, to the black's standing near him in the subway car. Similarly, during World War II identical rumors circulated among the French and Germans; instead of predicting Hitler's imminent downfall, Daladier's was announced. Rumors whose messages present dissonance or discontent for the group are either rejected and thus fall flat, or set back in the "right" direction.

Lastly, keeping tabs on a message over time allows one to observe *substitutions:* instead of a snake in a bunch of bananas, people talk about mygales or scorpions hidden in teddy bears imported form Taiwan or in Yucca trees. The signified remains the same, while the signifiers change. This evolution is precious to the analyst: it reveals, behind the multiplicity of version, the permanent common ground, the message's thesis, i.e., the rumor's *raison d'être.*

The addition of invented or confabulated details is part and parcel of the same logic: it is a question of getting across the deeper meaning or hidden truth. Moreover, as a rumor progresses, it encounters one new public after another. Each segment of the population has a specific vocabulary, particular symbols and stereotypes, and a way of thinking all its own. Just as a salesman adapts his patter to his customer, rumors adapt to the communication requirements of each new clientele [115].

Fidelity or Infidelity?

A particular question remains to be answered: how are we to reconcile these rumor content transformation modes with studies that document astonishing fidelity to content throughout the communication chain? Let us recall that Allport and Postman themselves were aware that rumors could preserve a message rather faithfully.

The more complicated and ambiguous the original message happens to be, the more it will evolve. This evolution is due to a search for meaning, i.e., elimination of the original ambiguity. On the other hand, a short coherent message has less chance of evolving. In laboratory simulations after four relays, a message is considerably reduced and has acquired a meaning: one thus observes considerable intra-chain fidelity. The ultimate form of invariance is that of slogans or dictums: these verbal encapsulations remain intact for years and even centuries, their few words representing a high concentration of meaning. Certain rumors can be reduced to slogans, e.g., "There is opium in Camel cigarettes."

Faithfulness to content depends essentially on the public's involvement in the message. The message can be either rational or affective [138]. In the first case, the message's content is taken to be important, but there is no identification between the relays and the message. This importance derives from practical and functional consequences, not from throwing into question fundamental values held by the public. This is true, for example, of rumors according to which "the Pope will come to visit our town during his next trip to France," or financial rumors like, "A takeover bid will soon be made for the Pernod-Ricard company." On the contrary, when the public feels emotionally concerned by a rumor, rational controls are let down: the rumor thus leaves behind the realistic plane, spiraling instead towards fantasy, speculation, and imagination. In July 1945, the village where the Chinese professor stopped presented such a situation. The war was drawing on and on (the event took place a few days before Hiroshima) and many of the village's young men had died in combat. The visitor was first and foremost Asian (and only secondarily Chinese), and thus obviously Japanese i.e., an enemy; his hostile presence could only be explained as espionage.

In situations of intense emotional stress, as we have already seen, rational controls are totally absent: nothing is too absurd to be believed; everything is plausible. This is seen for example in crowd phenomena or during social crises, when intergroup conflict reaches all-time highs. Thus the "explosive" Pop Rocks candy bore within it all the elements of conflicting values that set parents who were concerned to instill values of wisdom, composure, and utilitarianism in their children against marketing campaigns encouraging frivolity, rambunctiousness, and carelessness that are always latent in children. Pop Rocks was but one more provocative product in a long series of what parents perceived as aggressive acts by advertisers, merchandisers, and candy and coloring agent manufacturers. Thus one witnessed a total extremization of the rumor's content. It was already clear that Pop Rocks gave kids bursts of flavor. But according to the rumor, it was even worse: kids were literally exploding!

10

The Hidden Message

Introduction

Behind its apparent content, a rumor often bears a second message. It is the latter that gives intense emotional satisfaction as the rumor circulates. In fact, we essentially spread hidden messages of which we are unaware.

Since the beginning of research on rumors, analysts have wanted to build up classifications and typologies. Unfortunately, the latter relied too heavily on rumors' apparent content. To say that rumors about rat bones in Chinese, Turkish, or Greek restaurants belong to the family of contamination rumors, while those concerning Procter and Gamble belong to the family of conspiracy rumors obviously provides a first organization of the multiplicity of rumors, without, however, supplying any surplus meaning when compared with a direct reading of rumors. There is, in effect, a difference between surveying rumors and interpreting them. Interpretation alone gives access to hidden meaning and not simply a redundant version of one's first reading.

Just as the interpretation of dreams differs in accordance with the theory one adopts—Freudian or Jungian—there is no single key to the interpretation of rumors. Certain rumors become quite intelligible through a psychological reading, while others require a psychoanalytic interpretation, and still others can only be understood by taking into account local sociology. In any case, it is not the story itself that provides the key to its comprehension: a simple content analysis leads to a search for universal, unvarying themes. Interpretation of a rumor must incorporate the place, country, or culture in which it circulates as well as the rumor's particular public. As we shall see further on, the content of a rumor cannot be interpreted in the same way in Hungary as in the United States. Similarly, a rumor does not necessarily have the same meaning when it circulates among women as when it circulates among men. Using several exemplary cases, our analysis will reveal some of the functions rumors have in the groups in which they circulate.

145

National Superiority

During the month of May 1972, President Richard Nixon made a visit to Red China. This event, of considerable international importance, was even more important to the Chinese: the man who had been disclaimed for years, imperialism's henchman, was being welcomed by the Grand Helmsman, President Mao. Such an event could not fail to spark off rumors among the people: it was both important and ambiguous, and thereby demanded interpretation. Starting in July of 1972, a series of stories and anecdotes sprang up in China about supposed episodes of Nixon's trip [167].

On one occasion, while speaking with President Mao, Richard Nixon noticed a superb, ancient teacup—known as the nine-dragon teacup—on a table, and surreptitiously swiped it. His gesture was noticed by the guards, but they did not dare intervene as Nixon was China's guest. They mentioned it to Chou-En-Lai to ask his advice. Chou suggested that Nixon be asked to watch the famous Chinese circus perform. One of the circus' magicians had a copy of the stolen teacup made, made it disappear, and said he would find it in President Nixon's briefcase. Nixon was thus obliged to open his bag, and the magician took back the nine-dragon teacup and very deftly handed Nixon the fake copy.

A second rumor was set in a peasant village, and starred a peasant whose parents had been very wealthy property owners before the Revolution. One of the son's relatives, of unexceptional extraction, had risen to an important rank in the people's commune. The relative fell ill, and the peasant of upper-class extraction sent him a few eggs. Later the relative discovered that the eggs had been a sort of bribe; he ordered his peasant relative to make a public self-critique and be judged at a meeting. After the meeting, people recalled that there was on earth a very rich man—Richard Nixon—who was President of the United States and owned everything. He took a trip to China and brought many presents to President Mao. When he received the presents, Mao simply smiled.

Are such rumors grounded in some real incident of which they are an elaboration? One thing is certain: they were voluntarily created and propagated in China by the central administration. Leaflets were even printed up which were supposed to be discussed in people's communes. What did the anecdotes say and what was their function?

They showed the people how Nixon's visit was to be interpreted. Nixon was thus supposed to have come to seek Mao's aid, as he was going to have to face up to a further presidential election. That was why he brought so many presents (just like in the anecdote about the rich peasant's gift to his poor peasant relative): he wanted Mao to sing his praises. These rumors also strengthened the essential features of the Chinese people's self-image: the final victory of the clever, resourceful Chinese over malicious foreigners is inescapable. Notwithstanding, the Chinese know how to manage things gracefully so that no one loses face (as in the anecdote about the teacup).

Behind the façade of neutral and positive articles in the *People's Daily,* such rumors depicted imperialism as still nothing but a paper tiger: the Americans would never be able to beat the courageous and industrious Chinese, whether in a battle of wits or might.

The above-presented rumors had two functions: they explained and reinforced features of national identity. It was quite easy to understand them. The rumors to follow embody an appeal to symbolic discourse to express collective disarray.

The Return to Wilderness

We have already mentioned the rumors about venomous snakes being dropped into various French regions. Such rumors come back periodically in the French countryside. They designate ecologists as the agents of such plane or helicopter drops. What is the meaning of these snakes that whiz by our heads? And what are we to make of the rumors about wildcats wreaking havoc in farm areas? To be satisfied by a simple allusion to eternal fears, Middle Age legends about monsters, or the symbolics of snakes would be inappropriate here. A sociological analysis, however, will prove to be enlightening.

In November of 1982 [43], for example, in Noth, a small village in the Creuse region in France, a mysterious wildcat played at hide-and-seek: it was heard, felt, shot at, and tracked. The loss of the goats and calves it "savagely" attacked was sorely felt, but the beast was never found.

All of these rumors are unanimous: wild beasts have been sent down upon us [18]. As is true for most rumors, they allow for several possible readings, i.e., several levels of decoding. At first level, they reflect the acute disarray of the rural world—the world of those who are at conflict with nature, the same nature that a thousand-year battle had succeeded in pushing back, mastering, and making productive. Far from sensing that they are supported by government officials—those who make decisions that affect their lives—they feel abandoned.

For many years, incomprehension has been the rule between farmers and the central government in France. The coming to power of a socialist government in May 1981 exacerbated fears, as the socialists had a strong ecologically minded faction in their ranks. Now the ecologists are the farmers' obsession, as the former tend to want to supplant the latter in what grounds a farmer's identity: management of the natural environment. The rural world is terribly disgruntled by the appearance of ecologists in the French countryside. The sudden arrival of laboratory experts seems to farmers to be an insult to their own competence and centuries of tradition and rural experience, acquired the hard way—on the job.

It is thus telling that the "senders" of wile beasts should be imagined to be ecologists: they are the ones who pilot planes and helicopters. Flying airplanes overhead seems normal to the farmers: the ecologists have lots of equipment at their disposal as they are backed by the government—equipment that agriculture lacks. Moreover, one breezes over the countryside in a plane like one skims over a report. Unlike the farmers who know the nature report inside out, soaking their hands in it every day starting at daybreak, ecologists float in abstractions and make regulations in an irresponsible fashion. They are sorcerer's apprentices. Their decisions seriously harm those who truly know nature and who live in it: farmers and hunters. Releasing wild animals means killing off domestic ones; one makes unworkable the land it took so many centuries to learn to control [76].

For the rural world, nothing is more symbolic of the usefulness or uselessness of ecologists than the reintroduction of wild animals under their aegis: lynxes in the Vosges Mountains to the east, and vultures in the Cévennes in the south. Such acts are enticing to the city folk: to them, nature is a concept; the state of nature is what compensates for the artificial state of their concrete environment. While thousands of projects (with huge advertising budgets) are undertaken to reintroduce wild animals, the French countryside is perishing. Similarly, it is significant that in Noth, rumor connected the mysterious wildcat to a lady who had stopped at people's houses, asking them not to harm the beast and to call it Babette. Now Babette is Brigitte Bardot's nickname, and she has become a famous protector of animals and the public's beloved ecologist.

Thus periodically the French countryside begins talking of werewolves, the beast of Gévaudan, hordes of venomous snakes, and even crocodiles in the Dordogne River. In the village of Noth, despite witnesses, hunts, and nocturnal safaris, no decisive proof of the existence of the mysterious wildcat ever turned up. What is symptomatic at a certain moment is the desire to believe that is expressed by a community where a Beast is supposed to have appeared. What must be decoded is the mythical passage from the beast to the Beast, the transformation of an ordinary predator into the Mysterious Feline. Such Beasts are messages.

Behind the naturalist discourse, there is a social discourse that exposes the relations the rural world has with its environment. Ten years earlier, in the framework of a study on the wolf reputed to be lurking around Limousin, a region in central France [43], researchers cited a virtually automatic response by the inhabitants: "The wolves will come back again." This sentence is a symbol. The French countryside has been progressively becoming more and more deserted. Abandoned villages are an ever more common sight; the SNCF's (French railroad system) secondary routes are closing one by one. Wolves will no longer be afraid of the noise or of the increasingly rare presence of man. Nature is once again becoming hostile.

The Beast rumors express real helplessness. In the ruins of abandoned villages, people sense that the Beasts will return. At the deepest level, what many rural inhabitants fear is the return to wilderness if not to savagery: to say that Beasts are coming back is to make a judgment about social relations, or rather the lack thereof. To leave France fallow is to slowly choose the road that inescapably leads to the state of savagery.

Initiatory Reminiscence

Starting in January 1980, a number of young men who were doing their military service at the Mourmelon base in France disappeared. The mystery has remained altogether unsolved despite seven disappearances. Police investigations have continued indefatigably, though without turning up any evidence or confessions to date. Alongside the military police's meticulous work, local rumors quickly preempted other hypotheses. One claimed it was the act of a homosexual: the young men had been hitchhiking and were picked up and kidnapped by a German truck driver (the German border not being far from the base) in order to deliver them up to a Middle Eastern male-prostitution network. Another rumor sustained that the disappearances were due to criminal acts committed by a former legionnaire who had gone mad, living like a hermit in the dark forest around the camp (occasionally making him out to be a homosexual) [143]. Because of its protagonists (adolescent boys) and the place where it took place (a forest), this mystery recalls certain popular tales in which an ogre kidnaps children who get lost in the forest. At this stage in the game, it would be erroneous to claim that the rumor reproduces a tale. In reality, the rumor and the tale alike reproduce the same archetype—the same hidden, unconscious scenario. Even though it speaks of real concrete facts (in this case, the young men who disappeared from Mourmelon), the rumor draws largely upon the imaginary. In that, it is very close to the popular tale in its approach. One cannot thus confine oneself to saying that the crazy legionnaire and the German homosexual truck driver are the modern and realistic expression of the ogre of popular tales. The true question becomes: what is the meaning of the ogre himself?

Ethnographer Pierre Saintyves [227] and Russian folklorist Vladimir Propp [206], have found a link between primitive customs and popular tales. According to them, the characters in such tales literally embody people's memories of ceremonial characters in various popular rites that have more or less disappeared. On the whole, marvelous tales preserve the memory of primitive beliefs and rituals.

Thus in all primitive tribes, in order to become adults, adolescents have to undergo rites of passage, an initiatory period or adventure. Now all initiation rites have three phases. The first is that of abduction—the brutal ripping away of the neophyte from his family environment and his transfer to a sacred enclosure. The second phase is that of the symbolic putting to death (imprisonment, prolonged passing out, journey to the kingdom of death, struggle against a monster, physical torture, mutilation, and/or circumcision). The third phase is that of the rebirth of the hero who has survived.

Thanks to this ethnographic and ritualist perspective, one can associate many themes in popular tales with various states of rites of passage. The ogre recalls a character, the sorcerer, whose role is to terrify the neophyte, and even to submit him to semblances of death and physical and moral tests. The fabulous and terrifying forest, present in many tales (such as Little Red Riding Hood and Sleeping Beauty), is an initiatory forest, sprinkled with tests, a place where adolescents are transformed into adults.

In this perspective, one can see why the disappearance of young men from the Mourmelon base generated the above-mentioned rumors. Their content was predictable: every disappearance of an adolescent being akin to an abduction, i.e., the first phase of initiation rituals, it was normal for these disappearances to awaken fears and anxiety linked to the second phase of these rituals—the most dangerous phase of all—that of the tests imposed upon the neophytes by the sorcerer.

Moreover Mourmelon's physical appearance structurally reproduces that of initiations rites. One speaks, concerning the military base, of young men who are "called upon." Military service marks the end of adolescence and often brings about one's first long-term separation from one's mother. This distancing quite naturally leads to anxiety on the mother's part. The neophyte is brutally wrenched out of his environment. How will he survive the initiation?

The forest surrounding Mourmelon evokes initiatory forests, the site of all tests. The army and its isolated base are symbols of mastered instinctual power and channeled aggressiveness. But the contiguity between the camp and the forest allows a transfer to take place: the forest is thought to harbor unmastered asocial instinctual power, liberated destructive aggressiveness, and the repressed parts of our drives. That is why, once he leaves the military base and gets lost in the forest, the adolescent, a still-fragile neophyte, is threatened with the worst forms of corruption: homosexuality, punishment, and death. This age-old, universal theme dramatically resurfaced in the Mourmelon rumors.

Becoming an Adult

One of the most popular rumors in America is known as "the hook." Degh [69] found forty-four versions, most of which were circulating among college-age girls. In essence, the plot involves a couple in a car parked in a local lover's lane. The boy is hoping to make out (sexually) and turns on the car radio to put on some soft music. A news flash interrupts the music, announcing that a sex maniac has just escaped from a nearby mental hospital. One distinguishing feature of this man is that one of his arms is replaced by a hook. The girl is frightened and after much argument, convinces the boy to leave the area. The car pulls away quickly. Arriving at home, she gets out of the car and sees a hook hanging on her door.

Many interpretations have been advanced for this rumor. According to Degh, it aims at providing the thrill of a good scare. Dundes (84) made a very penetrating psychological analysis of its underlying hidden meaning and real function among college girls. The story summarizes teenage girls' fears about parking with their boyfriends. According to Dundes, the radio is the conscience-like voice of society, and from a girl's point of view, it says that "previously nice boys, when parked in a car on a country road, sometimes act like sex maniacs." The hook is a phallic symbol. The typical fear of the girl might then be "that a boy's hand, signifying relatively elementary necking, might suddenly become a hook (an erect, aggressive phallus). . . . One way of keeping a sexually aggressive boy at bay is to castrate him!" In fact, in the rumor story, the hook is ripped off just as it "had made contact with the girl's door." Contrary to many surface interpretations referring, for instance, to "the natural dread of the handicapped" or fears of mounting urban violence, the emotional *raison d'être* for these rumors lies in this age group's dating practices, and adolescent girls' first anxiety producing encounters with male sexuality. In the story, the girl is not so much afraid of what a man lacks, but of what he has.

Moral Education

A few years back, an anecdote, presented as though it were altogether true, went around Parisian dinner parties. Convinced of its veracity, the editor-in-chief of the newspaper *Le Monde,* published it as he heard it without seeking any further verification:

> Scene: a dinner party in Neuilly, the capital's most elegant suburb. One of the couples invited leaves their two children at home while they go out for the evening, the ten-year-old boy, duly lectured, keeping an eye on his four-year-old sister. He is to let no one into the house, to go to bed at nine o-clock sharp, and in the event of something unusual happening, the phone number of the friends at whose house mom and dad were eating is placed right near the phone. At ten o'clock, the phone rings: it's the little boy. Half crying, half laughing, and very excited, he says: "Dad, a burglar came in and I killed him." The father at first believes it is a fib, rolls his eyes and tries to calm his son down, but the details come streaming out and are quite alarming. "Yes, it's true. With your revolver in your desk drawer. He was a big guy with a mask over his face. He's here in the living room on the floor." At last the father gets worried and says, "I'll be right there." The burglar is indeed there on the living room rug. The police arrive. The body is turned over and the face is seen. Everyone screams: it is the twenty-two year old son of the friends with whom the parents had been dining. It happened a few weeks ago. No charges were made, court proceedings were dropped, and the case was filed away. [*Le Monde,* "Au Fil de la Semaine," July 2–3, 1972.]

An investigation interviewing journalists, the police, doctors, and hospital workers turned up nothing [50]. Moreover, the same story had gone around Australia ten years earlier. It had an anti-Catholic flavor to it there, as it was Doctor Mannis, the daunting Catholic bishop of Melbourne who was said to have used his influence to help the father hush up the scandal.

This rumor goes back even further in time. In *The Stranger* by Albert Camus, the character Meursault, while in prison, comes across a newspaper article relating a news item which was supposed to have taken place in Czechoslovakia:

> A man left a Czech village to make his fortune. After twenty-five years, he returned to the village, a rich man with a wife and child. His mother ran a hotel along with his sister in their native village. In order to surprise them, he had left his wife and child in another hotel, and went to see his mother who did not recognize him when he came in. As a joke, he decided to book a room. He flashed a wad of money. During the night, his mother and sister assassinated him with a hammer to steal his money; then they threw his body in the river. The next morning, when his wife came, she unknowingly revealed the traveler's identity. The mother hung herself. The sister threw herself into a well.

As early as 1613, a sporadically published paper, printed in Paris, put the following words on its front page: "The astonishing, incredible story of a father and mother who unwittingly assassinated their own son. It took place in the city of Nîmes in the Languedoc region in October of 1613." Similar anecdotes were published in 1848 and 1881 [235]. It is likely that someday, somewhere, the story was true, but that is of but little importance. What must be explained is the anecdote's amazing permanence in oral memory, and the reasons for its appearance at a certain moment in a specific place.

These anecdotes recount an eternal theme: tragic misunderstanding. Thinking one is doing something good, one does something evil. Such rumors seem to derive their eternality from the fact that they break taboos while immediately reinforcing them. They are parables or moral stories: behind the anecdote, there is a reminder of the commandments. Thou shalt never kill, for one always kills a fellow man, if not one's own child: one kills oneself in killing another.

These rumors also sustain that crime is everywhere nowadays, even in the very bosom of the most respectable families. They express worry about the anxiety-producing consequences of the return to individual justice—self-defense.

In the United States, rumors about fast-food restaurant chains are, as we mentioned above, classic. The protagonist is generally a woman who discovers, for example, a roast rat instead of the roast chicken she had ordered. We have seen that real facts are at the origin of such rumors. This does not, however, change the diagnosis: the rumor persists because it has become a moral tale. In effect, it is telling that such rumors involve a woman, i.e., a housewife whose responsibility it is to feed her family. The rumor reminds her that in neglecting her traditional role, she makes her family run risks: the rat is a form of symbolic punishment. The rumor more generally aims at women's liberation: thanks to new forms of nourishment, women are no longer obliged to spend hours and hours preparing meals.

Wish Fulfillment

One of the most widely diffused migratory rumor stories is the "Runaway Grandmother." It is popular in many parts of Europe as well as in the United States. The basic plot includes a family vacation on which an old grandmother (or mother-in-law) is taken along. During the trip, the grandmother dies. The couple decides to bring the corpse back home, but on the way, as they stop to eat at a restaurant, the car is stolen. In the European versions, more scare-value is added by having the family cross a border on the way home, the corpse often being hidden in a carpet roll strapped to the top of the car.

According to Dundes [84], this exemplary story is a reflection of modern attitudes towards the elderly. The new nuclear families hate to be loaded down with grandfathers and grandmothers. They do not live together any more. Since the elderly are clearly "unwanted," the story has a wish-fulfilling facet: the grandmother should die, so that the couple can be alone again and have a good time on vacation. The theft of the corpse is another wish-fulfilling facet. In the United States, unlike many other countries in the world, the family itself does not prepare the body for burial. Death has become taboo. In the story, the death of the grandmother burdens the couple because they have to take care of the corpse. As if by chance, the story eliminates the body.

Hungarian folklorist Degh [69] analyzes the story as a fear of ghosts. The disappearance of the corpse means she will not receive a decent burial: there is thus a chance that the grandmother will eternally come back to haunt the family, not having had an honorable burial. Is this interpretation as valid in the United States as in Hungary where ghostlore is rampant? Folklorists should not analyze lore as if there were no folk. The story's meaning in the United States is related to American laws and the American way of life. One of the few ways of quickly getting rich is to inherit wealth from deceased relatives. But without a corpse, there is no proof of death, hence no access to the money! According to Dundes, in the American version, the fear is not that the grandmother might return, but rather that she might not (p. 36).

Recourse to Magical Thought

We have already drawn attention to the surprising reproduction of the rumor known by the name of the "Cadaver in the Car." It was signaled in 1914 and in 1938 in virtually all of the countries involved in the war.

At first sight, this incredible story is simply a well-known type of rumor. In order to reduce latent anxiety due to the inescapable rise of German power, the rumor proposed an outlet: *taking one's desires for reality*. What one cannot hope for is collectively dreamt of in the guise of an anecdote.

In reality, hidden in the story is a cause and effect link between the two deaths: that of the passenger and the predicted death of Hitler. As Bonaparte shows [40], this innocuous anecdote is the direct expression of a primitive rite that one might have thought had disappeared thousands of years ago, but which resurfaces mentally: it is the ultimate recourse of so-called civilized peoples. Structurally speaking, the rumor describes a propitiatory sacrifice.

Among primitive peoples, human sacrifices seem to be deals: those who make the sacrifice thereby acquire rights over their gods. They pay before being gratified by them, in order to acquire their favor. That is the function of the sacrifice. The extreme prewar anxiety revived one of humanity's most archaic beliefs: civilized, Christianized, and disciplined man unconsciously turned back to magical faith. One must be able to have an effect upon one's destiny by offering up sacrifices, but not just any old kind of sacrifice: a human sacrifice—the dearest and the most taboo. God himself asked Abraham to offer up to Him what was dearest to Abraham: "Take your son Isaac, your only son, the son you love." The greater the sacrifice, the better one's chances to have the gods grant their favor and satisfy one's wishes.

Every sacrifice involves three protagonists: he who sacrifices (the one for whose benefit the sacrifice is made), the sacrificer, and the victim. In rumors, those who sacrifice are the future mobilized troops (and all of France through them). The sacrificer remains anonymous; he speaks and then disappears. He is Fate who makes the wounded man randomly encounter what will put an end to his life. The victim is a double of he who sacrifices: Abraham's own son or, in the rumor, the man who is also mobilized. Thus one sacrifices something in one's own stead, saving one's own soul by this small-scale holocaust. As for the car, it is the modern substitute of the altar or the stake: it transports one from life to death.

The rumor expresses a refusal to believe in fate: events cannot be inescapable. As governments seem to have lost control over our country's future, being sucked into the maelstrom of the imminent war, only magic can save us. It is significant that the rumor expresses the repressed: it goes beyond candles, ex-votos, masses said for peace, and prayers to God. Here the gods are invoked: one looks to Baal, Zeus, and other primitive divinities from before God's time. The rumor not only acutely reveals the state of collective feeling in 1939, it also provides a solution to them: a primitive sacrifice.

A second rumor, seemingly altogether different from that just discussed, proves to be similar at a deeper level: its hidden truth is identical. It too circulated on both sides of the front [40]. In many units of the French army, at the end of 1939 and the beginning of 1940 right up to the German attack, the soldiers complained that (potassium) bromide was being put in their wine (or coffee) behind their backs. This seriously decreased their passion and lovemaking capacity, dismaying them during their periodic leaves. Without denying that fatigue or anxiety related to expectancy during the strange war might have been determining factors in the epidemic of love fiascos, the rumor's theme and the scapegoat identified (the magic powder) were quite revealing.

In all primitive rituals, continence is supposed to have magical powers. Warriors believed that if they had intercourse before leaving for battle, they would be vanquished. This ritual is still present in sports competitions nowadays.

The rational explanation is generally put forth that continence has strengthening effects. But is this a physiological reality or the rationalized expression of a magical ritual? Taking into account the symbolic meaning of semen (a sign of power), to conserve it is to preserve one's power. Moreover, before wars, aside from continence, primitive rituals ordered a series of acts whose real physiological effect was to weaken the fighter, even if psychologically he felt invincible afterwards.

Just prior to battle, the bromide rumor revived the archaic commandment of continence. Continence is supposed to favor victory. Here again, it was a propitiatory sacrifice: a magical rite to convince the gods to be lenient. The soldiers acquired the right to conquer by sacrificing what was dearest to them: the possession of women. Buried by centuries of civilization and monotheistic religion, such continence is no longer desired or accepted as it was in tribal times: it was thus imposed by the authorities (those who controlled the soldiers' food supplies). In these two rumors, in different, far-fetched guises, the same archaic theme resurfaced. It circulated thanks to its being disguised as an innocent anecdote, and was spread with the vague feeling that it had some import that escaped the tellers. It was a ritual to ward off anxiety—a form of magical thought.

Magical thought is not limited to exceptional circumstances. It can be found currently, for example, in the theme of the president coming down with cancer. For an opposition party, this rumor functions as an incantatory rite: the word takes place of the act. In order for the Socialists' power to crumble in France—as the catastrophic predictions about what would happen after May 1981 were not borne out—only sorcery remained, invoked by a collective litany that now relies on cancer to make its wishes come true. An unforeseeable, sudden, and terrifying illness, cancer was the pagan, physiological expression of the divine push in the desired direction.

Satan's Return

The prophecy has been attributed to André Malraux that the next century will be very religious or will not be religious at all. The hypertechnology and hyperrationality of the modern world can only engender a rebirth of faith. That is its only chance for survival. The rise of religious fundamentalism, the creation of unidenominational republics, and the Khomeni phenomenon seem to be harbingers of his prophecy.

It is in this same context that one must situate the multiplication of Satanic rumors in the United States since 1978 [208]. The emergence of such rumors in the most religious states is not fortuitous. Since the failure of the Vietnam War, the United States has been witnessing deep geopolitical upheaval in the world. From its point of view, after decades of order, disorder seems to be everywhere. Within the country where technology is the most advanced, spiritualism has come back with a vengeance. After the wave of Hindu philosophies, young people now rally around new religious sects, the best known and wealthiest of which is that of the Moonies.

Rumors sound the return of witch hunting. Delumeau [77] has shown how the heretic hunting in Europe in the seventeenth century reflected the perception of a serious threat to Christianity. The great campaign to exorcize Satan was a defense mechanism, a reaction to the generalized feeling of insecurity. "Satan's agents" were denounced, whatever form they took— whether Jews, sorcerers, or heretics. Abroad, the conquistadors tried to convert the native Americans, whose cults could only be Satanic, like the religions of the Moors and the Arabs. It seems that the same fear has today seized backwoods America: the Midwestern states that have remained deeply religious.

The choice of companies to be used as scapegoats is interesting. Set up on American soil, they fill the bill: scapegoats are internal enemies that one must oust, Trojan horses that are fated to destroy the city from within. Mysterious and super-powerful, these companies were viewed as possibly responsible for the worrisome upheavals that sparked off the rumors. Up until recently, they were considered symbols of success, as the motors of the country's growth. Their designation as scapegoats is the sign of a *legitimation crisis*. In effect, it is no longer shocking to a part of American opinion to think that these companies in fact work against their country, that they pursue their own interests, even if in doing so, as the rumor would have it, they have to make a pact with the devil.

Multiple Levels of Interpretation

As these examples show, every rumor allows for several interpretations, i.e., several levels of decoding. At one level, one can consider that many rumors are but oral extrapolations of "what would happen if." For example, standing before a microwave oven, anyone with a bit of imagination might be spontaneously led to wonder what would happen if the family cat or a small dog were to inadvertently take a nap inside. Taking the hypothesis to the extreme, one comes across the theme of the "hot dog." Here we are not far from the classic funny stories of "the most incredible thing was" type (tall tales). Without refusing the value of deeper explanations, it should be realized that a part of rumors' popularity derives from their way of exploring the preposterous implications of things and objects around us.

A second level of interpretation links rumors to the recent history of the group within which they circulate. Starting in 1970, for example, the "snake in the blanket" rumor blossomed in the United States. Having bought a blanket through a mail order company, an American woman was horrified when she discovered, upon opening it up, a snake hidden inside. The rumor added that the blanket has been imported from the Far East. Depending on the variant, the woman either died or survived. The fact that this family of rumors appeared in 1970 allows one to associate it with the Vietnam War. It would be the symbolic expression of the fear of revenge by Far Eastern peoples, taken through imported goods.

At a more general level, one could point out that this rumor is ubiquitous. A manager at the French mail order company, "La Redoute," recently informed us of the existence of an identical rumor targeting his company: somewhere in France, a woman was said to have been bitten by a snake hidden in an imported blanket. He had taken the transnational rumor for a personal attack! The rumor's omnipresence proves that countries less involved in the Vietnam War enjoy circulating the rumor too, as if it harbored an important collective message. Is it a reference to the Western theme of the "yellow peril" that would be exacerbating the spectacular rise of Far Eastern economic powers?

But this rumor also belongs to the great family of contamination rumors, which also comprises all the stories about rats in Chinese restaurants (in France, Great Britain, and the United States), Yugoslavian restaurants (in Germany), and Greek restaurants (in Denmark). This very sizable family of rumors infinitely improvises on the theme of fear of the foreigner.

The question is still posed: which level must be used in interpreting rumors? In our mind, what is particular to rumors is precisely this complex mixture of meanings. Rumor stories are like palimpsests: they contain many different layers of meaning. For Klintberg too, "as successive layers are stripped away, fresh layers of meaning are disclosed." The Procter and Gamble rumor, for example, allows for the following interpretations:

- At a surface level it is a mercantilistic rumor [157] or a sign of fear of the powerful Moonies (where do they get their money from?).
- At a slightly deeper level, it belongs to the "David and Goliath" paradigm and is a sign of popular resentment against huge dominating corporations [102].

- It is a symptom of a legitimation crisis within American society and of a widening gap between the people and abstract economic forces.
- It is an updated and rationalized version of the universal myth of Faust.

Are all interpretations valid? To provide an answer, one needs a criterion. As interpretations are made *ex post facto,* predictive validity cannot be used. One criterion would be that of intelligibility. Obviously no interpretation can be said to be "true": however, some do make intelligible many of the details of the rumor story. We shall prefer, as epistemology recommends, a parsimonious theory accounting for most of the details of a rumor. For instance, the "alligators in the sewer" rumor may lead to endless discussion as to its meaning and emotional kernel:

- Does it give one a good scare?
- Is it a metaphor that means that under a thin gloss of civilization (the city), a world of violence, instinct, and aggression lives on (the jungle is just under the blacktop)?
- Is it a castration theme? Carroll [55] gives a psychoanalytic explanation that accounts for the continuing popularity of the story, and rules out true events as the source of this popularity. Carroll points out that in no article mentioning unexpected encounters with alligators in public places is mention made of their being "flushed down the toilet," the alleged elimination process. Furthermore, only one real account refers to sewers (*New York Times,* February 10, 1935). According to M.P. Carroll, the original stories have been modified so that they now clearly reflect castration themes. In psychoanalytic theory, an equation is made between penis and feces and between defecation and castration. Alligators themselves have a sexual connotation. This is why, unconsciously, the juxtaposition of "alligators" and "sewers" is particularly appealing to a modern audience. This explanation makes intelligible details that are not considered by other layers of explanation.

Another illustration is that of the spider in the yucca tree. This rumor spread all over Europe in 1985. One question arises: why did the story fail to circulate when it concerned cacti? Explanations of the yucca story which classify it in universal categories such as conspiracy rumors or fear rumors leave the question unanswered! Klintberg's explanation is that the yucca is a real phallic symbol [152]. And in fact, the story always casts a woman. Did the phallic form arouse subconscious associations and feelings among the tellers who, as it turns out, were mostly female? Klintberg adds that, in Swedish folk speech, the word "jucka" (pronounced exactly like "yucca") signifies "the body movement during copulation." Naturally this linguistic detail would not be valid in France or the United States.

In the interest of thoroughness, rumor interpretations should never forget the folk and the time. Of course there are collective or individual unconscious themes in rumors; but one must still explain why *this* rumor appeared in *this* group at *this* specific time. Mere content analysis is therefore not enough. Field analysis is necessary to complete the picture.

PART III
The Use of Rumors

11

Crimes, Investigations, and Rumors

Five Years in Prison Because of a Rumor

Rumors play a part in most legal rulings. Few cases illustrate their ubiquity and determining role as well as the case of Marie Besnard.

The scene is set in Loudun, a small town (a bit dead) with eight thousand inhabitants who are mostly somewhat well-to-do farmers in the Vienne region in France. The Besnard family, whose roots go back a long way in the region, was neither rich nor poor and enjoyed a good reputation. Late in life, Léon Besnard married Marie Duvaillaud, a young widow from a very good farming family, well rooted in the area, that made a very comfortable living: they were, in fact, rich but continued to live like farmers. To Marie, this marriage was a real step up, for Loudun was not the country for her, but a real town. Then the Second World War began, and the Germans occupied the region. One fine day in 1941, in a bus going from Châtellerault to Loudun, Marie Besnard chanced upon a woman of more or less her own age, Louise Pintou. The latter knew no one in the area, and Marie Besnard, kind-hearted as always, invited her to the Besnard home. Starting in 1942, after numerous visits, Mrs. Pintou virtually moved in with the Besnards.

The war ended. To help with the reconstruction efforts, Léon Besnard "inherited" a solid young nineteen-year-old German prisoner. The two women were moved by the young man: Marie Besnard treated him as if he were her own son, but Louise Pintou was more titillated, despite their difference in age. Thus the young German boy received the usual *substitutes* of affection—small gifts, handkerchiefs, candy, and so on—but nothing else.

One Sunday in October of 1947, the Besnard family and Louise Pintou went to one of their farms in the Liboureaux region. Léon worked hard in the morning, made necessary repairs, and took the animals to market. After lunch, he didn't feel well: he vomited and decided to go home immediately. As soon as he got to Loudun, he lay down. Three days later, on October 25, 1947, he died. The family doctors who knew him for years said he died of natural causes, after a bout of uraemia.

As chance would have it, during his last moments, Mrs. Pintou remained alone with Léon Besnard for a few minutes in his bedroom. Immediately following his death, Mrs. Pintou left the Besnard residence. She moved in with an old chap, Auguste Massip, in a not-too-far-off castle of sorts. Massip had courted Marie Besnard on several occasions to no avail, and highly resented her. What did Mrs. Pintou say upon arriving at the castle? "Léon told me, when I was alone with him, that Marie had put something in his soup at lunch in Liboureaux. Immediately after this avowal, made but a few hours before his death, I ran to alert the two doctors, but neither of them did anything. Léon died shortly thereafter."

This avowal was the spark. A whole slew of local, repressed desires and hatreds was about to be released. Everyone was going to take revenge. At last, the long-dreamt-of occasion had presented itself.

On November 4, Auguste Massip, no longer being able to resist the temptation, went to see the magistrate in Loudun. He repeated what Louise Pintou had said. A few discreet visits by police officers put the match to the fuse: people began wondering what was happening. It was all terribly ambiguous. The answer came from the castle: the death was suspicious, and Marie Besnard was the suspect. From the post office to the market, from Sunday mass to the coffee shop, and from one shop to the next, the rumor took hold of Loudun. Thus was born the accusation against the "Loudun Poisoner."

In growing, the rumor accused Marie Besnard of having administered arsenic not only to her husband but also to eleven other family members who had died many years before: her own father, her own mother, her first husband, Léon's grandmother, Léon's father, and so on. All these deaths which had been totally natural—due to extreme old age or illness—became suspicious, and Marie Besnard's arsenic was claimed to be the culprit.

Though no official accusation had been made, a police commissioner and an inspector felt that the case of their lives had just arrived, and that promotions were just around the corner. They thus took the initiative and spent several days questioning everyone in town. The rumor thus became part of the court's proceedings, and was heard as testimony. First of all, once someone has become a suspect, a well-known reorganization takes place of the details which had up until then been interpreted as insignificant. The reader had already seen this in many of the previously discussed rumors.

During her childhood, Marie Besnard, a devoted child, had discontinued her education to help out with the tough farmwork. She often went off alone to tend to the sheep. What was said in 1949 of her shepherding activities? "A shepherd who was rough with the animals and had probably *hung* one of the recalcitrant ewes." As her lawyers pointed out [93], this totally uncontrollable story, denied by the accused party and born of pure hearsay, nevertheless led the judge to worry that Marie Besnard might try to commit suicide in prison. Thus two "sheepdogs" were transferred to accompany her—prisoners whose mission it was to constantly watch her and try to make her confess! Everyone had his word to say about it, adding his bit of hearsay: no one saw anything, but everyone knew. The investigation's report was revealing: "Public rumor sustains that he [the German prisoner] had become Mrs. Besnard's lover, which sparked off violent disputes between her and her husband." "If she was misbehaving without it being seen, that was because she knew how to hide her acts." "She didn't keep good company, at least if one is to lend credence to appearances."

A philosophy professor who barely knew her declared that he believed she was guilty after having spoken at length "with the inhabitants who chatted rather openly with me." The report filed by the chief of the Châtellerault police mentioned: "At the end of 1940, a series of deaths began that public rumor rightly or wrongly claims to be suspicious".

After this accumulation of gossip and delayed slander, a presumably innocent woman was treated as though she were guilty: she was sent to prison on July 21, 1949, at the age of fifty-two. Twelve highly decomposed cadavers were dug up in the attempt to detect traces of arsenic.

The vague recollection of rumors turned all the details of her life against her. Even expert psychiatrists assigned by the judge to examine the widow Besnard could not shake off the influence of the rumors that made a criminal of her. They stated: "Marie Besnard is normal, so normal indeed that she is *abnormally normal*." During her 1954 hearing, without any evidence whatsoever, the rumor was the principal prosecutor: the police commissioner and inspector constantly referred to the rumor. They were its delegates.

Marie Besnard was finally released on April 12, 1954, on bail. She was totally acquitted on December 13, 1961. Imprisoned because of a rumor that led the police to zealously transform hearsay into presumptions of guilt, an innocent woman spent almost five years in jail. What happened to her could happen to anyone at anytime.

Delayed Revenge

In a small town or neighborhood, crime is never an isolated event: it is a social act that concerns the whole of the micro-society. It reveals the latter's history. In Loudun, the number of those who envied the Besnard family had been growing for most of fifteen years: their comfortable life made people jealous, certain of their furniture purchases had gained them secret enemies, and their neglected sycophants were terribly resentful. The army of disappointed and hateful townspeople was ready to spring into action at the first opportunity.

In such closed theaters where everyone is forced to rub shoulders, for better or for worse, desires to kill are never in short supply, though they are generally repressed. Faced with Mrs. Pintou's accusation, Marie Besnard quite simply replied, "I suppose that if Mrs. Pintou said I poisoned my husband, it's because she would have liked to have done so." With rumors, one accuses others of misdeeds one bears within oneself: anyone could have killed Léon Besnard, so why not her?

In Loudun, all of the rumor's necessary actors were present. The instigator was Mrs. Pintou. The apostles—those asked only to believe—were all those who were envious, disappointed, or jealous. The commissioner and the inspector were the opportunists: the rumor constituted an important case for them. What a great find: twelve murders disclosed!

Denials do not stop people from talking. A rumor is not like Sherlock Holmes, a pure brain in the service of truth. It is rather the prophetess of accumulated hate. It is not a question of knowing, but rather of "letting go" everything one thinks one knows that is in any way related to the case: in effect, one settles old scores.

At the hospital in Poitiers, on Tuesday, October 30, 1984, Nicole Berneron died in the operating room. A reversal of the respirator tubes necessary for the anesthesia was discovered. Was it a crime or an accident? No one knows even now. In hospitals, rivalry is latent and creeping: it became the fuel of incriminating rumors.

Overturning a Notable

Between January 1969 and January 1976, seven women and a man were assassinated in an identical fashion in the Creil and Nogent-sur-Oise regions in France. Committed at different times of day, the crimes seemed to have been the work of man who knew the area very well, and immediately disappeared, fading into the woodwork of the nearby streets. The absence of a culprit created an anxiety-producing situation for many years that was propitious for the persistence of rumors: who is he? why does he strike? what is the mysterious link between all of his victims?

Interestingly enough, the local rumors never adopted the hypotheses or insinuations of the press (*Le Courrier Picard, Le Parisien Libéré*, and *France-Soir*). The latter spoke at first of a mentally unbalanced man, and later of a railroad worker.

But in these towns, dominated by the French railroad company, this accusation was unacceptable: the rumor, being too dissonant, had to die out. Afterwards *Le Parisien libéré* identified a suspect: a North African plasterer who lived alone (*Le Parisien Libéré*, November 24, 1969). Six years later the paper made a further attempt to get its thesis of an immigrant worker accepted (*Le Parisien Libéré*, December 2, 1975). In both cases, rumor failed to adopt the North African.

These crimes seemed to be the work of someone who was very intelligent and yet highly disturbed. The "shadow killer," this "monster with cat eyes" (according to the description given by a young woman would had miraculously escaped from his clutches), had been scoffing at the police and investigators for seven years. That did not coincide with the image the two towns had of workers from the Maghreb.

According to the rumor, the killer was neither a worker nor a foreigner, but rather "a high ranking man" [35]. Several clues lent credibility to this thesis of the assassin-notable. First and foremost, the variability of the hours at which the crimes were committed suggested someone whose work schedule was rather flexible. He had to have ample time to watch and follow his victims. His sudden disappearances did not raise suspicion amongst those closest to him or his colleagues: he must thus have been a professional of some sort or other. Someone like that would never arouse the least suspicion in his family. But perhaps he had no family. That would make his crimes even easier to execute. Lastly, only a notable could evaporate into the population a few minutes after a crime with total impunity: notables are *a priori* above suspicion.

Thus the rumor's two favorite characters were the doctor who kills and the assassin-cop. Moreover, these two characters are accustomed to keeping records on their patients and fellow citizens. As for the dissonant indications (a bag and workman's tools, left by the killer on the scene of one of the crimes), they must have been placed there to throw investigators off the scent.

In the bedroom communities that Creil and parts of Nogent have become, rumors take on the flavor of underlying social tensions revealed by the crime and the free speech it released: misfortune comes from high ranking people who are thus untouchable. The rumors recreated the deeply rooted myth of an association between the upper spheres and the lower depths, the sacred and the mortal. This same myth runs through most rumors of white slave trading: if the police does not act and the government does not lift a finger, it is because they have sold out to those directing the loathsome commerce [114].

Notables, protected by their impunity, can move freely within the town and engage in the worst misdeeds, not against those of their own caste, but rather against the people. The symbolic content of the rumor makes it indissociable from the social context surrounding the crime space. Here again, if the hypothesis seems plausible, it is not uniquely due to movies like "Seven Deaths by Prescription" and "Investigation of a Citizen above Suspicion," whose protagonists were the medical body and a police inspector as assassin. The success of these two movies was itself the result of something else. They had mythical power: each of them represented the breaking of a social taboo—the doctor who kills and the protector who assassinates. In itself, the perennial nature of such rumors is a sign of a legitimation crisis.

The myth of the assassin-notable is a constant in provincial towns. In 1972 in Bruay-en-Artois, rumor took the notary public, Leroy, and accused him of having killed young Brigitte Dewèvre. In Poitiers in 1984, rumor seized the occasion to throw into question the social impunity of the medical *nomenklatura,* in a society in which "social problems are more and more medicalized" [35]. Every magistrate in small provincial towns knows of the eternal talk accusing the mayor or some other notable of going to orgies with underage girls or young boys, or of being involved in the seamier worlds of sex, money, and drugs.

In Caen, France, in 1980, several muggings and rapes took place in the space of a few short months, the culprits never being brought to justice. The rumor went into action, claiming that the senator-mayor's son was the guilty party. But the mayor, "wielding a great deal of power, would not let his kid be arrested." On January 15, 1981, on her way home from high school, the mayor's daughter, sixteen years old, was manhandled by two young men who plied her with questions so that she would admit to her brother's guilt. A few days later, the federal prosecutor was forced to act by making a statement indicating that the court had absolutely "no presumption or proof against anyone whomsoever." As for the senator-mayor, M. Girault, he brought a suit against X for slander.

In fact, in this all too calm city, rumors seem to arise not only from anxiety brought on by crime, but also from boredom and social frustration, as these two interviews attest. According to a trade unionist, "Considering the unemployment and the lack of possibilities, one becomes embittered", an ideal atmosphere for slander, especially when it targets a notable (*Libération,* January 28, 1981). A young man from Caen commented, "It's pretty disgusting, I agree, but it's also open war. The people who suffer from the crisis take revenge on those who are spared, like the mayor who is also a lawyer and a senator."

In Search of Myths

On December 17, 1976, the man who assassinated eight people in Creil and Nogent was arrested, after eight years of investigation. He was a rotating three-shift worker in Saint-Gobain-Rantigny by the name of Marcel Barbeault. His arrest concurred so little with the myth pursued by the rumor that the population remained incredulous, especially as the suspect constantly denied his guilt.

People had been expecting a dynamic personality, but got nothing more than a semi-skilled worker. Two months after his arrest, the rumor got its second wind: it was said that Marcel Barbeault had been released, that a judicial error had been made, and that the killer would return. The rumor was so rampant in February 1977 that the mayor expressed concern to the judicial police. That was normal: the isolated act of a worker is but a gruesome news item. It has no social import and transmits no message of any kind: it is not a myth or an exemplary story capable of becoming a contemporary legend. Today isolated murders interest no one, neither citizens nor the press.

The case of Bruay-en-Artois is exemplary in this respect. As Caviglioli pointed out,

[S]ince the notary public, Mr. Leroy, and his fiancée, Monique Mayeur, have been more or less acquitted, the town of Bruay has been dispossessed of its misfortune. It is a town that has been brutally deprived of a role which made it forget for a moment its everyday pain: that of a working class population overwhelmed by bourgeois justice. Bruay just lost everything: its class enemy, its Bluebeard [the notary public], its enigmatic female devil [Mayeur], its desire for vengeance, its hope for social revenge and its persecuted defender [Judge Pascal]. The notary public was the only rich man in town, the one who handled the people's money. It had to happen someday: not satisfied with taking the people's bread, he began devouring its children. It was a fairy tale full of horror, but was nevertheless tantamount to revenge for a great many of the townspeople's grievances. Since the affair ended, the miners of Bruay have felt abandoned, deprived as they are of their ogre and "ogress," of this miraculous nightmare that helped them bear their lives. The notary public will remain notary public, and the miners will remain miners. [*Paris-Match,* May 5, 1973].

Thus the rumor sought out the myth. One would nonetheless be mistaken were one to reduce the rumor to the reappearance of some eternal myth, like that mentioned above of the indisassociability of good and evil, of which the famous novel *Doctor Jekyll and Mister Hyde* is but one of many examples. When one studies a rumor several years later, or even when the rumor emerges in the national press, its local and historical aspects are neglected, while attention is focused on invariant elements of the collective unconscious. One wrongly glorified psychoanalysis at sociology's expense, and folklore at the expense of anthropology.

I Know Nothing, But I'll Say Everything

In a trial, the judge proceeds on the basis of rumors. Lacking direct witnesses, people are questioned who did not see anything but who have ideas or pseudo ideas. It is time for statements like: "It doesn't surprise me, because I remember when. . . . " In the case of Marie Besnard, we saw how collective memory brought out of the closet the old rumors about mistreated ewes. And, in Loudun, nothing was too absurd to be said about the young German prisoner who was doing farm work for Léon.

In big cities, life is anonymous. In villages and small towns, on the other hand, everyone knows everyone else; people have been observing and spying on each other for generations. Rumors get the jump on the judge's final decision. That is how most cases of incest are disclosed. Rumors arise from the more or less clear words of a presumed victim. They also arise from some signal: when a young girl leaves her family and her village, "it's because of incest"; if another girl shoots herself in the stomach, it is for the same kind of reason. Passing from girl to girl, from girl to teacher, and from teacher to social worker, the rumor is eventually told to the judge.

In the field of child protection, however, and in particular of abused children, we should point out the almost total absence of rumors. Indeed, the population proves to be too embarrassed to denounce what seems to be "a family affair." A true "conspiracy of silence" seems to grow up, censuring any vague impulse to talk. While censorship and secrecy engender rumors, self-censorship hinders their development.

The Media's Role

Many people do not want the police to know that they are witnesses, and do not spontaneously present themselves. On the other hand, they do not hesitate to speak to the press. Similarly, when a case drags out or becomes highly complex, the army of journalists sent out in the field must compensate for the dearth of real information by carrying out their own investigation. Suspense must be maintained whatever the cost, a true serial being made of the affair. The supply and demand of information must be balanced. Reporters' microphones pick up the slightest gossip which would have otherwise remained embryonic in form. Delivered up to millions of viewers or readers, what was but localized gossip becomes national information.

Today more than ever before, three fundamental rights are in conflict: the public's right to information, the accused person's rights (the presumption of innocence being reduced to naught when someone is accused in the media), and the legal system's right to calmly carry out its investigation so that the truth can be uncovered. There is a conflict between two pressures: the examining judge knows everything, but has no right to say anything, if he is to maintain the secrecy of the investigation. As for the journalists, they are asked to say everything though they know nothing. For the moment, the media are winning out. But, lacking information, they draw upon rumors, that black market that is always ready and willing to serve, but also to manipulate.

In Poitiers and in Bruay-en-Artois, the chronology of events was identical: a news item set off an accusatory rumor. An investigation was started up: as the judicial system remained silent, the rumor grew and grew. The press is there to inform: as the judge refused to talk, the press sought out the only source available, the rumor. What was, at the outset, mere hesitant and investigatory hypothesizing, was amplified by the rumor and then announced in all the media. It was a tough job for the magistrates and investigators to remain unaffected by the pressure. Certain charges were even deliberately deferred by examining judges so as not to give the impression that they have given way before journalistic rumors.

Crimes in Series

Before terminating this section on "crime," an urban phenomenon must be mentioned: series of crimes. In Saint-Germain-en-Laye, after the assassination of a young salesgirl on April 26, 1985, a rumor took off: it could only be one in a series of crimes. People very quickly began speaking about five victims. The mayor "was said to have received a letter announcing ten more." In this honorable, peaceful town, the rumor revealed a strong sense of insecurity: having been spared up until then, the town inescapably had to be affected, in its turn, by the "crime wave" and comply with statistical normality. The rumor filled in the gap between reality and fears: on the basis of one cadaver, it postulated a whole series of crimes, an hypothesis that had come to the fore again because of a televised broadcast, that very same week, of the movie "Fear in the City." Cinema has for a long time associated the criminally mad with the anonymity of large urban areas. In this movie, the one-eyed assassin pursued by J.P. Belmondo lost his glass eye. According to the Saint-Germain-en-Laye rumor, the "first" victim was supposed to have ripped away at her attacker's upper lip. Certain people claimed they had seen the lipless man. The crime had obviously brought anxiety-producing expectancy to the town: the point was to lighten it by, on the one hand providing the townspeople with a qualified criminal, and on the other allowing them to cry out all together.

Series of crimes are a considerable problem for the population: who will be the next victim? Faced with such an anxiety-producing question, the functional aspect of rumors is notorious. They set out to reduce anxiety. The first tactic consists in shattering the fated nature of the event by declaring that there is in fact no real series, but rather a simple addition of unrelated crimes. Thus during the eight year search for the Oise killer, from 1969 to 1976, rumors tried to introduce other potential assassins: friends, jealous lovers, and prowlers. By breaking up a series, it can be transformed into a simple enumeration of cases of delinquency and crimes of passion. To exorcise anxiety, rumors refuse reality and the inescapable proofs that a series exists.

A second attitude consists in seeking to predict by finding the link between the victims. In the case of the Oise killer, rumors first proposed the debauchery hypothesis: the exclusively female victims only got "what they deserved"; this amounts to what psychologists call "blaming the victim." The odious crime is transformed into a symbolic punishment, implying that there are no honest women in the town. Alas, the list of victims controverted this hypothesis. The rumor then had recourse to some physical feature: the victims were all short and brunette. Many women in Creil and Nogent dyed their hair for precisely that reason.

When the Investigation Gets Bogged Down: The Scapegoat

Whenever a traumatic event goes unexplained, its public does not remain passive, simply awaiting an official pronouncement. It seeks, through numerous discussions within the group, to forge its own answer or explanation. The latter is thus not the product of truth but rather of collective consensus.

What can be more traumatizing than a series of kidnappings of small children or young people? Apart from the pain and anxious worry of the families involved, everyone is able to identify with them and experience their concern. Fear of child-nappings runs so deep that many towns flare up at the least rumor of a disappearance, even when no one has disappeared.

Now in Mourmelon, the investigation answered the parents of the young soldiers who disappeared with total silence. The rumors were a response to this intolerable silence. Anxiety calls for something to dissipate it, regardless of what that something may be. The official silence was thus experienced as provocation or torture inflicted upon the parents. Hence the emergence of growing animosity and resentment. People do not understand how it is possible for an investigation not to uncover the truth immediately: does that mean that the army "is hiding something from us"? Frustration thus finds its scapegoat: the army itself has something shameful to hide, e.g., a black sheep in its own ranks [143].

The army in fact has the characteristics of a scapegoat, against whom the families' understandable animosity, frustration, and anxiety were turned. Nothing stirs up rumors like silence. For silence is a kind of message: it is interpreted as a refusal to engage in communication, exchange, or a relationship. It is like saying we don't exist!

The army's nickname in France is "the great silent one"—silent behind its walls, camps, and bases. Moreover, in the nearby Champagne region, the army does not have a good reputation. The Mourmelon camp itself is not at all integrated into its surroundings and remains marginalized. As there is a large military personnel and a camp, there are necessarily disadvantages: vehicles, shelling, and maneuvers create mini-strongholds of animosity, especially when, in the case of damages, compensation for repairs is delayed by endless administrative redtape.

Animosity was at its height when the army's behavior, though well intentioned, was interpreted as a sign of coldness, reluctance, and even criminal negligence. For example, the families were indignant about not having been alerted as soon as their children were suspected to be missing. The army thus seemed to be inhuman, cold and heartless. Yet the reason for the delay was altogether different: today adolescents lose their status as minors at 18; the recruits were thus full-fledged citizens, no longer under their parents' authority. Secondly, "late returns" of those on leave are frequent and, in the vast majority of cases, the recruits eventually show up again. The army's silence was in fact a sort of deliberate grace period.

Popular and Unpopular Rumors

Faced with a series of yet to be explained disappearances and years of investigation, rumors do not alight upon explanations at random. They must answer to two expectations: replacing confusion by order, and furnishing explanations that are socially acceptable to the group in which they circulate.

What one must understand in Mourmelon is why certain hypotheses explaining the disappearances never spread, though they were no less plausible than those adopted by rumors. Thus the hypotheses of real desertions and of crimes committed by a nonmilitary man very familiar with the region (or dressing up as a soldier) never had any currency. We cannot simply answer by saying that that was because they were not founded. To this day but one thing is certain in Mourmelon: no one knows exactly what happened. No hypothesis can be *a priori* discarded by the police investigation. The rumor—as a set of collective discussions—selected three explanations and discarded the others for essentially psychological reasons. Rumors only adopt satisfying hypotheses, rejecting scenarios that create dissonance. That is why the hypothesis of real desertions was rejected: not because it was false, but rather because it would have wreaked havoc in the town. To desert from the army is a crime: it constitutes an attack on the democratic values upheld by the nation. It amounts to reneging on one's duty. Desertion directly suggests a failure on the part of the families involved: their inability to inculcate basic values to their sons.

As this hypothesis was unacceptable to people, the rumors preferred to invoke an outside actor, a criminal hand that had deviated the sons from the straight and narrow; that put the onus of responsibility on an "other," not on the city, i.e., the families. No family could admit that one of its sons had deliberately deserted, for the family would then be partly responsible. As the hypothesis of a civilian criminal was also dissonant, it could not be adopted by the rumors. If he were a civilian, he would thus be a member of the town, living within its bosom. That would signal the corruption of the town, internal disorder, the worm in the fruit. That is why the rumors preferred to postulate a foreign actor: e.g., a "German" truckdriver or legionnaire (in reference to the "foreign" legion)—and, what's more, a hermit—or a soldier, i.e., someone from out of town. The scapegoat, let us recall, is always chosen for his marginal character, being outside of the group, or at its "border."

Insecurity and Politics

Series of crimes thus set off rumors of collusion: "the police know who the assassin is, but are protecting him." Anxiety is reduced: the assassin can no longer do harm, but the information must remain secret as it is compromising. As to the frustration of not being able to cry out for revenge, it is transformed into aggressiveness towards institutions that are unable to protect citizens, but are always ready and willing to bargain with assassins. In 1984, several elderly women were assassinated in their homes in the eighteenth arrondissement in Paris, and the police were unable to identify the assassin (or assassins). At the end of December 1984, a rumor going round the neighborhood announced that it was a drug addict, "not born in France," who was well known to those who frequented the Abbesses square. But the police could not arrest him because the socialists in power were stopping them from doing so. The authorities had decided to discreetly expulse the suspect and his accomplice (or accomplices), sending them back to their own country, as they were afraid of setting off a true popular riot.

The rumor drew its credibility from the amalgamation of two new kinds of inhabitants in the Montmartre area who were upsetting the neighborhood's equilibrium: drug addicts and immigrants. The rumor satisfied the powerless frustration of the elderly, stripped of all means of action. It also indicted the socialist government, suspected of criminal indulgence towards foreigners, an attractive hypothesis in a city with a conservative majority. In this context, one can not exclude the possibility that the rumor may have had a deliberately political origin. Maintaining a climate of insecurity can be an electoral maneuver: it suffices to maintain such a climate through rumors, and then to spread the latter through the newspapers under one's party's control.

In 1988, France witnessed the massive diffusion of a leaflet warning parents about tatoo stamps, highly prized by children, that were supposed to contain LSD in their glue. The rumor was known in the United States by the name of "Mickey Mouse Acid." Diffusion seems to have begun in Nice, whose mayor is known for his right-wing standpoints. Was the sudden appearance on the scene of this leaflet during an election year—the key period of the right/left face-off in the presidential elections—a simple coincidence or politically engineered to maintain a climate of insecurity?

12

Rumors and the Star System

Possessing a Bit of the Idol

There is no such thing as a star without rumors. A star already has a public, that of his or her admirers, venerators, and idolizers. In the eyes of this public, the star is the most important person around: their involvement with him or her is total. Fans live on identification alone: the star is their model and their source of identity. Alas, the star is distant, and necessarily so: one cannot approach the sacred too closely. The two conditions for the proliferation of rumors are thus present: great importance and considerable ambiguity created by the secrecy surrounding the star.

The savage adores wood and stone idols; civilized man adores flesh and blood idols, as George Bernard Shaw reminds us. The idolatrous fan wants to become one with the star, possess him or her, appropriate him or her physically and mentally. The star is the pivot point of his identity, his oxygen, his soul.

This "starophageous" desire is always frustrated: the star must remain inaccessible, beyond the grasp of the human world. But to maintain his crowd of adoring fans, there is a need for substitutes for this impossible possession. The rumor is such a substitute; another is the collection of physical traces of the star's passage. Unable to possess the star, the fan wants to possess at least part of him. Fan clubs are markets for objects that belonged to him, or were touched by her: Liz Taylor's lipstick, a strand of James Dean's hair, a bit of Michael Jackson's shirt ripped off at the "Palais des sports" concert hall in Paris, etc. The fetishization of reliques maintains faith, as does gossip.

The star does not possess his public: it is rather the other way around. The star has obligations to his public: to remain *its* star is a daily job. The public first of all wants to be repaid for its adoration, especially the fans, i.e., the part of the public that is most involved and most structured. The fan figures that he has rights: as one of the chosen, he wants special treatment.

The star's private life is public: a few patches are carefully exposed at the right moment by press agents and managers [10]. Overzealous journalists take it upon themselves to uncover other facets of the star's private life. In both cases, the result is the same: feeding the need to enter into the star's intimate world. Far from contenting themselves with movie images, the public is a constant Peeping Tom. Fans want more: their status depends upon it. They want to be those who contribute the indiscreet details, who leak information to those around them. They are the relays between the supernatural world of gods and heroes and the wider public. In this task of conveying between the two banks, the fan reminds us that he belongs to the world of the star: he is in the know. Bearer of the latest news, he gives the impression of living in great intimacy with his idol.

Rumors intervene at this point. To remain a star, one must manage one's secrets, engineer their timely leakage, and instill confidence. Transparency kills a star: a star is not a buddy. Total secrecy annihilates a star just as thoroughly: the public and fans become asphyxiated by the lack of information, and make themselves scarce. Carefully dosed mystery maintains faith. To make up for his powerless love, the fan wants to possess bits of exclusive information; he wants a momentarily opened window onto the idol's personal life. This imaginary appropriation substitutes for impossible possession.

Maintaining the Myth

Gossip does not have to be true. We prefer a story that does us good to a truth that gives us nothing. Good gossip feeds myths. Female stars represent archetypical lovers [187]. Thus gossip tells the uninterrupted saga of love. Rumors of engagements precede rumors of marriage, to better prepare the ground for rumors of conjugal conflict, reconciliation, and divorce. The quest for passionate love is permanent. Through these women, fans vicariously live the myth of Absolute Love that their drab lives have not allowed them to find personally.

The male star is a hero, and a lover as well. Gossip highlights both sides of his identity: Belmondo was said to have been wounded when he refused to have a stunt man play a dangerous scene for him; James Dean manifested his fury for life by constantly flirting with death: he supposedly participated in Mexican corridas. He was also reputed to be the lover of myriad stars and starlets. James Dean's whole life was construed as the brief passage of a superman whose days on earth were numbered. When he killed himself at the wheel of his Porsche Speedster on September 30, 1955, driving over a hundred miles per hour, rumor confirmed his superhuman status.

A superman never dies. According to the rumor, he was in fact simply disfigured in the accident and has been living incognito on a farm near Los Angeles. A whole legend has grown up around his Porsche [185]. After the accident, the wreck was purchased by the man who had kept it in running order for Dean: in taking it off the truck used to tow it back to his shop, the brakes let loose. A worker had both legs broken in the accident. The motor was then sold to a certain McHenry from Beverly Hills, a race car fanatic: he was of course injured in a race, shortly thereafter. When the body of James Dean's car was being sent to Salinas, the town where Dean was headed that fateful day, a sharp stab at the brakes by the truck driver threw the body out of the trailer: it claimed yet another victim and led to a pileup on the highway. Finally, thirteen years after Dean's death, the car disappeared, as if swept away by the wind. The legend forced one to wonder whether or not it had been taken back from the earth by some supernatural power, the same that had directed the superhuman destiny of James Dean himself.

When the Contract Is Breached

A tacit contract links a star to the public: throughout the star's life, he or she must play along with the myth that got him or her chosen. One does not become a star accidentally. A star is the coincidence of a physique with a personality type, the one the public expects at some particular moment. James Dean exploded on the silver screen because the shy actor played a character in whom a whole generation saw itself. It is the public's need for him or her that makes a star: part of the public, at a certain moment, needs a certain type of idol, endowed with very precise qualities. On the whole, the star contributes his or her divine physique to the role the public wants to have filled.

Once the merger has taken place between physique and character, a star is born; he must maintain his position, otherwise the public risks feeling gypped. The latter did not choose him because of his physique, but rather for his psychological function [149].

Negative rumors are a sign of a break: the star is deviating further and further from the terms of the tacit contract. He is violating the scenario for which he was selected. When Ingrid Bergman had a child with Roberto Rossellini even before marrying him, for example, it set off a general outcry. Ingrid Bergman had been taken as the incarnation of Joan of Arc, the role that consecrated her, endowing with all of her virtues. Every virtue has its star: the same holds good for movie and music idols as for patron saints in churches.

In France, the rumor about pop-singer Sheila was also a sign of disappointed expectations. When the pop magazine *Salut les copains* came out and rock music was in vogue, Sheila symbolized good high school girls; her songs were modern, but pure and reassuring. She was the very picture of the well-raised girl, following the straight and narrow path. Her vocation was very different from those of pop singers Sylvie Vartan and Françoise Hardy. She thus created very specific expectations in her public. Normally, her role would have required her to have a couple of boyfriends and few but stable relationships with them, all of that leading up to a straightforward marriage to a nice guy.

But Sheila's path was quite the opposite: not only did she maintain total secrecy about her private life—thus reneging on one of a star's duties—but, despite leaks, no public boyfriend was ever discovered, and still worse, she insisted on not getting married. This could only disturb the strongholds of her fans. Why this unexpected trajectory? Was there something impeding the female destiny the public had been promised? Later, when she was pregnant, Sheila remained very discreet: this contrasted sharply with the behavior of other stars who continually exhibit their swollen stomachs on television or the stage. Even a sex symbol like Raquel Welch proudly exhibited hers; the time when Petula Clark, while pregnant, sang while hidden behind a screen, is clearly long since gone. Nowadays, with babies being rarer and correspondingly more important, excessive secrecy seems suspicious.

As is always the case when important questions remain unanswered, rumors take up the torch and propose their own answers. Any single woman is ambiguous: alone, with no known boyfriends, taking care of things all by herself, Sheila's behavior was masculine in nature. Chosen to play the good girl, she adopted a masculine role. As everyone knows, the function makes the organ: rumor carried out an amalgamation between the failure to marry and the rather masculine type of career. If the singer had deviated from her expected path, that was because of some physical impossibility, some secret virility, previously disguised.

This mythical schema allowed the singer's professional and private lives to be fit into one single scenario. Which reminds us that a star does not belong to herself. She owes two things to her public: timely performances and permanence in the virtues for which she has been chosen. In not wishing to control rumors, one exposes oneself to the most uncontrollable rumors.

That is what happened to the movie actress, Isabelle Adjani. While she is the only real star of current French cinema, Adjani does not play the part of a star; she maintains total secrecy about her private life, grants very few interviews, and prohibits any pictures of her from appearing in the press without her explicit consent. This blockade tactic has aroused resentment on the part of all those who form opinion, wire newspaper columns, gossip, or spend their time trying to take pictures their papers will not be able to print. As for the public, it has neither pictures of her nor statements made by her; it has only more or less well-meaning hearsay. This situation made possible the explosion of a rumor that quickly ran the gamut of editorial boards and upper-class circles: Isabelle Adjani was supposed to be afflicted with "a serious illness." In January 1987, she was declared dead, people mentioning the very hospital where she died and her room number. The rumor got so out of hand that the actress was forced to appear on television to deny and try to hush up the rumors (see p. 233).

Images and Rumors

Adjani's case illustrates the existing relations between image and rumor. The Adjani rumors were, in fact, made possible by the image that the star had given of herself. In effect, through her roles, the actress had built up a very precise public image of herself. In all of her roles, she plays a passionate character, burning with intense ardor, who is pushed by destructive drives, and even self-destructive ones. This cinematographic image was taken for reality, and made the rumors of self-destruction through drugs, illness, and death plausible.

Many actors, when confronted with rumors, take someone to be responsible for them. They forget that rumors exist when people decide to repeat them to those around them. In order for them to do so, a rumor must thus seem plausible to them, i.e., compatible with the image they have of the actor. No one would ever believe that Catherine Deneuve has AIDS. In her movie roles, she acquired an image of respectability and class. On the contrary, her image made the rumors deliberately started by two television reporters credible, rumors whereby she had had a relationship with French Minister of Finances Pierre Beregovoy. The rumor did not target her at random. Even if, in Adjani's case, there was no dearth of people to start up or fan such rumors, the latter were readily believed as they corresponded to the image the actress had allowed people to form of her.

13

At the Factory and Office

Few conditions are as propitious to rumor formation as those of professional life, at the factory, the office, in businesses and administrations. One finds in these places most of the parameters that favor the emergence, diffusion and amplification of rumors.

The Inner Circles of Secrecy

Rumors flourish wherever one finds secrets. Secrecy, like censorship, increases the value of information and leads to an exacerbation of "desires to know more." As is classic in every market economy, a shortage leads to a black market, here one of information, a circuit of unofficial, unguaranteed, and unvalidated information, that is nevertheless immediately consumed and spread to the degree that the need to be informed has been frustrated.

Now even the most transparent business cannot be totally transparent. Secrecy is structural in the management of personnel, research, strategic options about a business' future, etc. Without being Lacanian, it is significant to point out that the first profession that comes to mind when one thinks of information diffusion is that of "secret-taire (the French word for "secretary," *secrétaire*, can be decomposed into *secrét* and *taire* [stay silent or hush up]. A job whose mission is silence can only inspire speech.

A Place of Anxiety

Rumors flourish when individuals have the feeling that they have lost control over their future. Everything is decided externally, without their input: nominations, pay, promotions, and layoffs. We find out only once everything has been decided—when it is already too late. Such an anxiety-producing situation can only be dissipated if individuals group together. Strength in numbers calms fears. Anxiety is also reduced when fear can be objectified, i.e., when one knows what it is one is afraid of—when one has a precise object.

Rumors have the following two functions:

1. As they travel by word-of-mouth, they oblige individuals to come together. They create the conditions and motivation for greater proximity and togetherness. People have to be close to each other to speak.
2. They give people something to talk about: they propose an anxiety-producing theme, and thus an occasion to objectify anxiety and fight it together. In the case where a rumor claims that a part of a factory will be shut down, that is enough for meetings to be organized and work stoppages to be planned.

Of course, the more an economic sector is in crisis, the more businesses in that sector are riddled with rumors. In a situation of economic growth, the dismantling of a machine would be interpreted as an announcement that a new, more efficient replacement has been found. In times of crisis, cries of total abandonment will be heard.

Businesses highly oriented towards sales are less sensitive to rumors. On the one hand, the salesmen are out in the field, and their communication network is thus loosely knit; meetings are impractical. Secondly, salesmen feel they have more control over their destiny: they see an immediate relationship, for example, between their efforts and their revenue. Their situation is thus very different from that of businesses' "sedentary" personnel such as office workers, blue-collar workers, executives, and so on.

A Locus of Power

In businesses, information is not in scarce supply—"official" information, that is. Its validity is guaranteed, of course, but it has been evaluated before being made public. It is information that someone has scrutinized to decide whether or not it should be diffused and in what form. Thus, despite efforts made by communication managers, in-house papers and informational meetings, rumors often persist.

It is enough, therefore, for confidence to be lacking in a business between management and personnel, for information to be considered suspicious, and for counterinformation to arise in the form of rumors. As unofficial information, they constitute a counterpower.

A recent survey done with a representative sample of 770 blue-collar workers, office workers and executives showed that while official information sources today dominate the communication horizon in businesses, they are far from neutralizing the grapevine. When asked which information source gave them a *lot* of information about the company's life; 22 percent of the people surveyed said "my direct supervisor or foreman"; 22 percent cited rumors; 21 percent the top-level management or boss; 15 percent their colleagues; and 8 percent the trade union delegates or representatives. Interestingly enough, when asked how much confidence they had in each of these sources, rumors received only 11 percent versus 77 percent for the direct supervisors, 74 percent for the top managers or boss, 64 percent for colleagues, and 38 percent for trade union representatives. The respondents who had the most faith in rumors were the bottom-of-the-hierarchy workers, those most lacking in power.

Informal Channels of Communication

In businesses, everyone is always surprised to notice that people often hear information well before official notification: this happens in the case, for example, of transfers, promotions, and so on. Curiously enough, official communication circuits seem less efficient that alternative circuits, which should come as no surprise.

To use an analogy, one can compare communication networks in companies to housing complexes. Working on the basis of blueprints, architects trace out pretty meandering paths that are supposed to aesthetically link, for example, different buildings in a residential complex. Now once the complex has been built, one soon observes paths that have been trodden by the inhabitants themselves, that more directly connect one building to another, and that avoid the aesthetic curves of the previously planned paths.

The same is true in companies: the planned channels of information flow take into account above all hierarchical considerations and power. Rumors constitute shortcuts.

Formal and Informal Groups

All the organigrams in the world cannot foresee the specific sociology of a company's personnel. They are conceived of in terms of logical criteria and respect for functional and hierarchical relations between individuals. In the official communication network, each individual is imagined not as a person, but rather as a position, status, profile, and hierarchical rank.

But another reality exists: that of informal groups, i.e., invisible colleges of sorts, that weave their own communication networks that have nothing to do with those foreseen in the organigrams. As instances of invisible colleges, we can cite groups constituted according to origin (e.g., the Polish, the members of a fraternity, etc.); school (e.g., Harvard alumni); and affinity (e.g., members of the football team). Now within these groups, differences in status and hierarchical rank lose their importance. Intra-group solidarity is created, along with direct communication between the group's members, protocol being thrown to the winds. Hence the propagation speed of rumors. Their speed merely evinces the existence of informal information networks.

As we see, rumors are inescapable in business. But too many rumors is a sign of organizational disfunctioning: loss of confidence, fear, political problems, too much secrecy, etc. The case of Renault illustrates this point.

Renault's Silence

There have rarely been as many rumors going around as during the weeks following Georges Besse's appointment to the directorship of Renault. The company's disappointing earnings had been such that Bernard Hanon, the former managing director, had been forced to resign. The government sought out Besse, a top-notch manager known for his effectiveness, who had already shown his mettle in setting the Péchiney corporation back on its feet. Anything could be expected from this man the media were presenting as Renault's last-ditch surgeon.

After his nomination on January 21, 1985, Besse made but two statements: "Savings have to be made," and "I will meet with everyone to determine his or her exact role in the business." He then maintained total silence for weeks on end. His silence opened the floodgates: rumors began circulating among blue-collar workers and office staff. Everyone was trying to surmise the frightful intentions of the merciless manager. Rumors went around that "he just shut down the cafeteria at the company's headquarters, on the Quai du Point-du-Jour [in Paris]," and "It seems that the cafeteria at Reuil-Malmaison [another office building] will be closed as well." According to the rumor told by ten o'clock coffee lovers and five o'clock tea drinkers, "he" had noticed that executives and office workers had a tendency to mistake cafeterias for offices.

Rumor had it that Besse had launched an anti-"excess" campaign. In Billancourt (one of the main Renault plants), he intended to close down all the prayer rooms. He was said to have made a surprise visit to the Leclerc supermarket right near the Renault plant to "nab" several workers who were doing their shopping during working hours, the upshot being a warning sent out to seventy-nine employees (notice once again how important it is, when information is emotionally charged, that it be propped up with realistic details such as this precise figure). On top of all that, Besse had supposedly gone to movie theaters near the Boulogne-Billancourt plant to check for "lazybones". It looked like old habits were going to be shaken up a bit.

To everyone's surprise, Georges Besse showed up at Renault headquarters driving a Renault Super 5, with neither a chauffeur nor a car phone. Most of the executives drove more sophisticated company cars, Renault 25's. A rumor went around that company cars would henceforth be limited to no-frills Renault 5's. And in fact, the minimal innovation imposed by the new director made real inroads. Those responsible for distributing company vehicles began frowning at requests, and within a few weeks were granting cars very sparingly. "Now they are lent to us far less often," one furious executive complained. At Renault, every change is now attributed to Besse (*Libération*, April 23, 1985). One evening, at the Quai du Point-du-Jour office, the lights went out, and people claimed that "It was Besse who cut the power."

Rumors were, of course, also running rampant about cuts in staff. Georges Besse had announced that he wanted to meet everyone, meaning everyone with some degree of responsibility. Through word-of-mouth, his intention turned into a desire to meet with every single employee: "During his factory 'visit,' he went to the nursing station at the Billancourt workshop, dressed as a blue-collar worker. As the health-care service was not fast enough, he fired the head doctor." As for cutbacks in personnel, rumors placed the number of layoffs in the 15,000 to 25,000 range.

It was in the assembly buildings that rumors had the most currency: at the bottom of the hierarchical ladder, where anxiety is highest, talk is repeated without due analysis. At higher levels in the hierarchy, rumors spread just as quickly, even when they are not believed—they constitute the "latest stories" one tells one's colleagues in order to exorcize worry through laughter. Whether they were believed or not, this succession of mini-events, rumors and stories contributed to building the "Besse" myth. Rivers are made up of small streams that run together; similarly, mini-rumors make a reputation.

A Trade Union Weapon

As we have already seen, rumors constitute a counterpower. In business, management's media are silence, memoranda, house organs, press releases, and lectures. Rumors, leaflets, and trade union bulletins are the media of workers' organizations. What are the various uses of rumors?

Rumors mobilize people. At Renault, for example, the CGT (the dominant local trade union) regularly starts up rumors that Séguin Island, where the main Renault plant is located, is going to be sold. Seemingly arising from the base, these rumors allow the union to mobilize union sympathizers; they strengthen its image and do wonders for its public relations. When delegates from the personnel are to be elected, union delegates start rumors among immigrant workers that if they are not reelected, immigrants' social advantages will be partially eliminated. In 1984, in a castle not far from Paris, the directors of one of Renault's branches met with foreign representatives to negotiate possible trade relations and lay the groundwork for industrial cooperation. The meeting seemed ambiguous to the unions; the latter thus started a rumor that the branch was going to be sold to foreigners. At that point it was child's play to organize a march around the castle and disrupt the worrisome secret negotiations.

Rumors condition people's minds; they create and maintain a desired climate. This was the case in the many rumors portraying Georges Besse as a man who was going to make deep cutbacks and go right to the root. The rumor about the Renault 5 company cars aimed at unsettling executives by throwing into question their "already acquired rights"; the one about the prayer rooms aimed, rather, at Muslim immigrants. though the two rumors may well have been spontaneous, they certainly could have been part of a deliberate communication plan.

Rumors work against plans; they take the initiative and organize resistance; they oppose passive acceptance of decisions that have already been made, of which those who are affected are generally informed when it is already too late. Thus in 1985, at the moment of the renewal of the commercial cooperation contract between Renault and the USSR, Renault threatened to suspend a contract concerning the sale of equipment and engineering materials, as the USSR was making too low an offer. Rumors then went around announcing sizable layoffs: if the equipment was not sold, the machine tools sector would be devastated, and employees in that sector were likely to be fired.

The rumors forced the Renault management to break the silence and dispel doubts: the rumors announced what was patently false in order to force the truth out of hiding. By constantly starting up alarming rumors, the unions tried to guess what the company's managers intended to do: it sufficed to examine which of the rumors were denied and which of them were not. Using this tactic of constant fire, they managed to reverse their usual relationship to management. The latter lost its lead concerning information diffusion: it could only react to rumors started by the unions. The problem was serious: to regain the upper hand and stop being backed into a passive role of denying or confirming, the management might have been tempted to adopt a policy of total silence—"no comment." But in doing so, it would have encouraged the persistency of the rumors, if not exacerbating them: silence would have been interpreted as a sign of embarrassment at having been found out.

Management itself sometimes uses rumors as an experimental tool. It wants to know what the reaction at the base would be to a particular unpopular measure, i.e., to know to what extent the troops would mobilize if the measure were implemented. A rumor is thus started: management has but to observe the speed and strength of the union's reaction.

The Management of Internal Communication

While they control their external communication (their advertising and their public image), businesses have realized that they are totally unarmed when it comes to internal communication. A proliferation of rumors is generally indicative of this deficiency. Thus a new functional position has appeared in company organigrams, that is directly involved in general management: manager of internal communication or human relations. This manager's job is not to eliminate all rumors, but rather to stop certain rumors from coming into being. To eliminate all rumors would be a utopian goal, based on the false hypothesis that rumors are harmful. They are, instead, above all a mode of expression and a way of acting upon one's environment. Moreover, considering businesses' social organization and the conflicts that characterize it, rumors are unavoidable: they are the product of social structure and power relations. The number and content of rumors are excellent atmospheric barometers [65].

One can nevertheless prevent certain rumors. An examination of the tactics used by internal communication managers shows that these managers espouse the ideal of transparency. As rumors are born of under-information, over-information, or mis-information, their strategy consists in excising the roots of these three factors by an open information policy. The new manager at Renault's Billancourt plant, for example, has opted for frank, direct communication with employee representatives. He never misses a meeting with trade unions and announces his decisions very clearly. When, for reasons of provisional confidentiality, he cannot reveal his rationale for certain decisions, he does not avoid the problem; the reasons for secrecy are explained, as well as the date at which secrecy will be dispelled.

A manager of internal communication edits his company's house-organs. His job is to explain the company's major decisions, but also to point out facts that are all too often considered minor by management. For purely managerial reasons, the Valéo group, for example, decided to sell its headquarters: it was less expensive to rent the space than to freeze capital in such an unproductive way. Such decisions are generally considered to be of too little importance to figure in in-house informational sources. But this is a mistaken view. Office workers and blue-collar workers have a hard time deciphering strategic diversification plans; they are, however, very sensitive to signs that are near at hand, tangible and highly symbolic. If one does not watch out, the discreet sale of the company's headquarters may turn into a rumor of bankruptcy: "The company is being sold!" A similar event took place at Renault: the manager of a foreign subsidiary sold his personal house to buy another. It was interpreted as a sign that he was leaving the country, and that Renault was pulling out altogether. Such mini-events must be announced in advance if one is to avoid rumors [64,66].

Career Management

In every organization, there are at least two communication networks. The first, formal network, is symbolized by the company's organigram. The second, informal network, can never be found in any document, but nevertheless exists. Practically speaking, the latter is an irreplaceable source of secrets, especially concerning the company's most prominent figures [75]. This channel is ideal for finding out:

- Who rates and who does not.
- Who is going to be promoted and who will not.
- What the future organization will look like, before it is officially announced, allowing employees to take the necessary precautionary steps.
- Who is going to be transferred;
- What positions are going to be created and who is in line for them—that allows individuals to perhaps apply before the list is officially closed by using word-of-mouth to suggest their names.
- What one's own image is in the company—people are reluctant to answer frankly when directly approached. Thanks to anonymity, however, rumors give the answers one is seeking without beating around the bush.

This second communication network is known in France as "hall-radio" for horizontal communication, and "carpet-radio" when the rumors come down the hierarchical ladder from top management. It is not simply a source of information; it is also a source of influence with rumors as intermediaries. Take the case of an executive who would like to be appointed to a newly created position: a rumor can incline those who might never have thought of him to consider him for the job, and it can also discredit his competitors. Career management involves managing one's internal and external images: rumors have their say in that realm.

14

Rumors in Marketing

Introduction

In the commercial world, not everything is permitted—not officially at any rate. In France, for example, comparative advertising is not authorized. Nor are salesmen supposed to openly denigrate competing products. But too much is at stake for rumors not to become part of commercial strategies and communication plans.

Destabilizing the Competition

In the field, word-of-mouth is the sales medium. It is through face-to-face contact that clients and suppliers communicate. Every time a salesman comes to see one of his clients, an opportunity presents itself of surreptitiously slipping a rumor into the conversation that throws into doubt the reliability of competing suppliers. Nothing is stated openly, everything being merely understood: a salesman can easily "rumor" pseudo-information, disguising behind a tone of well-meaning confidence. "I heard from one of my friends who works for X that the company is undergoing a bit of restructuring. Is the news trustworthy? I don't know, but I thought I'd better let you know." When a buyer has but one supplier, his high degree of dependency entails risks. Production could be interrupted if his monopolistic supplier succombs to a strike or delivers his goods late. Clients are therefore generally very sensitive to rumors about their exclusive suppliers—the information is too important to be neglected.

The slightest fact can become the basis of a rumor. If a business loses one of its best salesmen to a competitor, people are likely to say: "He's not the first, according to my sources, to leave in the past few years, and perhaps it's just the beginning." Thus a localized event—the resignation of a salesman—is presented as a sign of a hidden problem announcing problems to come in the company. In the current economic context, salesmen for big companies often bet on the Achilles' heel of smaller competitors, i.e., their fragility. Rumors about a supplier's forthcoming bankruptcy run rampant. A salesman suggests that a small business is likely to go bankrupt because he hopes to pick up an extra client thereby. If the rumor gets spread around, it becomes self-confirming. Worried at the prospect of seeing one of their suppliers go out of business in short order, buyers prefer suppliers who are sure to be alive and well for at least ten years to come. In such a case, the cancelling of orders spurred on by the rumor can in fact drive the targeted supplier out of business. In everyone's mind, the rumor was thus accurate.

In the business world, every buyer feels abandoned by his salesman. Once a sale has been concluded, resentment and grievances accumulate, just like after the initial euphoria of marriage. Rumors find particularly suitable ground among frustrated and abandoned buyers: rumors provide a simple explanation for a set of details and situations that have been unpleasant for the buyers, as, for example, the salesman's less frequent visits, fewer invitations, and smaller New Year's gifts. The buyer projects his resentment: he thus takes hold of a rumor that opens his eyes. His supplier was hiding something from him.

The fact that the slightest event can be negatively exploited by rumors influences company decisions. In 1984, for example, when the Grands Moulins de Marseille came out with the *banette* (an improved version of the French bread, the *baguette*) the company wondered whether it should invest in a television advertising campaign or not. It decided to stay away from television, as the budget could only sustain a short-lived campaign. Their competitors would thus have been able to start a rumor presenting it as a "shortened" campaign, i.e., a sign that the *banette* was not selling in bakeries, and that it was thus wiser not to buy it.

In the permanent, underground war aiming at undermining big companies' reputations, France has a serious handicap: the financial and international economic press is written in English, when it is not altogether English in extraction. Due to the linguistic barrage and their paucity of journalistic relations, the French are unable to start insidious rumors in this influential press at the right moment.

Underground Struggles

We have already spoken about the case of sugar in chapter 8. Having consumed natural sugar for centuries, the Western world then set about using synthetic sweeteners. Year after year, the sales of aspartame (an artificial sweetener) showed geometrical growth. The problem for sugar producers was to figure out how to eat away at the growth of the new substitute products. A first approach consisted in using regulations to limit the competitors' market penetration. A second, defensive approach consisted in trying to rid natural sugar of the flock of false rumors that had sprung up around it. Another tentative approach, more offensive this time, consisted in starting a rumor to discourage consumers from switching from natural sugar to sugar substitutes. There are enough paramedical journals, revolving around health issues and nutrition, in need of good material that one could easily insert a few alarming articles on the hidden dangers of using sugar substitutes, sustaining, for example, that they may be carcinogenic.

Thus every company and every brand has its weak spot, an Achilles' heel that can be exploited by rumors. To take an example, part of the capital of the mail-order sales company, Les Trois Suisses, is German owned. Now mail-order clients tend to be rather xenophobic, preferring to buy French products. They do not realize that Les Trois Suisses is partly German owned. This could constitute fertile ground for rumors, if it were exploited by its competitors. Similarly, most French drinkers of Heineken beer think that Heineken is an imported beer. And in fact, for many years it was brewed in Holland, and its success in France is largely based on its image as a beer "imported" from abroad. But without any fanfare, Heineken has set up a brewery in France, in the town of Schiltigheim, a suburb of Strasburg. The very basis of Heineken's image is no longer true. A competitor could very well have an interest in exploiting this fact by starting up a rumor.

Many brands wind up being targeted by rumors. Certain of the rumors arise spontaneously for, as we have already seen, the social body at times reacts defensely towards innovation. Others are probably intentionally started. Still others, while arising spontaneously, are encouraged by those in whose interests they happen to be. Since it was bought up by the powerful Perrier group, the Roquefort Société, number one in the market, has been targeted by rumors: its cheese is said to have become industrialized, to have lost its purity, and its authentically rural and even artisanal character. Naturally, even if the less important brands of roquefort cheese were not really behind the rumors, they took advantage of and encouraged them. To give another example: since its creation, the shoe polish, Baranne, has been plagued by rumors. As opposed to what its intense advertising campaign claimed, according to the rumor, the polish "dries out leather." This argument is spontaneously employed by small shopkeepers who sell competing brands that do not advertise.

In Belgium, every Belgian would claim that Stella Artois beer gives you headaches. What was but a rumor ten years ago has since become part and parcel of common knowledge: it is difficult to say whether this rumor was planned or whether Stella Artois, the market leader, quite naturally inherited rumors about beer in general. The rumor even went so far as to claim that Stella Artois beer made people impotent. Now that was at the very same moment that a new competitor, Jupiler beer, was being advertised as "a man's beer"—a tangential if not a direct reference to the rumor. Today, Jupiler is the number-one beer in Belgium.

The many products listed on the "Villejuif" leaflet clearly suffered from willful manipulation on the part of consumers [144]. Moreover, it is no accident that the leaflet is now circulating in other countries: the competitors of French business have every interest in having it circulate.

There is a way of criticizing products that is very close to rumors: jokes. They circulate very quickly in the groups concerned because of their comic effects. And while they aim at some particular company or brand, they also allow one to laugh about it. In 1985, for example, while Bull (the largest French computer company) was making a spectacular recovery, the following story was going around computer circles: "Do you know why Bull's logo is a tree? Because it's the only computer that's for the birds!" The intention behind the joke is quite obvious: it denies Bull's transformation and reminds one of technological fiascos from a few years back. It was a defensive maneuver aiming to perpetuate Bull's former image.

Word-of-Mouth Stimulation

Consumers have more confidence in what their friends and neighbors tell them than in advertising and salesmen. Thus all manufacturers have asked themselves the same question: how can one start up rumors about one's own products in order to increase sales?

In reality, the question has more to do with word-of-mouth stimulation than with rumors. Let us recall that rumors and word-of-mouth are not identical. In the very concept of a rumor, it is understood that a truth that has heretofore been hidden has been accidentally revealed, unbeknownst to the company, and perhaps even against its will. That is why most rumors are black, and why they are a competitor's ideal weapon.

There are, nevertheless, favorable rumors: they provide a sales argument that was not wished for or to which one cannot openly admit. In Martinique and Guadaloupe, for example, the Vittel mineral water company sells a great deal of "Ricqlès," a mint-flavored soft drink. According to the local inhabitants, Ricqlès has aphrodisiacal qualities. Were Ricqlès to sell as much in France as in the French Antilles, it would be the number-one soft drink in the country. But in order to do so, Vittel would have to somehow start up a rumor in France that Ricqlès is a high-powered aphrodisiac.

Word-of-mouth does not connote something that goes unsaid, or some sort of message that is diffused without certain people being aware of it. On the contrary, most manufacturers openly wish the public would adopt and spread its advertising arguments, i.e., that the public would become a media-relay.

Of all sources of influence over consumer choices, word-of-mouth is both the oldest and the most effective. Informal conversations about brands, products, and stores give precious information to consumers faced with difficult decisions. And word-of-mouth tends to come at just the right time: one can engage in it when one has a specific need for advice ("what movie should we go see tonight?"; "what kind of clothes should we buy to be in style this summer?"; and so on). Moreover, it emanates from people in whom one has total confidence, i.e., who can hardly be suspected of wanting to "sell" one on something.

There is no dearth of studies showing the influence of spontaneous word-of-mouth on consumers [11]: one out of two people purchasing household appliances consults friends and family before buying, and one out of three buys a product and a brand that he has seen at a friend or relative's house. Word-of-mouth thus contributes to accelerating or slowing down the sales of new products: the first buyers naturally speak of their reactions to those around them.

Generally speaking, the more a product is involving, constitutes a risky purchase, or is extremely innovative, the more spontaneous word-of-mouth grow up around it. Thus it should come of no surprise that household appliances, cars, and fashion articles are very much subject to this form of media. In the United States, Wilkinson blades were largely promoted by word-of-mouth: shaving is an important subject for men, and Wilkinson blades constituted real progress in shaving technology. On the contrary, for low-involvement products [238], media and shelf space play a predominant role. Only 8 percent of purchasers of a new toothpaste mention word-of-mouth as a source of information, while 28 percent mention the sight of the product on the shop shelves, and 25 percent the advertising that appeared in the media.

Word-of-mouth is very important in the service sector. Unlike products, services are invisible or intangible. How is one thus to evaluate whether such and such an insurance company is upfront, or if a particular car mechanic is a trustworthy professional? Only the experience of others can provide a convincing message: word-of-mouth communicates the lessons of their direct experience with the service in question. It is not astonishing, therefore, that 42 percent of the population use word-of-mouth as their source of information when they choose a mechanic to tune up and repair their cars [138]. Services also create the highest degree of proselytism: consumers spontaneously seek to share their discovery with those around them. This is due to the human contact that takes place during the service: one develops affective relationships with one's baker, banker, mechanic, insurance broker, hairdresser, doctor, and so on.

Satisfied clients appropriate their service providers, and begin talking about them as "their" mechanic, "their" doctor, "their" hairdresser, etc. In speaking of them, they speak a bit about themselves: in valorizing their gem, they valorize the discoverer. The clients of Club Med are its most ardent salesmen.

Furthermore, while product quality is stable, due to the standardization of production, services can be of very variable quality. A restaurant, for example, can rest on its laurels and let the quality of its service slide. While it will continue to benefit for another whole year from the number of stars it received in the fine dining guides, rumors will immediately warn people of the recent decline in value. The public is thus quite attentive to rumors about services (hairdressers, restaurants, dry cleaners, banks, insurance companies, etc.). People convey information that seems to be utterly recent [207].

Generally speaking, word-of-mouth is especially influential during the last stages of a consumer's decision-making process; when one must opt for one product or brand or service provider among many. Conversely, media and advertising play their parts essentially at the beginning of the decision-making process: when a consumer begins to formulate his purchase problem, looking into what is available on the market, where it is available, and at what price. Thus the media contribute information, and word-of-mouth provides an appraisal. Advertising tells us that a movie has just come out; word-of-mouth tells us whether it is worth seeing or not.

For marketers, word-of-mouth constitutes both the carrot dangled in front of a donkey's nose, and a stick with which to beat him. It acts like a stick when the product is unsatisfying. In that case, consumers start up counter-advertising—negative word-of-mouth. Moreover, they have at their disposal consumer associations that widely diffuse their views in the media. One may recall the cases in France of the unreliable Kléber tires and motorcycle helmets, and the Fichet locks that were not as unpickable as their advertising suggested. When, on the contrary, a product is excellent, word-of-mouth speeds up sales.

Certain companies rely exclusively on word-of-mouth to promote their brands. The Abeille brand furniture polish in France, for example, does not advertise, unlike its competitor, Favor. Women who use the wax (in paste or spray forms) on their furniture are generally very concerned about their housework and the maintenance of their homes: they are the spontaneous converts for products that seem more effective to them. An old and well-reputed brand, Abeille is part of their affective environment: they speak of it with fervor to those around them.

Up until 1981, Tupperware did not advertise in France. The company sold its hermetically sealed plastic containers by word-of-mouth alone, and by direct contact between consumers. Tupperware depended on 12,500 home-makers who praised their products to their friends, neighbors, colleagues, and relatives during organized meetings. Each hostess thereby spread Tupper-ware's products to those around her by her own word-of-mouth. Every year, 700,000 such meetings took place, and 7 million women were contacted. Similarly, the Weight Watchers company, promoting weight-reducing diets, relies largely on proselytism by individuals who have successfully used the rules of nutritional behavior recommended by the company.

It would nevertheless be erroneous to consider word-of-mouth and advertising to be exclusive choices. Advertising stimulates the need for information that is then taken up by word-of-mouth: "what is one to think of the latest movie?" "what is one to think of Peugeot's most recent car?" Advertising gives substance to word-of-mouth because of the notoriety it confers on the brand or product, and notoriety is reassuring. On the contrary, less advertising in the media can reduce the frequency of word-of-mouth. Thus, when the latter is very negative, a brand will try to stay out of the public eye for a while. After the incident that hurt Tylenol so badly, no advertising for the drug appeared in the media for over a year.

The cinematographic industry has adapted especially well to word-of-mouth. When a producer foresees that a movie may be targeted by negative word-of-mouth, he makes sure that it's shown in a great many movie theaters at the same time. Attracted by the advertising, the public stampedes to see the film before word-of-mouth has had a chance to make the rounds. The distribution tactic thereby forestalls the predicted effects: the movie has already made the considerable box-office showings before its reputation can be tarnished by word-of-mouth stemming from opinion leaders and the first spectators. But there are also active approaches to controlling and directing word-of-mouth [79].

A few years ago, in the United States, public relations agency W. Howard Downey and Associates (based in New York, Chicago, Atlanta and Toronto) was offering an unusual service: its employees could, at a client's request, get word-of-mouth going, i.e., get people talking about a particular person, product, or event. In the afternoon, the firm would send quite a few of its employees down into the subway by pairs. Each pair would begin talking in such a way that other passengers could hear everything they were saying: e.g., when the crowds would begin to crush into the subway, they would not stand right next to each other, but would rather leave space for a few passengers in between them. The same procedure would also be used in elevators, stadiums, or movie lines.

To focus the public's attention and set off word-of-mouth related to advertised products, a frequent ploy is to use a two-step mechanism known as a "teasing campaign." One tries to arouse curiosity: the prototype was the well-known "Myriam" campaign in France (a billboard poster of a pretty, topless model, saying: "tomorrow I'll take off everything"). At the first stage, the ad poses a mysterious question without mentioning any brand at all; at the second stage, the answer is given. One hopes thereby to involve the public, to incite it to discuss the mysterious question and create collective suspense setting off word-of-mouth.

To stimulate word-of-mouth, businesses also use the organized leak technique. More than a year before it was available, for example, IBM let it be known that a new IBM computer was about to come out. IBM thus announced an important and yet ambiguous event: no one knew exactly what the new model would be able to do. The mystery encouraged rumors and word-of-mouth, which was precisely what IBM was hoping for. The operational result was that many buyers decided to wait until the new model came out, rather than purchase a competitor's model right away.

A Privileged Target: Opinion Leaders

In spontaneous conversations about brands and products, not all individuals play the same role. Certain people have influence over those around them, even if they are not aware of this fact: they enjoy giving their opinion, and their opinion is even sought out. Such people are opinion leaders [209].

The discovery of the key role played by opinion leaders in influence phenomena dates back to the 1950s. Up until then, the social scene was (and still is too often today) understood as a two-man show: on the one hand there were the media, and on the other that massified entity known as "the public." According to this conception, the media were supposed to have a direct influence on the public—that simple agglomeration of individuals. According to another conception, it was clear that certain individuals could influence others: the opinion leaders were considered to be political or social elites who served as sources of inspiration and identification for the "masses." In both cases, influence was direct and vertical: from top to bottom, from the media or the elites to the public.

Work done by American sociologists and political scientists [147] since that time has shown that the influence of the media is not direct: it must pass through the filter of people who, in their immediate circles, function as leaders, without, however, enjoying any privileged status [147]. The concept of opinion leader thus cannot be limited to an elitist or statutory acceptation: such leaders are active within restricted groups (e.g., groups of friends, relatives, connections, etc.). Opinion leadership is not vertical, but rather horizontal; it takes place within each group, in a very informal fashion. We all have around us, in our immediate circles, people whose advice we solicit about particular subjects. In effect, opinion leaders are specialists. There is no such thing as a leader in everything, i.e., an omnispecialist. Depending on the subject, we solicit the advice of different people. These key people serve as relays, intermediaries, and filters between the media and their circles; they inform and evaluate [120].

Who are the opinion leaders? As opposed to the elitist and statutory conception, nothing objectively distinguishes an opinion leader from his social circle. Yet he has a higher degree of involvement in a given subject (e.g., politics, cars, fashion, cooking, home maintenance, or whatever). As he is more involved, he is more informed and more open to specialized media about his subject of interest and to other opinion leaders. As we thus see, interpersonal influence by word-of-mouth moves from relay to relay, an information receiver becoming a leader for his own circle, and so on and so forth. It is a process with multiple stages.

The discovery of the essential role of opinion leaders has had repercussions on business communication strategies. Using the elitist conception of opinion leaders, companies used to try to acquire (in the original meaning of the term) favors from these social and cultural "locomotives." To put a new product on the market, companies offered it to the small world of stars and people who create fashion. Every advertising campaign included generous coverage in *Vogue* magazine, the latter being proud to provide contact with leaders, not followers. Indeed, *Vogue* was read almost exclusively by people who were considered at that time to "make opinion . . . fashionable men who determine what will be fashionable . . . who are ready and willing to adopt a novelty item and spread it." The Rubik's cube, for example, a brain teaser with different colored sides, was launched by sending it free to 1,200 celebrities in politics, the arts, the performing arts, and the press. This vertical conception of influence relied on the mechanism of social identification, and was primarily applied to products with a great deal of value as signs (alcoholic beverages, cosmetics, perfumes, restaurants, hotels, and so on).

To get the renowned Belgian beer, Abbaye de Leffe, off the ground, the advertising agency hired to do the job paradoxically decided not to advertise. The paucity of the budget (approximately $40,000) would have covered no more than a two-page color ad in the magazine, *L'Express*. Instead, they sent, free of charge, superb wood cases, each containing four bottles of the beer, to several thousand people who were considered to be opinion leaders and social locomotives, able and perhaps willing to spontaneously proselytize and proclaim the qualities of their "find" [127].

In another realm, manufacturers have always been aware of the influence of those individuals who are designated as experts on particular subjects. In the case of tennis racquets, for example, champions recommend racquets to professionals; tennis pros recommend racquets to ranked players, and the latter recommend them to ordinary players. There is thus a status ladder. The promotional policy adopted by tennis racquet brands therefore concentrates on certain recommendation levels in order to reach the bigger target; the public at large. Similarly, in industrial marketing, companies have tried to influence those who have the greatest influence in deciding what products will be purchased for their businesses. A salesman's role is to identify all those who participate in the decision-making process, and to try to persuade the most influential among them.

This strategy of targeting social leaders and experts is quite well known nowadays. But the wider concept of opinion leader draws attention to the process of influence among friends. In order to form their own opinion about something, certain people wait until they have first spoken with the individual who, in their circle, advises them about such matters. In order to influence the public, companies try to identify opinion leaders, i.e., these linchpin relays, so as to directly give them exclusive information, thereby recognizing their role as opinion leaders, and the needs that that role creates. The case of the French mail-order company La Redoute is exemplary in this respect: it illustrates how a company was able to modify its procedures after having recognized the wider scope of the concept "opinion leaders."

Formerly, La Redoute conceived of the "public" (the clientele listed on its five-million name file) as a mass, without any internal communication network. La Redoute sought to stimulate word-of-mouth by making the same offers to everyone. In their catalogue, for example, they included a "coupon-for-a-friend." The idea was to incite their already-existing catalogue-receiving clientele to talk about the company with their friends and convince one friend to take advantage of the special offer reserved for a friend.

Since that time, La Redoute has discontinued its policy of extension through friends. All of its word-of-mouth stimulation activities are now aimed at opinion leaders. It would be pointless to incite nonleaders. The social influence network exists independently of La Redoute, and it could no longer be neglected.

How is one to locate opinion leaders if they have the same social characteristics as those around them? The first method used was that of a self-evaluatory questionnaire: on the basis of a number of questions, those listed in the file were asked if they viewed themselves as leaders in relation to those around them concerning certain areas of interest. The second method began with the observation that leaders, being very involved in a certain field, tend to show behavior that is characteristic of highly involved consumers:

- They are the most loyal buyers.
- They consume a great many products in the category in question.
- They use all the services proposed by the company.

Once they have been identified, the opinion leaders are targeted for specialized communication. As we have already seen, one does not approach very involved people in the same way as one approaches uninvolved people [138]. The former, because of their expertise and their role as leaders, expect selective, exclusive communication adapted to their level, answering their informational needs. In order to be a relay, one must have information to relay. While communication directed at the public at large is limited to presenting pictures and strengthening notoriety, communication directed at leaders must be very informative: it must reinforce the idea they have of themselves by providing them, for instance, with a plethora of details about products and services.

In order to accelerate the friend-to-friend spreading process, mail-order companies make special "sponsorship" offers. The idea is to stimulate leaders' natural proselytism by offering them a gift if they manage to convince a large enough number of people in their circles upon whom they have some influence.

The marketing of products for children also relies heavily on word-of-mouth processes and opinion leaders. Many candies and toys are put on the market without any advertising: they count on talk during recess at school, recess being the most propitious period for word-of-mouth [139]. Such products spread like wildfire in schools. Similarly, many manufacturers try to create new media in order to communicate with children: television is costly and fleeting, and the press is less than perfect. Thus we see a true explosion in the number of clubs. Created in France in 1982, the Barbie Club, for example, now has 350,000 active members. This astronomical growth is due to the success of sponsorship campaigns aimed at girls. Each club member who introduces new members receives a small gift from the famous Barbie doll. That member thus plays an active role as an opinion leader in relation to her girlfriends.

The Case of Luxury Items

Luxury items have a particularly great need for social recommendation. Although it may be possible to detect the opinion makers in a town, one cannot easily turn them into salesmen. They would refuse such a role because of their status, and for fear of losing all credibility. The strategy to adopt thus consists in not trying to put a product under their noses, but rather to bring them into the brand's universe in an exclusive and privileged way. Several fine luxury brands have, for example, revealed their secrets to a hundred people that a sociometric analysis had shown to be very influential in one hundred towns in France. These people were brought to Paris, met and spoke with the creators of the product lines themselves, visited the production centers, and so on. The goal of this privileged treatment was to familiarize them with the brand's value system. Returning to their hometowns, they were quite naturally led to speak of the brands with their friends and acquaintances, as it is flattering to have been invited to see Yves Saint Laurent, Oscar de la Renta, or Karl Lagerfeld. Later on, the companies asked their advice about new products, and occasionally for the advice of their personal friends. Selling was never mentioned on any occasion whatsoever, the results being but all the more impressive.

15

Financial Rumors

Introduction

For the public at large, financial rumors correspond to mythical phenomena. The very term "finance" immediately conjures up spectacular buy-out operations on the stock exchange, historic crashes, insider information leading to the swift amassing of colossal fortunes, and so on. It is true that the stock exchange is seen as a small closed-off world, that is completely opaque and thus totally mysterious. It is a perfect blank screen upon which people can project their dreams and their wildest imaginings. Financial rumors have a two-fold hold on the imagination. We have seen to what extent the very word "rumor" smacks of heresy; if we add the smell of money and big capital, the whole becomes totally mythical.

The study of financial rumors poses certain particular problems that make it both very difficult and all the more fascinating. These rumors are very localized and fleeting. As opposed to text, talk does not linger: it starts up (amidst those present), spreads and vanishes. It is thus very difficult to have at one's disposal a recapitulative review of rumors.

In addition, the Stock Exchange, like any other shares market, is a universe which claims to be rational. The whole of today's financial community functions in accordance with a theory known as "market efficiency," derived from the work of the Chicago School. Financial markets are supposed to correspond to ideal market phenomena; thanks to the media, telex machines, and Reuter (the British press agency), everyone has the same information at his disposal instantaneously, and can thus act rationally. The very notion of financial rumors introduces the hypothesis of a certain irrationality in the behavior of financial operators. It allows us to suppose that not everyone really benefits from the same information. For these two reasons, studying financial rumors is, in and of itself, unsettling to market theorists.

The phenomenon is alive and well, notwithstanding. *The Wall Street Journal* now has a permanent column entitled, "Heard on the Street." The column informs everyone of what is being said in smaller circles.

It is quite normal for there to be financial rumors. The operators are, of course, experts and professionals, but having early access to information can, in this context, have considerable monetary value. Legend has it that the Rothschilds made their fortune because they were the first to find out that Napoleon had been defeated at Waterloo. Their having been the only people to know (and to believe) this particular bit of information was supposed to have allowed them to purchase shares, on London's financial markets, that would necessarily take a sizeable leap once the news was made known and officialized. According to the legend, they also diffused the rumor that Napoleon had won to create a landslide among the stockholders, willing to sell at any price. Even if it is but a legend, it illustrates how rumors operate.

The Inevitability of Rumors on Financial Markets

By concretely examining financial rumors, we will see why, theoretically speaking, financial rumors are inevitable. In theory there is no room for rumors in the world of high finance. Financial markets are supposed to represent models of rationality. Each person, thanks to the Reuter press service, for example, has access to the same information as his neighbor; well-informed, he thus has all the data needed to make optimal short- and long-term decisions. Books on financial theory all aspire to an ever more sophisticated model of decision making: equations and statistics are given to eliminate the human factor. Moreover, with a *Wall Street Journal* under his arm, a stockbroker takes himself for a paragon of rationalism.

In practice, the Stock Exchange and other financial markets run rampant with rumors. Our purpose here is to show why this is in no way abnormal or pathological. Quite simply, the Stock Exchange and other financial markets contain within themselves most of the parameters that favor the natural blossoming of rumors. We will take them up one by one.

The Future Is Silent

Wherever there is secrecy, there are rumors. Secrecy of sentencing makes for judiciary rumors, medical secrecy makes for medical rumors, and censorship makes for political rumors. Now every financial decision made at the Stock Exchange is a wager or gamble on the future. Everyone knows that while it is easy to predict the past, predicting the future is a perilous art. The future is silent, remaining the most impenetrable of secrets.

To uncover its secret, it is well-known that chairmen of the boards of businesses, and often big businesses, consult futurologists—modern versions of the ancient oracles; other consult gurus and fortunetellers. Whenever a burning question requires an urgent answer, people find some way or another of soothing their uncertainty. The impenetrable wall of the future leads us to consult "experts" endowed with a sixth sense. It also makes us hypersensitive to the least indications that reduce the uncertainty of forecasts, even indications that are but tangentially related to the problem. Hence the attention given to rumors that seek to give meaning to the slightest market fluctuations.

What Is Scarce Is Dear

At the stock exchange, as at the horse track or at war, to find out something before the others is a source of profits, winnings, and victories. The more information is shared among many, the more the hope for profits is diluted: when everyone has bet on the winning horse, the winnings are moderate. Official financial information meted out by companies, official statements, press conferences, newspaper articles and telexes are at everyone's disposal. In theory, this is a case of perfect competition.

The quest for windfall profits and exceptional financial gains thus leads people to be sensitive to what runs alongside official information: exclusive information, i.e., what is not explicitly stated, information leaks, and talk that takes the "it seems that ... ", or "I heard from a reliable source that ... " form. The Securities and Exchange Committee relentlessly tracks down insider information, but to no avail. The demand for bits of exclusive information and tips that no one else knows of is too overpowering. Companies are too large and too human for nothing to filter in about future announcements of dividend payments, planned diversification, and divestment.

Testing Rumors

Paradoxically, nothing is more difficult than to keep a secret to oneself. Having heard about a scoop whose reliability is unclear, an operator hesitates before embarking on the adventure alone. He needs to reduce his uncertainty and subjective risk: thus he speaks of it to a small number of people whose expertise is widely recognized. In doing so, he of course spreads the information, thereby reducing his hoped-for profits, but at the same time he can better access his chances of success or failure; how could he know all by himself? It is wiser to speak confidentially with a few chosen colleagues, who will be happy to hear the news.

At the stock exchange, as at the horse track or at war, to find out something before the others is a source of profits, winnings, and victories. The more information is shared among many, the more the hope for profits is diluted: when everyone has bet on the winning horse, the winnings are moderate. Official financial information meted out by companies, official statements, press conferences, newspaper articles and telexes are at everyone's disposal. In theory, this is a case of perfect competition.

To Each His Own Expert

Financial markets are not egalitarian. The world of finance is stratified: at the top one finds the Brahmans, *viz.* the experts whose opinions count—that is why they are called opinion leaders. At the bottom are those with minimal savings who are isolated, underinformed and uncertain. Between the two groups stretches a network of sub-Brahmans, mini-experts, local experts, and ordinary people with a passion for stock market speculation who spend hours poring over the latest prices. Even the latter enjoy some prestige on a local level, granted by those who know even less than they do, who have no keys to market activity, and who, in short, are not initiated into the market's workings.

Now the psychology of human relations reminds us that every individual tries to maintain the status to which he or she has been raised, assuming some advantage is derived from it. Experts continually act like experts: they talk, they give advice, and make recommendations. Those who listen to them have but one concern, and that is to take advantage of the expert's prestige: they talk about what he said to those around them, showing thereby that they belong to, or at least have secret links with, the innermost circles ("I heard it from so and so that ... "), i.e., the insiders.

We thus see a cascading of relays, each individual playing the role of opinion leader for a few others, right down to the bottom of the ladder. At the bottom, the small investors, overwhelmed by the technicality of market functioning, lend credence to what they are told. They go along with their expert, without realizing that his opinion and his "information" are often simply based on rumors started by experts higher up the ladder.

Short-Lived

The particularity of financial rumors is that they are generally short-lived. That is quite normal. In everyday life, many rumors last for years; this is because no one has a vital interest in seeking out or revealing the truth. To give an example, people who hear the rumor that Procter & Gamble has ties with the Moonies (its logo being a crescent moon) generally do not try to find out whether it is true or false. The rumor confirms their views that there is some sort of secret alliance between Reverend Moon and big capital. Similarly, as the rumor does not affect the sales of the company's product lines, Procter & Gamble has not gone to any great lengths to let the truth be known.

At the Stock Exchange, events themselves rapidly clarify the situation, denying or confirming rumors. Furthermore, once a rumor takes on a certain magnitude, journalists pick it up and carry out an investigation, questioning officials from the company at issue. Thus rumors are short-lived, except when the officials, by their silence or ambiguous answers, merely encourage them.

Listening to the Whole World

Stock exchanges are affected by what happens in Washington, Moscow, Tokyo, Beirut, and so on; that is why there are so many rumors going around them. Finance is linked to politics, and politics affects the future. The financial analysts, being in constant communication with their foreign correspondents, scattered the world over, the slightest suspicious event in new Delhi or Johannesburg is quickly transmitted to Wall Street and the Brongniart Palace in Paris. It is then dissected, interpreted, blown up, and transformed into rumors which then function like a tocsin: they spread the news of danger. The next day, official information snuffs out or confirms the rumors.

A Mechanical Phenomenon

Taking the financial futures markets as examples (the CBOT in Chicago, the NYMEX in New York, the LIFFE in London, and the MATIF in Paris), short-lived rumors can be found there everyday. This is a logical consequence of the structure of these markets, built as "information processing machines." For instance, around the MATIF's floor, there are 150 traders, telephonemen, etc., all assembled in a closed space. More than a thousand telephone lines have been installed to link that space with all the banks that intervene on the "futures" market. These banks are themselves linked by the Reuter press service to the whole world.

Two situations are thus possible: either information exists and the machine efficiently and immediately processes it, or there is no information in the pipeline. In the latter case, as "nature abhors a void", the machinery will take hold of the least conjecture emitted anywhere concerning the next foreign trade deficit figures, and transmit it at once.

Crises and Panic

Rumors do not create crises or panic. Operators seek information first when the stakes are very high. It is information that generates crises and panic: "Wall Street just crumbled!".

Instead, rumors often accompany and accentuate panic. In crisis situations, anxiety is high and the future looks even more horrible than the present. Everyone is listening for news, whether it be true or false, as long as it is news: anything but silence!

But whenever anxiety is high, people feel the need to get together and communicate with each other in order to reduced their anxiety. Sharing fear is a well-known therapy. Thus people talk a lot during crises, each person exchanging his impressions, speculations, conjectures, and hypotheses with his interlocutors. Word-of-mouth is the privileged means for the exchange of rumors, and true or false news, which, in the end, only have one purpose: to keep the lines of communication open.

Crisis situations simply exacerbate the causes for the existence of rumors during "calm" moments: in such situations there is more anxiety, higher risk, a greater desire to foresee the future, a multiplication of new experts (due to the failure of the previously accredited experts who had not foreseen the crisis), more communication, and a greater sensitivity to the slightest indications. In crisis periods, one order disappears. Before being replaced by another, subjectivity, mimicry, and even a certain unscrupulousness hold sway. A rumor is more than a yell, it is a rallying cry.

In order to more concretely examine financial rumors, we will distinguish the commodities market from the classical stock market. In the former, we will examine the example of traditional raw goods, in particular the famous case of sugar, as well as currencies.

Commodities and Dollars: Rumors in Action

The 1974 Sugar Crisis

In 1968, the average price of sugar in France was 200 FF per ton. It gradually rose to 1,000 FF in 1973 and 1,650 in early 1974, rising to a record high of 8,150 FF on November 22, 1974. This sharp upturn was due to the conjunction of several factors. First of all, sugar constitutes a market with a structural imbalance between production and consumption. In 1974, a number of experts had made very pessimistic forecasts about upcoming harvests: according to them, the imbalance was going to get worse. In addition, there were rumors going around about different countries' expected behavior: the Philippines were expected to stop exporting, and purchases were expected by the United States, Japan, and Russia. In Paris, the forecasts and rumors gave rise to a great deal of unthinking speculation, instigated by certain careless commissioners. These speculations considerably magnified price fluctuations. Alongside that, certain manufacturers started up a press campaign designed to make people believe in a sugar shortage in order to have higher ceiling prices granted by the European Economic Community. Then, in early November 1974, the Polish government imposed an embargo on 120,000 tons of sugar. The conjunction of the forecasts, the press campaign, the rumors, the rise in stock prices and government decisions led to a very severe stock price inflation, where rationality gave way to carefully encouraged dreaming and imagination.

On November 22, 1974, the market underwent a sudden turnaround. The stock prices could not continue to rise indefinitely, and several operators decided to cash in on their gains. In effect, the feeling that things had gone too far sparked off alarmist rumors inciting people to immediately cash in. That was the beginning of the fall: by December 2, sugar prices had fallen to 6,200 FF, and by February 15, 1975, to 4,200 FF. On October 18, 1975, sugar no longer cost any more than 1,530 FF per ton in Paris.

What should be gleaned from this rumor-related crisis is the following: the rumors that preceded the spiraling price climb simply reinforced an already speculative movement. The rumors were given indirect support by the press campaign organized by sugar producers themselves. The reversal on November 22 corresponded to a "crash" phenomenon whereby operators realized the overinflated nature of the speculative movement, cashed in and thereby set off a rush to sell. Rumors thus expressed the anxiety of those who were afraid of losing their shirts. The rumors took on exaggerated importance, and contributed to creating an atmosphere of panic. It is in such contexts that rumors reach extreme proportions: operators no longer know who to trust, become sensitive to every bit of talk, however extravagant it may seem, and lend more credence to subjective information than to verifiable facts [2 and 148].

President Reagan's Influence on Sugar

During the second week of March 1985, the New York Stock Exchange was booming. A rumor was going around that import taxes on sugar, foreseen for the end of the month, would not be imposed, and that the American government was even thinking of eliminating these taxes, which were very substantial and had been hampering the sugar industry for some time.

Behind the rumor there was probably an administration official who had spoken in confidence to a representative of an agricultural lobby. On the basis of the rumor, sugar prices got the jump on "information" that was to be taken up, a few days later, by the Reuter Agency, and even then only conditionally stated. The rumor was officialized, but the market had already taken it into account a few days beforehand.

A Chinese Plane Gets the Dollar Back Off the Ground

After plummeting for several days down to 7.06 FF, the dollar made an upturn on all markets on February 21, 1986. Sudden tension on the Tokyo market was at the root of this: a press agency release had just announced that a military aircraft coming from the north had just penetrated into South Korea's airspace. A red alert had been set off because of the incursion. A rumor started up immediately: the North Koreans were said to have begun an attack against the Western bastion. In reality, as was later revealed, the plane had been piloted by Chinese military personnel who had wanted to leave Communist China. The rumor only lasted a few hours but had repercussions on other financial marketplaces.

A Few Rumors That Should Have Been Believed

By 1974, the Soviet Union had been exporting sugar for years. Nevertheless, a rumor started up in Paris that a Soviet official would be coming to Europe in order to negotiate sizable sugar purchases with the European Economic Community (EEC), another net exporter. The rumor was immediately interpreted as meaning that there had been bad harvests in the USSR for the year, and suggested that considerable imports might be necessitated due to the Soviet Union's domestic demand. Given the USSR's previous trade situation, none of the Parisian stockbrokers believed the rumor, and sugar prices consequently remained stable. They were mistaken: since 1974, the USSR had become a net importer of sugar. The rumor circulated because it was unexpected news; but it was judged to be highly unlikely and thus had no effect. At the time, due to the lack of precise information on the perennially top-secret level of Soviet harvests, the USSR's past as an exporter excluded any hypothesis of a reversal in tendency.

In January 1985, the dollar made a record climb, exceeding 10 FF to the dollar, and reaching a high of 3.45 DM. In February of 1985, the dollar hit 10.70 FF, after a week of continual gains. Rumors began going around exchange circles that certain central European banks would intervene on the exchange market to put a halt to the depreciation of their national currencies. The rumors succeeded in slowing down the dollar's dizzying climb, but could not stop it altogether. None of the foreign exchange brokers in any of the exchange markets believed the intervention would take place. Their belief was based on the fact that similar rumors a few years earlier had turned out false, as well as on the fact that the few attempts to intervene that had been made in the past by central banks had had no impact (as, for example, the interventions on the part of the Banque de France, which had not been able to stave off devaluations of the franc).

On February 20, 1985, foreign exchange brokers in all the major stock exchanges were dumbfounded as they witnessed an abrupt stop in the dollar's dizzying climb, and even a slight drop. A concerted intervention by the main central banks had led to an unprecedented selling off of dollars. Once again, misled by their subjective assessments of the probability of the event, the foreign exchange brokers had not lent any credence to the rumor [137].

At the Stock Exchange

The managers of private portfolios rush around on the stock market floor, their daily concern being to optimize their rate of return, capital gains, and profitability. In such a context, where the risks are lower than on the commodities markets, everyone is listening for privileged information, tips, and information that was supposed to be kept secret but that leaked out all the same, i.e., stock market rumors. These rumors are quite natural: a need to foresee as carefully as possible and a concern with seizing the fleetingly right moment create a permanent demand for information. Rumors satisfy a part of this demand. One might nevertheless be tempted to encourage them, and even to set them off. In such cases, rumors are linked to the malevolent intentions of those who have an interest in propagating certain information in order to bring about a change in share prices.

Information Delays

In one case [62], a rumor sprang up on the basis of an event that was independent of the will of the agents intervening on the financial market. On September 28, 1984, the Clause company in France informed its shareholders by mail, as well as by the press, of a possible increase in their shares' dividends. Nevertheless, the mail was delayed by postal system strikes. It was not until October 10, that the figures, with a few inaccuracies, appeared in a weekly paper. The most groundless rumors went around about the new dividend figure. In order to silence them, the stock market regulatory commission asked the company to publish an official statement. It only appeared, however, on October 28! Delays are very common in the publication of earnings: in many cases, these time-lags are intentional. Thus, in a 1985 report, the regulatory commission condemned this practice (*La Vie Française,* April 29–May 5, 1985). Whether it is a question of announcing substantial earnings (as was the case of Roussel-Uclaf which had called a meeting of its board on Friday, April 6, 1984, but waited until the following Tuesday to publish in the press a statement of a sharp rise in earnings) or of losses and the elimination of dividends (as was the case for Maisons Phénix) these delays allow for "insider trading." The people who know that the company is going to distribute dividends can benefit by quickly buying bonds while their price is still low. Such information also filters in through rumors.

Information within Companies

After a long period of secretive management, companies have changed their practices. Presidents set up more and more meetings for their executives to keep them abreast of the company's doings. In its October 1983 bulletin, the French stock exchange regulatory commission explained how its inquiry, sparked off by sudden trading of SCOA stock, revealed that the trading had coincided with a meeting of two hundred executives on September 9. The management had clued them into movements allowing them to better assess the prospective gains for the financial year ending September 30. What the executives told others led to rumors at the stock exchange, allowing traders to act before the gains had been officially reported.

There's a Takeover Bid in the Air

Since the high-impact BSN-Saint-Gobain bid in France, the public has been aware of the principle behind takeover bids, a frontal method for taking control of a company. It is an everyday phenomenon in the United States. Rumors regularly announce that one company or another is going to be the target of a takeover bid. All experts know the typical profile of companies that succomb to takeover bids: underrated companies that underutilize their financial capacity. It therefore suffices for there to be unusual trading for a rumor to burst out and accuse a "raider." A raider is someone who, having identified a particular company, purchases its stock little by little. At a second stage, he presents himself openly to shareholders and proposes to buy the remaining shares at a particularly good price. His objective is to hold in his hands a high enough percentage of the company's capital to take control of it, sending the management packing. Such rumors constitute a terrible message for the existing bosses: they insinuate that someone thinks he can do a better job than they can in running the business!

On the other hand, one might have an interest in encouraging the rumor that one company will soon be sold to another in order to prop up stock prices. Since early 1985, for example, everyone at Wall Street has known that the Sperry computer and aerospace company has been looking for a buyer. Rumors regularly indicate a buyer that is generally a firm that has declared its intention to diversify. At that point, Sperry stock prices that had started to waiver restabilized—which was probably the precise objective of those who started up the rumor.

That is exactly what happened at the Paris Stock Exchange in October of 1985. On the stockmarket floor, it was being said that a worldwide giant, no other than Coca-Cola, had decided to "make itself a present" of Pernod-Ricard, a mythical union of the symbol of America and the national aperitive.

The rumor spread far and wide, being relayed by the economic and financial press, as well as several nationwide daily newspapers. A conjunction of facts did, in fact, make the rumor believable:

1. In order to change its image, the Pernod-Ricard group had been extending its activities into the soft drink sector, which now represents 40 percent of its turnover. But the soft drink sector is less profitable than the alcoholic beverage sector. Thus, theoretically speaking, an extension of this activity was supposed to represent a financial risk.
2. After the two new soft-drinks it brought out on the market with heavy advertising, Pacific (a nonalcoholic pastis) and Brut de Pomme (an apple-flavored soft drink), the group had been discreet about its profits from the sales of these two products. This discretion, generally well advised, was perhaps a bad idea given the circumstances: the investors wanted to know.
3. The Pernod-Ricard group had been designated by the economic press as the most dynamic company for 1983. Now once a company has made it that far, it is scrutinized so much by specialists that the slightest sneeze is blown up and interpreted as a sign of decline. In fact, after three years of growth in earnings, in 1984 the company showed a decrease: the summer of 1984 had not been a hot one, and sales for every company in the business had been poor. Moreover, the group had made a great many investments that year.

4. The Pernod-Ricard group distributes Coca-Cola in France. The two groups thus already knew each other.
5. Lastly, Coca-Cola's problems in the United States, with the flop "New Coke" had constituted, could explain why the group wanted to strengthen its position in Europe.

Thus from a strictly financial point of view, the rumor had nothing theoretically implausible about it. Hence its success. In fact, Pernod-Ricard's bonds showed some fluctuation. Moreover, the press did not deny the rumor. On the contrary, certain reporters stirred it up still more: "All of that is far from being clear, and Pernod-Ricard's management is dragging its feet ... ; but there is a rattlesnake just around the bend," *L'Echo des Halles* pronounced.

It was true that the chairman of the Pernod-Ricard group, answering the accusations with humor, had made a denial that might have seemed ambiguous: "Pernod-Ricard's capital is relatively well protected ... even if we wanted to sell out to the Americans, it is not clear that we would obtain authorization from the state .... I am not a salesman ... in life, everything is a question of price." This conclusion, said in jest, led to his having to reiterate his denial, the second time in more categorical terms. What was clear was that Pernod-Ricard's stock went up. Was the rumor started by a speculator? It seems likely.

Even if many a rumor is premeditated, it is often difficult to identify its source. But it is occasionally possible. The first Thursday in September of 1980, Wall Street was shaken by an alert: Ronald Reagan, the Republican candidate for presidency was said to have had a heart attack. The immediate result of the rumor was that the market closed with a serious blow to the Dow Jones (*Le Matin,* September 10, 1980). According to Don Dorfman, a reporter for the *Chicago Tribune,* the rumor had been deliberately started by a New York stockbroker. Expecting a decline in prices, the stockbroker had put an option to sell. But the decline had not materialized. Prices instead had gone up, and the broker stood to lose five million dollars. Then the idea struck him of starting up a rumor about Ronald Reagan having a heart attack. The news flew around the trading floor and then all of Wall Street. Due to the ensuing drop in prices, the broker was supposed not only to have broken even, but to have made himself a tidy sum. On the whole, it was a rumor that was worth its weight in gold.

16

Political Rumors

Introduction

In schools of political science, there are no courses on rumors. This is a mistake. There is no such thing as politics without rumors. The very essence of rumors, as we have shown above, is that they involve speech that takes place outside of the field of official speech. They constitute a counterpower. It is thus altogether natural for rumor is to proliferate in the field of the conquest and management of power.

The Advantages of Rumors

In the arsenal of tools used in political warfare, rumors have a number of advantages. First and foremost, they allow one to avoid exposing oneself directly: others speak in one's stead, becoming the willing or unknowing bearers of rumors. The source remains hidden, impenetrable, and mysterious. No one is responsible, yet everyone knows the rumor content.

Rumors are the media of what goes unsaid: they allow one to bring up in public subjects that the political tradition forbids one to mention openly. Thus unlike the Americans, the French are in general ill at ease when health problems are brought up; they constitute a taboo subject that cannot be publicly discussed. Thus it is a frequent theme of rumors; they cast doubts on a man's ability to remain in office, and his ability to rule lucidly and serenely.

Rumors require no proof. Public opinion is often founded more on impressions than on facts. Accusations alone suffice [261]. Rumors require no full staff meetings either. They can be gotten going in small committees. That is why they are a favorite weapon of conspiracies. The Markovic affair, is an example of such a case. Exploding in October 1968, it was supposed to mar the reputation of presidential candidate, Georges Pompidou, and his wife. For months, editorial boards were constantly talking about the "well-known pictures taken in a villa near Paris during the summer of 1966," which everyone could describe though few had seen. According to the prefect of police, Rochet, who was then director of the DST (the French equivalent of the FBI in America), "The silence kept by people around the future President of the Republic, the photographic montage spread around Paris, and the problems encountered in trying to uncover the source of the scandal, all pointed to the fact that a very worrisome conjuncture had taken place, and that there was a true network of accomplices from the Ministry of the Interior, the Justice Department, and a pro-Gaullist clan" [14]. The former minister of the interior under General de Gaulle, Raymond Marcellin, also believed that the Markovic affair had been orchestrated by several of Georges Pompidou's personal enemies [174].

Let us add that rumors allow the conspirators to remain anonymous. They are the only undertaking in which one can play a two-fold role: no one speaks in his own name, and everyone simply repeats the rumor. It is difficult in such cases to separate out one's real friends from one's fake friends.

The last, but not least, of the advantages of rumors is that they cost nothing. Compared with the millions of dollars laid out for advertising campaigns whose effectiveness is often doubtful, rumors are a weapon with no direct financial price tag. Once set going, they are relayed by the media, which diffuse it free of charge.

But they also have their disadvantages. Unlike advertising campaigns in which one can control one's message down to the last comma, and its dates and times of appearance, rumors escape one's control, their results being somewhat chancey. Moreover, it sometimes happens that a rumor gets turned around onto those who started it: a well denied false rumor allows the target to forestall future rumors. By killing one rumor, one kills off all the others as well. Thus François Mitterrand brilliantly dissipated the rumor that accompanied the beginning of his first seven-year term in office, that he had cancer. He pointed to his scientifically laconic clean bill of health published every six months. And he replied with disarming humor: "It seems that there are a lot of heads of state who are ill, and I have the impression that many people would like to add me to the list. I do admit to sneezing now and then, but other than that ..." (*Le Matin*, September 25, 1981).

Uses of Rumors

As elections approach, everything is worth a try in the attempt to destabilize bothersome future candidates. Rumors are ideal weapons in primaries—struggles between people within a single party.

In every war, one finds that rumors concern one's allies more than one's enemies. Aggressiveness towards the enemy has an authorized outlet: death. On the contrary, fratricidal combat being held in contempt, internal dissension and inimity must necessarily use the hidden media: rumors. The same phenomenon explains the harshness of rumors in medical and legal circles. In the two professional groups, there is a great deal of competition for positions of power, but one cannot openly attack one's peers. He who dreams of being the dean of the order can, however, count on rumors to mar a "colleague's" reputation.

In the political realm as well, slander often derives from one's own political "friends." Georges Pompidou's candidacy for the presidency, after the departure of General de Gaulle in 1969, was bothersome to the Gaullist clans. They did not make any bones about turning to their advantage the assassination of Stefan Markovic, Alain Delon's friend and body guard, to attack the future presidential candidate. And it was in order to strip Jacques Chaban-Delmas of whatever chance he may have had of winning the presidential elections in 1974, that someone sent a copy of his tax returns (showing that he did not pay any taxes) to the satirical newspaper, *Le Canard enchaîné*, and spread rumors about the death of his first wife.

When it comes to local elections, the bipolarization and harshness of the competition are such that rumors come especially form the adversary's camp. In 1984, Langenieux-Villart, public relations director at city hall in Grenoble, France, under the Gaullist mayor, Alain Carignon, published a 415-page guide called *Gagnons les cantonales (How to Win Local Elections.)* Two years earlier, a comparable guide, *Gagner les municipales de 1983 (How to Win the Municipal Elections in 1983)* had been published. These guides aroused emotion, especially the chapter devoted to the correct usage of "word-of-mouth." The press was indignant that people would openly teach others how to use rumors *Dépêche AFP*, no 251755, November 25, 1984, Grenoble). But the guides merely officialized a practice that was well known and utilized by all political parties. It is true that in Grenoble, reading the guide could only recall to mind rumors that had persistently circulated during the 1983 municipal elections. For at that time, a local, anonymous rumor had sustained that the incumbent socialist mayor, Hubert Dubedout, had a Kabyle (Algerian) mother and was related to a rich merchant of Maghrebin extraction, a certain Mr. Boudoudou (the rumor played off the similar pronunciation in French of their last names). Hubert Dubedout lost out to Alain Carignon. To what extent can his defeat be attributed to the rumor?

The other main use of rumors in politics, as in business, is to feel out public opinion. It is a way of suggesting that one is interested in a certain portfolio or position of responsibility. It is also a management tactic: when a minister wants to assess what kind of reaction might be aroused by a certain decision, he sets a rumor circulating and decides what to do on the basis of the reactions he sees or hears.

During the campaign for the French legislative elections on March 16, 1986, President François Mitterrand declared that he would not speak again after his televised speech given on March 2. Nevertheless, during the week directly prior to the elections, a rumor was insistently spreading: the president might prematurely resign if the opposition had a large majority. Mitterrand had never publicly spoken of resigning; he let the rumor play out its last card to convince legitimist voters. The rumor was on the front page of *Le Monde* on March 19, and of course all the other media had to comment upon it, which spread it even more widely. Thus while Mitterrand had nothing said officially, everyone knew.

Lastly, provocation is often the real goal of rumor starters. They preach what is untrue to find out what is true, or to create a favorable psychological climate and thereby put pressure on those in power.

Thus on February 11, 1986, a rumor starting in Tel-Aviv quickly hit all Western capitals: as Gorbachev had released Chtaransky, the dissident Jewish mathematician, Nelson Mandela, the black leader in the anti-Apartheid struggle was supposed to be shortly released in South Africa. President Botha was claimed to be about to put an end to Mandela's twenty-three years of captivity. People were thus expecting that Mandela would at last be freed on February 12 or 13. Nothing of the kind happened: Botha refused to give in. The rumor had created suspense and focused the attention of the whole free world on South Africa, making the South African government's obstinate refusal even more visible, and thus isolating it still further.

The Main Themes of Rumors

The analysis of political rumors shows that such rumors amount to infinite variations on a small number of themes, seven as it turns out, that one might call the seven cardinal sins of rumors. We will present them one by one, though the order in which they will be presented has nothing to do with their frequency, as any attempt to measure their frequency would be rather difficult to carry out.

The first theme is that of the invisible hand, occult power, or secret society that is pulling the strings of power. This theme follows logically from the conception of political life as a stage. It postulates a marionette stage where the strings are manipulated by invisible hands. Behind the electoral staging and a democratic façade, in reality there is an occult power or hidden arm unbounded by the harness of parliamentary procedure and universal suffrage. The secret society theme is a constant in the French political imagination. Every society that is somewhat closed and mysterious can become a scapegoat; this happened to the Jews (e.g., the rumor of the conspiracy of the Sages of Zion) and the Freemasons. These groups were considered to be really running the country, regardless of the administration that was supposedly holding the reins of power. Such rumors promptly remind people that those on the other side are all Freemason brothers [114].

In the United States, the influence of the underworld, and above all the Mafia, on the White House is a theme that spurs on rumors. Thus, it was said that Richard Nixon ended the Vietnam War in order to be able to start up relations with the People's Republic of China and thus open up the Chinese market to American industries, especially those controlled by the Mafia. This thesis was sustained in the play *Secret Honor,* made into a film by Robert Altman. Similarly, according to another rumor, Marilyn Monroe did not commit suicide. Indeed, it was known that the star had been seeing Robert Kennedy since 1950; he was then heading a committee studying American trade unions. According to Kennedy, the trade unions, and in particular the most powerful among them, the truckers' union directed by Jimmy Hoffa, had direct links with the Mafia. By way of reply, Hoffa was said to have bugged Marilyn's house in order to mar Robert Kennedy's reputation, and even John F. Kennedy's, by creating a sexual scandal. The United States is still a very Puritan country, and such rumors can do serious damage to one's reputation. Marilyn Monroe was supposed to have been assassinated in order to hush up the political scandal.

Backwoods France is still very sensitive to rumors about freemasonry. People got pretty fired up when, in February 1977, *Le Canard enchaîné* published an article with the following title: "He wants to become a Freemason: Giscard knocked at the door of the lodge." According to the article, President Giscard d'Estaing had asked to be admitted to the "Mozart Lodge" located in the sixteenth arrondissement in Paris. The information was denied. The president had, of course, had some contact with high-ranking members of the Freemasons, but so had his predecessors at the Elysée (*La Correspondance de la presse,* February 21, 1977).

On the left, conspiracy imaginings are dominated by the Trilateral Commission, created at David Rockefeller's behest, that includes highly-visible people from the financial, economic, political, and academic worlds in the West. This commission is often denounced as "an occult power in which international financial forces make and break Western governments" (*Le Monde,* May 30, 1985). Such rumors, and an article in *Le Monde* (May 30,

1985) as well, have also insisted on Raymond Barre's open participation in the Trilateral Commission.

To what does this obstinate will to find "the clandestine conductor," who secretly rules the world, correspond? According to Gauchet [110], it is an expression of anxiety about totalitarianism. For many people, "the limits within which legitimate government arising from universal suffrage is contained are absolutely unbearable. These people must reconstruct an immense power backstage, for which these derisory politicians are but a mask." Rumors thus disclose this grab for power. It expresses a totalitarian fear: in the wings, there are perhaps people who prefer not be weighed down by the law and republican democracy.

The second theme of political rumors is that of secret agreements. They sustain that there are meetings and arrangements that secretly link political adversaries, thereby contradicting their public stances. The slightest indications are taken up by rumors answering such questions as: "Why do you think François Mitterrand made a courtesy visit, on July 6, 1984, to his enemy, Giscard d'Estaing, during an official trip to Auvergne?" It is self-evident: the president and his rival were deciding how to divide up the electoral pie for the 1986 legislative elections.

This theme of alliances stems from the myth of politics as a stage. On stage, candidates argue and inveigh against each other; in the wings, as everyone knows, they dine together and are invited to the same cocktail parties [173].

The three following themes (third, fourth, and fifth in our discussion) make up a trio: money, illness, and sex. There are countless rumors about hidden fortunes, scandalous accumulations of capital, profits made off of the sweat of the community, etc. Léon Blum was supposed to have gold crockery! Edgar Faure was supposed to have received a million from the Sultan of Morocco! Laurent Fabius was supposed to have purchased a luxurious residence in Cléguer, near Lorient!

Sex has lost some of its vigor as a theme for rumors. Strip-teases have become everyday sights on prime-time television in France. Sex is less and less secret or taboo; it is thus gradually becoming less and less subject to rumors.

While a certain sort of love life is accepted, deviant sexuality is not at all tolerated [91]. In provincial towns, reputations are ruined by rumors of politicians being seen with underage girls or having homosexual relationships. Similarly, a new theme has arisen because of tension related to immigration: politicians are claimed to be going out with immigrants. During the 1983 municipal elections in Roubaix, a rumor accused Pierre Prouvost, the Socialist party candidate, of having "knocked up an Algerian girl." To what extent did the rumor contribute to Prouvost's defeat?

The theme of illness is one of rumors' favorites. In the most recent American presidential elections, Ronald Reagan used innuendo against Michael Dukakis when he said, "Look, I'm not going to pick on an invalid." As it is badly viewed in France to publicly question a politician about his health, this task has been taken up by rumors. In Western democracies, voters increasingly demand to know everything about the health of those in power. In the United States, the procedure has become institutionalized: even the candidates who are simply nominated by the Republican and Democratic parties must publish the results of their most recent check-ups. The time is long since past when a president could undergo an operation on a boat, as President Cleveland did in the 1800s. Everyone was in the know about the slightest change in Ronald Reagan's bump on the nose. In letting it be known officially that he had a tumor, Ronald Reagan stopped rumors dead in their tracks.

The sixth theme is that of double talk: a politician's real intentions are claimed to be the opposite of what he publicly announces. The persistence of rumors about Communist party-affiliated Georges Marchais's real attitude during World War II is an example of this. It is true that the initial pact between Stalin and Hitler corroborated the rumor's hypothesis. Recent history, the resistance, and collaboration constitute further fertile ground for rumors. Similarly, to counter the gentle image that extreme rightist Jean-Marie Le Pen is trying to acquire, rumors have drawn upon his recent past: his involvement in the Algerian War.

The last theme is that of immigration. Like the preceding theme, it concerns treason. France of the 1980s is quick to lambast a politician suspected of complicity with immigrants from North Africa. This was the case during the 1983 municipal elections in Grenoble and Roubaix: rumor attacked two candidates from the Socialist party. Such rumors are by no means new. At the very dawn of Edgar Faure's political career, when he ran for office in the Doubs region in France for the first time, he was attacked by a similar rumor: it was sustained that his name was in fact Lehman, but that he wanted to keep his Jewish background a secret! In our time, the scapegoat has changed.

These are thus the seven dominant rumor themes. The list is, of course, not necessarily exhaustive. Nevertheless, it becomes clear why the Markovic affair, for example, was so dangerous. One and the same rumor contained several of these main themes: death, deviant sexuality, the underworld, the star system, the presidency, and a foreigner—the very ingredients of modern detective stories.

How to Create an Image

Rumors targeting politicians are not started by accident. They seek out each politician's weak point, exploiting his Achilles' heel, and thereby acquire a great deal of credibility—they seem plausible. On the other hand, it is as if, behind the apparent diversity of rumors targeting one and the same person, people were attempting to create a certain image of him through successive brushstrokes. Thus the examination of rumors started up about the best-known French politicians allows us to reconstitute the intentions that lie behind them, i.e., the portrait that they try to paint. Table 16.1 lays out the intentions behind each rumor. We will take a few examples.

It is very telling that two of the rumors about Valéry Giscard d'Estaing, while he was president of France, involved a slap in the face. The first rumor related that, coming home one morning at dawn after a late-night fling, at the wheel of his movie-maker friend Vadim's sports car, he had forced a milk truck that was passing his way into a ditch. An argument broke out, and the truck driver was said to have slapped him. The second rumor casted Michel Piccoli, the movie actor. The actor was said to have slapped d'Estaing at a party one evening because Mrs. Claustre was wasting away as a prisoner held by rebels in Chad. The rumor was denied by Michel Piccoli, just as Marlène Jobert had always denied having had relations with d'Estaing. She only met him once, in a restaurant on the island of Djerba, a coincidence that was exploited in certain papers to insinuate plenty more.

What is interesting in the milk truck rumor is not that d'Estaing fought with the milkman, but rather than the milkman slapped him. The act seems highly improbable: either the milkman had recognized the president or he had not. If he had not, he would have been far more likely to hit him with his fist. Nowadays, slapping is out of style. This detail is thus a highly significant construction.

The former president was often accused of being haughty; his kind of dignity got on people's nerves. That gave him a certain fragility, and the rumor went straight for it. It reinforced his image as a noble or monarch (thus hardly to be suspected of harboring democratic or popular leanings), while at the same time humiliating him. The rumor said: this royal man is the kind of guy one might slap shortly after his nomination. The story was iconoclastic and desacralized the president.

Generally speaking, rumors aimed at constructing an image of Valéry Giscard d'Estaing as a sort of Louis XV, a frivolous, fun-loving, egocentric king. Moreover, there were even certain posters that depicted him with a crown. Furthermore, his kingly behavior was not always altogether responsible: he disappeared at night without anyone at the Elysée knowing where to reach him. France was thus often without its head of state to make urgent decisions that might have arisen.

TABLE 16.1
How to Create an Image

Target	Image to be Created	Typical Rumors
Valéry Giscard d'Estaing	Frivolous king	-- Secret nighttime affairs -- Milktruck rumor -- Relationship with Marlène Jobert
	Haughty	-- Michel Piccoli's slap
	Egocentric	-- Bokassa's diamonds -- Greek domanial forests
P. Mauroy	Fun-loving	-- Frequents hotspots at night in his red Ferrari -- Emptied out the wine cellars at the Matignon residence before leaving
M. Rocard	Hesitant	-- Many rumors at the outset, none of which were confirmed -- His wife convinced him to resign from the administration in 1985
J. Chaban-Delmas	Double-talker: Not very upright	-- The man of the "New Society", who pays no taxes -- Mystery around the death of of his first wife
G. Marchais	Double-talker	-- Worked at the Messerschmitt factories in Germany during World War II
R. Barre	Fake Gaullist	-- Did not join the free French forces in 1942
	Extreme-right sympathizer	-- Participates in the Trilateral Commission
	Moscow's man	-- Soviet sympathies
F. Mitterrand	Worn out	-- Cancer
	Machiavelli	-- The attack at "l'Observatoire"

The portrait that people try to paint of François Mitterrand is very different: he is portrayed as a Florentine prince—a shrewd politician willing to do anything to extend his reign. This portrait was encouraged by a variety of books about the president. The most famous of them, written by Catherine Ney, attempted to show that François Mitterrand was not a true socialist, but rather an ambitious man. In the rumor about his having cancer that followed his acceding to the presidency, this idea was also present: having reached a ripe old age, and having obtained wnaι he had wanted, François Mitterrand was ready to die. The rumor had the scenario of François Mitterrand's life end in style and splendor.

Michel Rocard's enemies within his own party built up an image of him as hesitant, hardly capable of making important decisions, and thus not presidential candidate material. Many rumors announced that Rocard was going to make an outburst, become rebellious, and say what he really thought. Thus on November 22, 1984, *Le Matin* in Paris entitled an article: "The Rocard rumor. Talk is going round that the Minister of Agriculture is going to make a big stink on *l'Heure de vérité* ["the Moment of Truth," a television show] and then leave the administration. But in fact, Michel Rocard has not decided anything." Later, when, as it had been announced, he resigned because he disapproved of the decision to abandon the two-round majority rule system in France, rumors suggested that he had in fact been heavily influenced by his wife—proof that he was a spineless man.

Thus, every politician, to the extent to which he becomes dangerous, must logically be attacked by rumors at some point or another. Since 1984, operations aiming at creating or fanning rumors against Raymond Barre, for instance, have been mounting. Because of his Gaullist tone, his positions against his political "friends", and his refusal to be involved in cohabitation with President Mitterrand (had the opposition party won the legislative elections in March 1986), Raymond Barre became the man to attack, for leftists and above all rightists.

At the end of 1984, in the RPR's innermost circles, a file was circulating about the Inter-France press agency that had been financed by the Germans during the Occupation. A man by the name of Raymond Barre was found on the lists, and a rumor pointed out that Raymond Barre's doings between 1940 and 1946 were unclear, and the extreme rightist, Jean-Marie Le Pen had been very tolerant towards him! In reality, when the information had been verified, it was another man by the same name who had worked for Inter-France, a Raymond Barre who was fifteen years older than the French politician (*Le Monde,* May 30, 1985).

A little-known fact was pointed out about Raymond Barre in the same file.

His seemingly upright father had been brought before a court of assizes, after having been accused of fraudulent bankruptcy and forgery in trade accounts. The rumor naturally omitted to mention that he had been acquitted. What's more, Raymond Barre's parents had gotten divorced, and the former prime minister had not seen his father since the age of four. But the main attack concerned his behavior during World War II on Reunion Island in the Indian Ocean. In 1942, the free French Forces opened up a recruitment office in the town of Saint-Denis-de-la Réunion for those who wanted to join up with the British. Unlike some of his friends, Raymond Barre did not sign up—at his mother's behest. He was eighteen years old. The Gaullist clan constantly exploited this fact to undermine his legitimacy.

On the left, in 1985, in an article on the "hidden Barre", *Le Monde* published the same insinuations: "He can swear all he wants to his staunch Gaullist faithfulness, and that he was moved every time he heard the General's speeches when they were rebroadcast by All India Radio, but nothing will undo the fact that he failed to provide the first service record that could have grounded his legitimacy" The same article also insinuated that Raymond Barre had been very "marked" by rightist riots that took place while he was visiting Paris on February 6, 1934. Now at that time, he was not yet even ten years old! Lastly, while appreciating Barre's eclecticism and curiosity, the article emphasized his official participation in the mysterious Trilateral Commission.

Each of these rumor seeds and still others resurfaced in February 1986, in the midst of the campaign for the legislative elections, in a brochure with a revealing title: *The Other Face of Raymond Barre*. Who was the publisher? It was an unknown publishing house, created for the occasion, Avenir International. To accelerate the rumors and expose them publicly in the media, the brochure must have been massively and freely distributed to notables and journalists.

The planned organization of rumors does not only concern the highest-ranking presidential candidates. It is also a reality at the local level. The author of the already mentioned guide, *How to Win Local Elections,* at least had some merit in that he described in print the different procedures to be used depending on the image one wants to project of oneself.

1. You want to show that you are an active man? Tell people of and circulate detailed schedules of your work with government agencies.
2. You want to prove that you are a sincere candidate? Tell people and have other people say what you refuse to publish about yourself, for fear of laying it on too thick.
3. You want to show that you are disinterested? Tell people and have other

people talk of the risks you are taking by being a candidate (in your profession, for example).

4. You want to show that you are loyal? Tell people and have other people talk about what you refuse to write about your adversary.
5. You want to show that you have an instinct for contact? Tell people and have other people tell a few anecdotes about your life.
6. You want to criticize the cost of your adversary's campaign? Tell people and have other people mention the prices of the documents that have been distributed.

For a rumor to take, it is naturally out of the question to organize a meeting designed to "train" one's "informers": an impression of propaganda and manipulation would be given thereby. One must proceed by successive, innocent-seeming discussions with people, without even giving the slightest clue that something is going to be expected of them—quite the contrary! In one's careful selection of the first mouths, ten to fifteen people will suffice, and the mechanics of rumor spreading will be well underway. In effect, the political world is the only world endowed with so many loudspeakers, i.e., rumor "professionals" [54]:

1. The class of political journalists, former deputies, political attachés of ministerial offices, attachés of employers' federations, and newspaper gossip columnists dreaming of a new Watergate, in whose interest it is to dream up or confirm scandals.
2. Those people in whose interest it is to create or exploit rumors: political party apparati and foreign embassies. They give the decisive push that accelerates rumor processes.

Rumors circulate all the more quickly when the political world is a microcosm probed by all editorial boards, and scrutinized from every angle by parliamentary journalists, press attachés for ministers, communication advisors, and the editors of the many "confidential letters" who, afraid of being left behind in the dust, prefer to press on ahead and spread rumors to their readers. Correspondents of the provincial press spread rumors to the rest of France; foreign correspondents spread them to London, Bonn, Washington, and Damas. Rumors thereby reach their full public magnitude, and are ready to be claimed for a certain side and exploited.

PART IV
The Anti-Rumor

17

Controlling Rumors

Introduction

Can one smother a rumor? What means can be used? What is the effectiveness of denials? Such questions become crucial for any individual, group or organization that suddenly finds itself faced with "false" rumors whose effects risk being negative, if not downright dramatic. Let it be said right from the outset: there is no magic recipe for controlling rumors. It is only through a precise definition of the situation that one can make a diagnosis and offer up recommendations.

Procter & Gamble and the Devil

In the fore mentioned case of Procter & Gamble, what were the company's reactions to the rumor accusing it, in 1980, of being owned by the Moonies? It began by responding very directly by reminding people of the historical origins of its logo, designed in 1882, and of the structure of its capital assets: obviously no one could single-handedly own Procter & Gamble. The phone calls slaked off, and the crisis seemed to be over.

In late 1981, however, there was a new onslaught of phone calls. This time callers wanted to know whether the company was really possessed by Satan or not. Little by little, the wave of anonymous letters and calls grew to such enormous proportions that the company received 15,000 phone calls during the month of June 1982 alone.

Right from the outset, Procter & Gamble had decided to react discreetly, without using the mass media. There was no need to alarm shareholders or provide an occasion to distributors to become more demanding about the commercial conditions proposed by the company. An explanatory report was first sent to sixty-seven influential leaders of religious public opinion, and later to 48,000 religious organizations to alert and sensitize them to the problem. As the anti-Procter crusade (with a call for a boycott of their products) had a religious side to it, it was important to communicate with the leaders of these communities, as they were the only people would could exercise some control over their followers.

Faced with a persistently increasing number of calls, the company resolved to call upon the media. On June 24, 1982, Procter & Gamble made a press release in which the primary leaders of fundamentalist movements argued against any possible connection between the company and Satan. The most powerful reporters from newspapers and magazines in the United States were invited. The press coverage was impressive. The director of public relations for Procter & Gamble appeared on the famous morning television show "Good Morning America," but carefully avoided, despite invitations, to appear on Phil Donahue's very popular television broadcast. Indeed, one version of the rumor had been based on a supposed appearance of one of Procter & Gamble's managers on the Phil Donahue show, where he supposedly declared quite openly that the company paid 10 percent of its profits to Satanic churches. By avoiding the Phil Donahue show, Procter & Gamble hoped to unvaryingly contradict the rumor on that precise point: as opposed to what the rumor alleged, no company executive had *ever* appeared on that show.

Alongside its massive press campaign, Procter & Gamble decided for the first time to sue six people who had been distributing leaflets on the Satanic nature of the company and inciting people to boycott its products. Among the people sued, there were two distributors of products made by Amway, a competitor in certain of Procter & Gamble's markets: the motives of rumor-mongers are not all related to belief, but can, as in this case, be strictly opportunistic; such people profitably exploit rumors about their rivals. Lastly, Procter & Gamble hired fifteen telephone operators to clear up the misconceptions of all callers [7,157].

By July of 1982, the monthly call figures had dropped below 6,000. But little by little, the figures once again climbed, reaching an average of 15,000 per month in the space of a few short months. In the end, after four years of hassel, thousands of anonymous letters and hundreds of thousands of phone calls, the gigantic company, showing an annual turnover of more than twelve billion dollars, decided in April of 1985 to take its logo off all of its products, thus putting an end to a practice dating back to 1882. The logo has since only been used at the Cincinnati headquarters and on the group's stationery. As the rumor had been based on the Satanic look of the logo, the company did away with the offensive symbol.

Will the disappearance of the symbol put an end to the rumor? In France, the brands that replaced the European codes ("E" plus a number) for their food additives by their real names (e.g., sodium orthophosphate) on their food packaging were, strangely enough, soon taken off the "Villejuif" leaflet, as if this rumor were only responsive to variations of pure form.

In responding to the rumor, Procter & Gamble might conceivably have adopted other strategies:

1. Silence. This approach is adopted by politicians who view with disdain the more or less remotely controlled slander thrown at them [33]. Can one assume that the Procter & Gamble rumor would have stopped by itself? That would have hardly been likely in the short run, as it was spreading everyday into new religious strata of the American population. The rumor's potential market was very large, and could have been fed with unspent fuel for a long time to come. While the first people affected by the rumor would have tired of it, newcomers would have been overwhelmed by the revelation.
2. Geographical concentration: the rumor did not have the same penetration in every state. The company could have focused its efforts on the key southern states where the rumor had been very widely diffused.
3. In terms of advertising, as the Procter & Gamble company is a master in the art of televized advertising, a solution could have been found in this realm. They would have had a clear advantage in being able to control what was communicated to the public, but on the one hand, the cost would have been considerable, and on the other that would have risked alarming those who had not yet heard the rumor. Moreover, the advertising would have brought the name "Procter & Gamble" into the public eye, something the company had been avoiding for a century. The company has never sought to make its name known, and has exclusively promoted the reputation of each of its brands. This was shown by a survey done [3] in which 79 percent of the Americans interviewed were unable to list products manufactured by the company. As for the others, they were most often mistaken in the products they mentioned. These figures are important as they show that the management's fear of a boycott was perhaps exaggerated. In order to boycott Procter & Gamble, people would have had to know which products they made. Moreover, only 4 percent of the people interviewed said they had been purchasing less of the company's products. On the whole, and from a strictly economic point of view, the strategy of remaining silent was probably the wisest, but the most difficult to maintain psychologically. The company's employees, salespeople, and distributors were all expecting action to be taken by the management.

In Canada, in 1984, in order to combat a rumor accusing the famous beer brewers, La Batt's, of being owned by Pakistani shareholders, the company oriented its advertising campaign for this beer around the theme of the "Canadian heritage," showing La Batt's deep roots in Canada's history. While they were also advertisements about the beer itself, the theme indirectly addressed the rumor. At the same time, La Batt's extended its patronage of the arts activities and its sponsorship of local and national sports teams.

McDonald's also took advantage of its TV advertising, as one of the fronts in a counterattack that also included activity directed at journalists and local franchises. Restaurant managers posted a letter from the minister of agriculture certifying that McDonald's satisfies the norms of the food safety and quality service. A public relations campaign demonstrated the rumor's absurdity from an economic point of view: a pound of earthworms is five times as expensive as a pound of beef! Alongside that, a TV campaign praising McDonald's hamburgers heavily stressed the message: 100 percent pure beef!

Orléans: The Anti-Myth

The case of the Orléans rumor differs from that just mentioned in several respects. The Orléans rumor was localized in but one city with 88,000 inhabitants. Secondly, the rumor was first replied to on June 2, 1969, only three weeks after the rumor got started in junior high schools. Thirdly, the counterrumor was effective: the rumor died out by mid June, leaving behind a myriad of mini-rumors, before repression ("It's better not to talk about all that") and progressive amnesia ("Me? I never believed it") took place. By mid June, the clientele of the shopkeepers targeted had been fully restored.

On May 30, 1969, M. Licht, owner of the Dorphé shop, the first store to be accused by the rumor, made an official complaint to the police about anonymous slander. On June 2, the regional daily press joined the fray: they not only related the events, but also attacked the rumor vehemently, speaking of "odious slander" (*La Nouvelle République*) and of a "campaign of deffamation" (*La République du Centre*). That burst the bubble: the rumor, which had up until then remained underground, was deliberately brought to the surface in order to be ousted and bring on public shame. This change of perception modified the status of the rumor's relays: from anticrime watchdogs, they became the willing henchmen of anti-Semitism. Spreading the rumor lost its prestige value and inspired instead a negative image.

On the local level, the Bishop of Orléans, along with many associations, political organizations, and trade unions published a whole stream of reproving statements. At the national level, antiracist organizations and associations of former concentration camp prisoners followed suit. From June 7–10, 1969, the Parisian press made final attacks in articles appearing in *Le Monde, L'Aurore, L'Express,* and *Le Nouvel Observateur.*

Faced with such a counterattack, the rumor first sparked off an anti-counterattack. The myth of the white slave trade absorbed the anti-myth: "the local press, associations and the local elected officials had all been bought off by the Jews." The same was said to be true of the Parisian press which, as everyone knows, "can be sold off to the highest bidder." By trying to encompass too much, the rumor burst, like the frog who tried to swallow an ox.

Why was the counterattack so effective in Orléans in 1969, in Amiens in 1970, and in La Roche-sur-Yon in 1984, and why has it been less effective thus far in the case of Procter & Gamble in the United States? What are, generally speaking, the key parameters that must be taken into account before deciding whether it is wise to counterattack, and if so, in what manner? Let us recall for the record that the means used by Procter & Gamble, while considerable, were mere homeopathic doses on an American scale. On the contrary, the wave of statements, demonstrations, and articles in the press from June 2–12, 1969, in the city of Orléans alone constituted a considerable campaign. Hence our first conclusion: as long as a fire remains contained within a limited area, it can be rapidly extinguished. On the scale of the United States, the fact that Procter & Gamble began receiving phone calls constituted proof that the rumor had begun some time before and had already had the time to spread. The people who called at the beginning were "friends," i.e., people who did not really believe, but who expected to be reassured by the company in which they had faith. As we have already mentioned, a person targeted by a rumor usually finds out too late, and it is usually a friend that tells him [212]. In Orléans, M. Licht only found out about the rumor on May 23. And even then, it was presented as simple slander going around about him personally, and not as a vast rumor about white slave trading targeting six well-known shops in the center of town. As the rumor's real scope was underestimated, no reply was made for several days.

Isabelle Adjani: Live Denial on Television

On Sunday, January 18, 1987, in order to put a stop to rumors running rife about her health, Isabelle Adjani, the movie star, decided to make an appearance, after two weeks of absence and an information blackout on the part of her lawyer. Sunday morning, ratio stations announced that the star would appear in person on the evening news at eight o'clock—prime time on

French television. Thirty-eight percent of French people over eighteen saw Adjani on the news that evening [145].

Visibly moved, she spent ten minutes denying the false rumors that had forced her to appear that evening before the public. Next to her, the president of the French medical board attested that the actress was in fine health. Lastly, the star announced that she would sue anyone and everyone behind the rumor. The very next day, every paper, magazine, and radio station was talking about the TV show, and unanimously supporting the actress. This talk in the media brought the rumor to the attention of 57 percent of French people, at the same time as its denial. An opinion poll carried out by the author of this book a month after Adjani's television appearance revealed that half of those 57 percent believed the denial, while the others had reservations (see table 17.1 below).

TABLE 17.1
Post-denial Opinion of Those Who Heard the Rumor
along with Its Denial (n = 1032)

I believe that she is really ill, denials notwithstanding	2%
I would not be surprised if, despite the denials, she were really ill	5%
I do not know what to believe: is she really in good health or is she ill as the rumor sustains?	39%
I believe the denials: the rumor is groundless. Adjani is in good health	51%
No opinion	3%
Total	100%

At the behavioral level, so much noise was made about this rumor in the space of a few short weeks that it actually "killed" the topic. No one dared mention the Adjani rumor at parties for fear of being thought obsessed with the idea. The tremendous noise had given way to silence, if not belief. By the summer of 1989, two years later, time had taken its effect. Adjani is alive, well, and beautiful. Her latest movie, "Camille Claudel," was a success. Few people still believe she is ill. In any case, the rumor is now totally obsolete. Moreover, her case has constituted a good prophylaxis against rumors about well-known public figures. Whenever one attributes illness to someone, feelings of uneasiness, if not outright resentment, are aroused. The topic has now somehow become taboo. This is part of the aftermath of Isabelle Adjani's televised denial.

18

Denials: A Perilous Art

Less Valuable Information

Denying does not suffice. Denials have a number of handicaps as to their value on the information supply and demand market.

1. They do not constitute hot news. They are expected. Someone who is attacked says (or has someone else say for him), "I am innocent." What constitutes real, surprising, unexpected news is when the accused says, "Yes, I did it." Denials are often truisms. In a case of unfounded rumors that accused a brand of tuna fish (made by the Saupiquet group) of food poisoning in July 1985, the denials published by the press were more discreet than the articles about the tuna alert, which is only normal. Saying that "tuna is not dangerous" is noninformation and altogether banal, while saying, "Watch out: canned tuna may be dangerous" is a scoop!
2. Denials are cold, almost kill-joy information. They defuse the imagination, plunging us back into the banality of reality. Denials suppress stories of whose truth we are not altogether sure, but which in any case have an effect when they are told, spurring on a wide variety of commentaries and passionate elaborations. Let us recall: *se non è vero, è bene trovato!* Thus we understand that, in the papers, denials are about as welcome as a fox in a henhouse. Either the paper never spoke of the rumor, in which case the denial does not deserve much space, or it spoke of it because it was pleasing, and in that case denials can only displease: thus it will be granted but little space, and will be easily missed, tucked away at the bottom of some page or other.

If the denials come from official authorities at a high level, it naturally becomes virtually necessary to print it. This is also true if it has deep social implications. In Orléans, for example, the authorities—the mayor, the prosecutor, and the prefect of police—never publicly adopted a stance

235

concerning the rumor. On the other hand, the denials made by the many local and national organizations revealed an affair whose implications for social balance were extremely important. The denials brought to light a truly fundamental problem: that of the progressive return of latent anti-Semitism. In so far as such, the denials constituted important information: hot news.

Information That Wears Out

One of a rumor's strengths lies in its repetition. One day you hear it in one place, and the next day somewhere else. The versions evolve, are enriched, refined, and become more precise.

In order to be effective, denials should also be repeated. Alas, in the form of an authentic declaration that must be conserved in every respect, denials cannot be expected to be printed more than once in the press. One reads a paper or listens to news on the radio, not in order to reread what has already been announced the day before, or, still worse, a few weeks before. When the victim of a rumor tries to have another denial broadcast, he discovers that his denial has become obsolete before the altar of novelty. Occasionally, however, due to activism or a spirit of religious crusading, a denial may be republished in certain papers. But the relays themselves tire: "we've already given to that cause!"

To win the public's attention in a fail-safe way, one can always buy advertising space. To snuff out a rumor of a child being bitten by a snake hiding in a bunch of bananas, for example, the manager of the supermarket targeted by the rumor bought more than half a page in his local daily paper, *L'Alsace,* On July 30, 1982. He formally denied the rumor therein and offered a reward to anyone who could provide information as to the rumor's origins. In 1984, in the conservative Midwest in the United States, a rumor began claiming that Stroh Beer, a very popular beverage in the area, was secretly financing Jessie Jackson, the black democratic presidential candidate, in his electoral campaign against Ronald Reagan. By way of reply, *Stroh Beer* bought full page ad space in the number one selling daily in the area, the *Chicago Tribune* [157].

Selective Exposure

One of the paradoxes of persuasion campaigns is that they seem to affect those who are already convinced more than those who are not yet convinced [138]. Indeed, except when we are certain of our opinions, we avoid taking the risk of hearing information that would throw into question our ways of thinking, when they concern highly emotionally charged subjects. This phenomenon of selective exposure explains flight from messages that one knows are opposed to one's own beliefs, when it is a question of subjects with a high degree of affective import.

The figures corroborate the hypothesis of flight on the part of the people targeted. Of the Americans who had heard the rumor about Procter and Gamble but did not believe it, 83 percent declared that they had seen, read, or head the company's official denials. Only 54 percent of those who believed the rumor or had reservations about it remembered having been exposed to the denial. In Orléans, given the barrage of denials printed in the local and national press for ten full days, it would be unlikely for someone not to have been exposed to them.

In the poll that followed Isabelle Adjani's denial [145], people were asked whether they had heard the rumor prior to the denial, whether they had watched the televised denial, and whether they had read magazines echoing her live denial. There were no difference between subgroups as to viewing of the TV denial: exposure rates did not vary in accordance with age, sex, or social class. As expected, prior exposure to the rumor was highly selective: exposure was correlated with age (young people being more exposed than older people), social class, and educational level (the higher strata being the most exposed). The pattern was the same for magazine exposure. The magazine denials, unlike the TV denials, reached a selective audience.

The choice of medias thus allows one to get around the problem of selective flight. But here we come upon another paradox. The best media and the perfect times to reach the people one wants to convince are not the best from the point of view of communication. In other words, the press—the media most given to selective exposure—is the media that best transmits messages. The opposite is true of prime time radio and television shows such as TV news.

That is why it is useless to try to explain at great length one's position on television. Arguments go in one ear and out the other, and, in the worst of cases, are simply misunderstood. Television must be used as a visual medium maximizing source effects as part of an emotionally persuasive strategy. When watching TV, people generally decode visual cues and make attributions on the basis of what they see: their views are dependent on whether they think the incriminated person looks sincere, deeply hurt, etc. On the whole, in rumor processes, people believe on the basis of what they hear; in the case of televised denials, they decide on the basis of what they see.

Television watching tends to be somewhat peripheral as people often do other things at the same time: their presence in front of the set is not constant, nor is their attention very sustained. They pick up a few words, phrases, and images here and there. If it is announced on the radio, for example, that: "According to certain rumors, Procter & Gamble has links with Satanic Churches. This is but pure invention. The rumors are entirely false," part of the viewing audience may very well accidentally only hear the beginning of the statement, and conclude that the station has thus confirmed the rumor. Thus it is not advisable to repeat a rumor when one makes a televised denial.

The psychology of memory teaches us that concrete concepts are more easily remembered than abstract ones. Thus, when people hear a denial of the following type: "Product X is not carcinogenic," some of them "remember" afterwards that X *is* carcinogenic. Indeed, the negation is easily forgotten: heard together, the concepts "X" and "carcinogenic" have been stored right next to each other in one's memory, and quite naturally remain associated.

The press minimizes such problems of truncated interpretations: the reader can read and reread at his own rhythm, without being overwhelmed by the unstoppable flow of images and words. Alas, he can also decide not to read, if his belief in the rumor brings into play his deepest values, thereby leading him to be highly selective in exposing himself to messages. For many rumors, the degree of involvement is, fortunately, rather moderate. And even in the case of highly emotionally charged rumors, one cannot speak of a homogeneous public. Certain people are far more involved than others in a rumor. Those who are less involved should be accessible to the press [266].

The Boomerang Effect Denials May Have

Recent studies on rumors and denials show that *one can be affected by a rumor even if one does not believe it* [264]. On the other hand, one can be negatively influenced by a denial, even if one believes it [260].

This is an important finding, for in any denial campaign, there are in reality two communicative actions that take place: one makes people who are *not* yet aware of the rumor aware of it, and one tries to influence those who are already aware of it. Thus Procter & Gamble's press campaign in June 1982 resulted in spreading the rumor to a wider segment of the public. In the southern states where the rumor started, word-of-mouth and sermons were the main channels through which people heard of it. On the scale of the United States as a whole, those who knew of the rumor heard it essentially from the press. And the majority of the inhabitants of the northern states (60 percent) found out about it *after* the denial campaign began. In Orléans, the press campaign also spread the rumor considerably in the suburbs and nearby cities (and to the city of Amiens, no doubt).

This poses a key question: is denial by simple refutation strong enough not to contaminate those who first hear the rumor along with its denial? In medical terms, does it vaccinate such people against the rumor or does it, rather, allow the rumor's kernel to filter through? If the latter is the case, what kind of messages permit one to avoid this risk and completely innoculate people who thus learn of the rumor?

In an experiment on different strategies to adopt in order to reduce the persuasive effects of rumors, students were asked to watch a preview of a new televised serial [254]. As often happens in the United States, the program was interrupted by commercials, one of which concerned McDonald's restaurants. During the McDonald's commercial, a female student in the group (who was, in fact, one of the experimenters) said aloud to the other students in the viewing room: "This McDonald's commercial reminds me of the rumor about earthworms and McDonald's—you know, it seems that McDonald's puts earthworms in its hamburgers."

In the experiment, there were four different groups of students that attended four different sessions where the following scenarios were played out:

1. In the first group, called "rumor-only," after the experimenter-accomplice had announced the rumor, the official experimenter in the room reminded everyone that there was supposed to be no talking during the viewing.
2. In the second group, called "rumor-plus-refutation," after the rumor had been announced, the official experimenter said, "Oh that's just old wives' tales, it doesn't hold water: anyway, earthworms are too expensive—$8 a pound! What's more, the minister of agriculture did a study and found that McDonald's uses 100 percent pure beef. So let's keep it quiet now, if you will." As we see, the experimenter used the same arguments as those put forward by McDonald's itself.
3. In the third group (called "rumor-plus-dissociation"), the experimenter said to the student accomplice, "This may seem strange to you, but last week I went with my mother-in-law to the famous French restaurant in Chicago, 'Chez Paul,' and we had a wonderful sauce made with earthworms. Well, please keep it quiet now."
4. In the fourth group (called "rumor-plus-reassociation"), at the end of the viewing, an evaluatory questionnaire was passed out on the serial (as in the three other groups) with, in addition, three question about meals at McDonald's (the food is good/not good; it is what I like/not what I like; I will surely go eat there/not eat there). But in the fourth group, unlike the

other three, before answering the three questions, the students had to indicate on the questionnaire where the McDonald's they usually went to was located, how many times a year they ate there, and if it had an outside eating area or not.

What were the results of these four approaches? (See the figure below.)

Figure 18.1
McDonald's and Earthworms:
The Effects of Anti-Rumor Communication

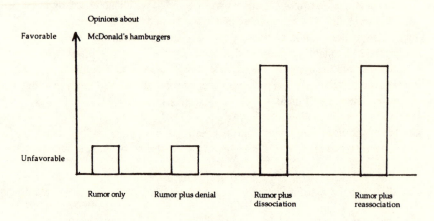

(From A. Tybout et al. *JMR*, 1981)

As can be seen, presentation of the rumor followed by denial had the same negative effect as presentation of the rumor alone! The two other tactics, however, annihilated the rumor's effect.

One should not conclude from this experiment that denials are never effective. In this study, only one form of denial was tested. Generally speaking, denials appear in the media—on TV or in the written press—and that gives them a degree of credibility that the experimenter perhaps did not have.

Whatever the case may be, the experiment is full of lessons about the formation of opinions and the influence that a rumor one does not necessarily believe can have on one's opinions. Indeed, a subsidiary question students were posed two days after the experiment revealed that all four groups considered the rumor to be totally unfounded.

The study of information processing explains why a rumor can have effects even when one does not really believe it. Indeed, after having been exposed to the rumor about McDonald's, for example, the students had in their memories new information that was associated with that company. Asked their opinions about McDonald's, their opinions were based on the positive and negative thoughts that came to mind. As it was recently acquired, the worm/McDonald's association was one of these spontaneous thoughts. Now this thought was unpleasant. It thus generated a less favorable opinion than if no such unpleasant thought had come to mind. The students were affected *not because they believed* in the worm/McDonald's association, but rather *because it came to mind*.

Case studies corroborate this interpretation. In early 1981, in Great Britain, a Kentucky Fried Chicken restaurant fell prey to the classic "rat in the fried chicken" rumor [243]. The manager noticed that even his regular customers stopped coming for a number of weeks because, although they did not actually believe the accusation, "the very thought of it put them off."

This theoretical framework also explains why, in the similar cases, the refutation of a rumor is ineffective. The refutation leads students to repeat the rumor to themselves, thereby reinforcing the earthworm/McDonald's association. Even if the refutation were effective to the point that the thought, "McDonald's hamburgers do not really contain earthworms," would easily come to mind again, this latter thought still cannot suppress the association, which is in fact mnemonically strengthened due to repetition.

In this theoretical perspective, in order to defuse the effects of a rumor being told to people, one must maneuver the situation such that:

1. Either the negative information (e.g., earthworm) not be stored in their memories at the "McDonald's" address, but rather elsewhere.
2. The negative information (e.g., earthworm) be positivized:
3. Or when questioned about their opinions about McDonald's, they have in mind other thoughts than the negative one implanted by the rumor.

In the experiment, the third group (rumor plus dissociation) was an example of the implementation of the first two tactics listed above. In saying, just after the students had heard the rumor, that he had tasted a wonderful earthworm sauce in the French restaurant, Chez Paul, in Chicago, the experimenter facilitated storage of the "earthworm" information in association with "Chez Paul" rather than with "McDonald's." Moreover, he made the information "earthworm" less unpleasant.

The fourth group (rumor plus reassociation) was subjected to a maneuver designed to make information come to mind about McDonald's which might not have come to mind spontaneously. Once present, this positive information strongly influenced the students' opinions about McDonald's hamburgers.

Denial Transparency

Research on the effects of innuendo casts still more light on the problem of denials. Innuendo about a person can be described in terms of two critical features: a statement about a person, and a qualifier about the statement. According to these criteria, statements such as "Isabelle Adjani may be very ill," "women have not been disappearing in this store," and "is Procter and Gamble linked to the Moonies?" are all innuendos. Denial is one kind of innuendo. An experimental study [206] examined the persuasive effects of direct assertions, simple questions, and denials on an audience's impressions about someone. In addition, half of the experimental audience received the message from a high credibility source, the other half from a low credibility source. The results are straightforward (see Table 18.2):

TABLE 18.2
Mean Impression Negativity as a Function of
Source, Credibility, and Headline Form

Source Credibility	Headline Form				
	Assertion	Question	Denial	Control	
High	4.65	4.28	3.54	2.84	
Low	4.12	3.97	3.56	3.12	

Note: Possible range was 1 to 7, with higher values for greater negativity of impression. (From D.M. Wegner et al., *JPSP*, 1981).

Innuendos were certainly less persuasive than direct incriminations, but they nonetheless left a negative impression. Simple questions proved to be rather damaging. Even denials had a negative impact when compared to control statements (i.e., neutral assertions about the person). An analysis of the effect of source credibility revealed that innuendos continued to have impact even when the source of the innuendo had low credibility. This finding seems at odds with typical findings of research on source credibility. However, source credibility only plays an important role when the audience: (1) lacks involvement (and uses peripheral yielding cues instead of thoroughly processing the message [57]; (2) lacks the competence needed to understand the topic and relies on experts; (3) forms opinions in order to adhere to some reference group or to identify with a reference person. None of these conditions was present in the innuendo experiment.

Why do innuendos leave damaging impressions? Why do even denials damage one's image? One reason may be that people see through denials. People, unlike computers, have no "reset button" to erase their memories. Denials do not erase impressions, but rather accompany them. People process information cumulatively. One piece of information does not delete another; they are added together. This is why it is difficult to leave out information that is known to be false. There are other explanations of the effects of innuendo [260, p. 338]: generally speaking, statements are more salient than qualifiers. They are more imaginable and more easily accessed by memory. The audience also makes attributions about the statement itself: "Why would someone deny something if it were not a real possibility and not something altogether ridiculous?" [265].

What Does Reality Prove?

Many rumors dissipate because they cannot stand up to reflection or a logical examination of their details. Others, however, are unaffected by rationality [262].

Indeed, the more symbolic content a rumor has, the less the details provided by the rumor count in and of themselves. The details are considered to be what they are: substitutable signifiers. If a particular detail is not realistic, that does not prove that the whole of the narrative is false: it suffices to replace the defective detail by another that is more realistic but has the same meaning.

Would the rumor of the snake hiding in a bunch of bananas that bites children, for example, suddenly be discredited if it were found out that this snake cannot kill someone in a minute? It seems unlikely, and an interlocutor who believed the rumor would quickly claim that it was not that kind of snake, but rather a more lethal one. Similarly, in the United States during World War II, it was a frequent occurrence to accuse one or another social group of getting its members exempted from military service. When statistics proved that this was not the case, the most frequent response was: "Yes, but they got themselves the easier jobs going in the armed forces!" [5]. Thus while the signifiers are interchangeable, the signified remains stable. It may not be *the* truth, but it express *a* truth.

The resistance of certain rumors to facts sometimes surprises observers. For a rumor to spread, it must survive the legitimate objections inevitably raised by the first people who hear it. Reality must thus at least not have been an obstacle to the rumor. In itself, therefore, the proliferation of a rumor as absurd as that about McDonald's earthworms proves that the rumor is able to surf on the surface of reality and absorb the counterarguments that people put forward.

A rumor is not bothered by one or two details that seem somewhat abnormal. In many rumors, content takes precedence over form. The person who spreads the rumor generally does not try to stick to the precise message he has heard, but rather to persuade his public, and is willing to correct or improve the message in order to do so [193]. He will be altogether ready to concede here or there that abnormalities have slipped into the narrative. It is because rumors are supple and malleable throughout their construction that they are so at ease when faced with objections bearing on details.

Rumors also know how to turn proofs and counterarguments around. In Amiens and Orléans, all the facts put forward to contradict the rumor were used to proved that it was, in fact, founded. The initial silence of the newspapers, inaction on the part of the police, and the official absence of people who had disappeared attested to the will of high-ranking people to hush up the affair, bought off, as they were, by the henchmen of the white slave trade. Thus a well-known connection was demonstrated between the lower depths and the upper circles. No trap doors were found in the incriminated shops: that was because the owners, having been tipped off by their friends in high places, had boarded them over. Every fact brought forward was immediately turned around: it did not mean what people had thought it meant. Thus facts turn out to be of little import: for it is each individual's system of beliefs that gives them their meaning.

By denying a rumor, one is not simply asking people to add a further piece of information to their repertoire, but rather to alter their entire worldview. Believing a rumor is largely a process of self-persuasion: one is not convinced by others, but rather slowly assimilates the rumor if it clears all the hurdles of one's natural skepticism, and if it reinforces one's general perceptions. Rumors rarely convey merely neutral or entertaining information: they are emotional and are linked to people's cognitive structures. That is why we see such vehement reactions when people find out that a rumor story they had taken to be true was, in fact, false. It is not a simple problem of saving face, but rather of defending a whole attitude structure or worldview.

When the Truth Is Unprovable

Aside from the problem of prejudices that use any and all facts as grist for their mills, regardless of how contradictory they may be, certain rumors pose a far subtler problem: no fact can ever *prove* that they are false. What fact could irrefutably demonstrate, for example, that Procter & Gamble does not send money to the Devil's henchmen?

The problem of proofs and refutations has been studied for a long time by philosophers of science. According to Karl Popper, a theoretical proposition cannot become scientific unless the operations by which it can be tested are specifiable. It is empirical verification that gives a theory its validity. To be valid, a theory should be falsifiable.

Every rumor is a proposition that links a characteristic to a person or object. Certain propositions can quite easily be denied by facts, as they present themselves in a verifiable form, i.e., in a form in which they can be put to the test. In June of 1979, for example, the city police forces in Nice were assailed by phone calls from worried citizens: a rumor had spread that a tidal wave was due to hit Nice on June 24 and that an earthquake was to follow on August 23 (*Le Monde,* January 9, 1983). The rumors could be verified by simply waiting until the appointed days: a natural test of the predictions was not long in coming.

Certain propositions, however, cannot be refuted by empirical tests, as they involve concepts that cannot be directly or even indirectly measured. Every rumor involving the Devil poses serious problems of refutability, if one wishes to bring forth facts with real relevance to the accusation. The same is true of rumors that express hostility towards a group, and that claim, for example, that the members of some particular group receive, during wartime, all the easiest jobs in the armed forces. The proposition is irrefutable in the sense that the decision whether a particular position is laid back or not tends to be rather subjective.

Aside from such extreme cases, certain propositions can only be confirmed and others can only be refuted. During wartime, for example, rumors that take one group or another as scapegoats abound. It is said, for instance, that "there are traitors in that group." Such a proposition can only be confirmed, for even if, after several investigations, no traitor has been found in that group, that does not altogether eliminate the possibility that one will be found during a subsequent investigation. The rumor accusing the famous Stroh Beer in Chicago of secretly financing Reverend Jesse Jackson's political campaign was also of this kind: no investigation could realistically speaking have refuted the rumor. The latter could thus only be confirmed.

Conversely, the Achilles' heel of most denials is that they can only be refuted. After having heard a denial of the "Villejuif" leaflet, for example, assuring the public that citric acid is innocuous, and is a very ordinary ingredient in natural oranges and lemons, a man who was interviewed replied, "Perhaps we'll find out some day that citric acid was in fact dangerous."

Generally speaking, propositions asserting that something does not exist suffer from a terrible handicap when it comes to verifiability, or—to use Popper's terms—falsifiability. How can a business, for example, prove that it does not finance a particular political party? The only convincing denial would consist in saying, "No, we did not send that party a million dollars, but rather two million"! Situations that are unbalanced as concerns confirmability or refutability are frequent occurrences, and they explain the persistence of rumors: no proof can logically put an end to them. The case is thus never closed, forever remaining in abeyance.

Thus we are led to recognize a fundamental paradox: belief of a denial obeys the same logic as belief of the rumor itself. In both cases, one has to take someone at his word. The problem of extinguishing rumors is, first and foremost, a question of people: the answer to the question "what should I believe?" depends on the answer to the question "who is speaking?" Without a credible source, anti-rumor combat is doomed to failure.

Finding a Credible Source

In its denial campaign, Procter and Gamble asked for help from well-known religious leaders (e.g., Jerry Falwell, Billy Graham, etc.). To prove that she was in good health, Isabelle Adjani asked the president of the French medical association to testify on her behalf on television. Research on source persuasion enhancement has encouraged such behavior, although appealing to credible sources is not a panacea, as we have already seen. In any case, experts, credible sources, and opinion leaders have a major advantage: they have access to the media and can attract an audience's attention if and when one decides to make a formal denial.

Recommending the use of credible sources to spearhead denials amounts to a statement of the obvious, but it is sometimes impossible to carry out. Indeed, the proliferation of rumors often attests to a loss of confidence in official information channels, and in the authorities themselves. In countries where information is subject to censorship, rumors abound; now what official statement could ever hope to snuff them out? To do so, a miraculous purity, lost ever so long ago, would have to be reinstated.

And yet the task is not impossible: in reality it is not a question of acquiring credibility, but rather of discrediting one carefully chosen rumor, and thereby discredit other rumors past and future. That is what is known as disinformation. Consider the following example: on Saturday, December 19, 1981, at 5 P.M., the radio station "France-Inter" announced that a prominent figure in Polish activist Catholic circles, Tadeusz Mazowiecki, had died in prison. Though it was not officially confirmed, the information seemed reliable [203].

The news very quickly sped around the globe, and Polish authorities proffered not the slightest denial of the news which, notwithstanding, dealt a serious blow to General Jaruzelski's image. In the West, headlines and commentaries in the press proliferated, deploring the suspicious death (in prison) of this prominent person. In reality, by not denying it, the Polish authorities let the rumor spread in order to ridiculize it all the more when they deemed the right moment had come. At the same time they hoped to ridiculize Western journalists who are so quick to relay the slightest rumors going around Poland. A few days before the end of the year, a representative of the Polish government formally denied Tadeusz Mazowiecki's death, and derided the Western press. In doing so, he undermined the confidence people had had in rumors up until then, and thus increased the government's relative credibility [237].

Choosing One's Timing

In her anti-rumor strategy, Isabelle Adjani picked the right moment. Accused by the rumor of having a "serious illness," she totally disappeared from the public eye for a few weeks between the end of 1986 and early 1987. That led to the expected result: the rumor grew, stirred up by her disappearance. The rumors quickly went from illness to death; people even mentioned several hospitals and precise room numbers. That was the moment Adjani chose to reappear on television: January 18. Indeed, while it is difficult to deny rumors of illness (Michael Dukakis, the Democratic United States presidential candidate, discovered how difficult such rumors can be to dispel), life effectively denies rumors of death. By choosing a propitious moment, Adjani was able to snuff out all the rumors at once.

It might be sustained that she acted too early, as her denial campaign made the rumor known to 57 percent of French adults. This figure should, however, be compared with the 26 percent who had already heard the rumor. And this latter figure would have naturally continued to grow due to word-of-mouth diffusion of the rumor. Through her massive denial campaign, the star made overt what had thus far been covert, and instead of being a passive bystander, and even a victim, she began to control the situation.

The Mobilizing Function of Denials

Problems of timing cannot be detached from the internal function of denials, i.e., their function within a group. A denial can be a great relief to a company's employees, a political party's partisans, or a movie star's fans.

Denial is sometimes an essentially internal communication decision (even when it is outwardly voiced). In all rumor problems, one is tempted to think in simplistically dualistic terms: "they" and "me"! There are actually four groups of people: one's enemies (those who will always believe the rumor as it confirms their attitudes); the uninvolved (those who pay little attention to the rumor); the hesitants (those who do not really know what to think); and one's allies. By remaining silent, one grants the rumor a monopoly on voice, and the hesitants will thus be progressively influenced by the rumor. Furthermore, this gives one's allies no support or leverage. In corporate rumors, for example, the attacked company's employees are the first to be questioned by their friends and relatives. It is essential that they feel bolstered up by a clear corporate position on the subject. To remain silent or wait too long to make a denial would be a mistake.

Former President Valery Giscard d'Estaing made such a mistake in not acting immediately to stop rumors claiming that he had received diamonds from ex-Emperor Bokassa. His silence strategy was a mistake for two reasons:

1. First, because the rumor was not groundless. Had he acknowledged it at once, the gift would not have been viewed suspiciously.
2. Secondly, the rumor was not spontaneous, having been started by political adversaries. They would not stop their campaign: the rumor was thus likely to last a long time, and this was in fact the case. Proper diagnosis of the type of rumor with which one is faced is essential for proper anti-rumor decision making.

19

Changing a Rumor's Image

Introduction

The more a rumor has an emotional basis, the less a reality-related strategy is operative. Reality rarely suffices to set the public's imagination afire: why would one thus expect reality to be able to put the fire out? A key to the problem of extinction is pointed out by one of the founders of contemporary social psychology, S. Asch. His idea can be simply stated: people do not change their perception of objects; it is rather the objects of perception that change. In other words, a reversal of public opinion can only derive from change in a rumor's very identity.

Depositioning Rumors

An analysis of the backlash that began in June 1969 against the Orléans rumor provides a clear example of how a rumor can be dislodged or depositioned: the rumor's identity was changed, i.e., its position and the public's perception of it were modified.

At the outset, the rumor's identity was that of a spontaneous warning to the people against the organized kidnapping of the very symbols of the city: its young girls. It then became more precise, accusing foreigners, i.e., Jews working in the very heart of the town, of being the masterminds behind the kidnappings. Its initial identity only allowed it to attract the attention of people who felt directly threatened: the female population of Orléans.

The reply to the rumor consisted in publicly exploiting the anti-Semitic side of the rumor, thereby endowing it with an unacceptable identity. The Orléans rumor was thus "positioned" as implying a true anti-Semitic conspiracy, an organized clan, slanderous operations, and the return of demons that France had chased away in 1945. Such a rumor thus could not be attributed to the innocent imagination of a junior high school virgin; it could only stem from underground action on the part of a resurgent anti-Semitic group. An official complaint therefore had to be made against X—which is what M. Licht, the first shopkeeper accused, did, as did many antiracist associations as well.

These complaints reversed the relationship between the townspeople and the individuals targeted. To begin with, the rumor portrayed victimized citizens, whose most precious fruits were being stolen away. According to its new identity, the town's citizens were no longer innocent relays, but were rather being manipulated by neo-Nazi resurgence. By not attacking the townspeople, the new identity allowed them to save face, and helped decrease their defensiveness. The new identity, virulently proclaimed by associations, federations, and unions, and confirmed by the media, thus allowed the rumor to be silenced, not because people no longer believed it, but because it became unseemly to speak of it.

A Negative Reflection

Every rumor gives people a certain reflection, impression, or image of the person who spreads it. In Orléans, for example, revealing to others that a white slave trade was operating at the very heart of the town gave a real boost to the narrator's image, increasing his social standing. The psychological benefits derived from such announcements are one of the essential motor forces behind the spreading of rumors. The new identity founded on an anti-Semitic conspiracy transformed these benefits into disadvantages, as one cannot openly present oneself in public as an anti-Semite without running the risk of social disapproval. It is of little importance whether the inhabitants of Orléans still believed the rumor or not; the fact is that very act of speaking about it became socially discouraged.

In Orléans, the anti-rumor actions were carried out spontaneously and were improvised, no plenary sessions having been called to decide upon a strategy and to create a body to control its implementation. During World War II, in the United States and Europe, this was not the case: the problem raised was to limit as far as possible the spreading of many rumors.

The strategy adopted consisted in endowing rumor-mongering—the very fact of speaking about rumors—with an antipatriotic identity: it was made to look like a potentially traitorous act, involving collusion with the enemy. In order to do so, as in Orléans, the hypothesis was spread around that rumors that were unhealthy for the morale of the population and for national cohesion were being masterminded. The mastermind was no other than the Axis' propaganda department. It is true that many rumors going around the United

States were heard in the form of news on Nazi radio shows broadcast in English and directed at the United States. This does not prove that the rumors stemmed from Axis radio stations: perhaps the latter were simply relaying already existing rumors. Whatever the case may have been, spreading negative rumors was equated with working for the famous "fifth column," the presumed source of such rumors.

Spreading rumors was made to look like a serious crime for another reason: the potential grain of truth hidden in a rumor could provide crucial information to infiltrating Nazi agents. The "fifth column" was thus the ubiquitous receiver of every rumor, and that meant a sizable potential risk for the Allied Forces.

As we see, the strategy adopted by the Allies turned rumor-mongering into a socially unacceptable practice. Rumors were thus endowed with a despicable identity: whether stemming from the enemy or picked up by the enemy, they could have disastrous consequences on one's group. To give rumors this identity, the warring Allies mainly relied on anti-rumor posters:

- In Great Britain, one such poster portrayed two women chatting, sitting next to each other on a train-car bench. Two rows behind them, one saw caricatures of Hitler and Goering. The slogan on the poster reminded people that, "You never know who's listening! Loose lips sink ships!" Another poster declared: "Speak less ... you never know," it showed a man half dressed like a civilian, like anyone else, and half dressed like a German officer.
- In the United States, a poster showed a dog with a sad expression on its face, lying on its master's empty armchair. On the wall, there hung a folded flag, an unmistakable sign of the master's death. In large letters, the following few words were printed: " ... because someone talked." Another poster showed a young smiling Marine leaving with his platoon. At the bottom, it was written, "If you say where he's going ... he might never get there!" A third poster showed a little girl tenderly holding in her arms a picture of her father who had obviously been mobilized: "Don't kill her father with idle talk."
- In France, a poster bearing the words, "Advice to those on leave: a good soldier keeps his lips sealed," showed a soldier whose mouth was a zipper. On another poster, one saw a civilian and a soldier talking together in a café. In front of them, a water pitcher is listening in, the pitcher bearing Hitler's face.

As we have already mentioned, this whole strategy against rumor-mongering is nevertheless plagued by an enormous Achilles' heel: how can the public recognize rumors? How can it distinguish information from rumors, or innocuous news from potential secrets? It cannot. We come across the same problem, on an operational level, that we already came across on a conceptual one: how are rumors to be distinguished from other related phenomena? How can one identify a rumor?

Here again we see how much more closely the concept of rumors is related to judgment, i.e., to subjective evaluation, than to objective reality detectable by any outside observer. The problem does not arise when one decides to attack a specific rumor: its identification is made by referring to its content. A few key words suffice to define what is in question here: "earthworms in McDonald's hamburgers," "Procter & Gamble's Satanic logo," "Jane Fonda's death due to aerobics," etc.

Inventing a Hidden Enemy

When attacked by rumors, victims often make official complaints about person X. These are not simply juridical acts, they are essentially mythical in nature. For first of all, most rumors have no identifiable source, or at least no source that would admit to being the real source: would any of the girls in Orléans ever believe that their innocent fantasy-based confessions were used as springboards for the rumor? Secondly, to make official complaints is to attack. A rumor then takes the mythical form of shadow boxing. The complaint about X postulates that X exists, i.e., that this unknown person has a physical body, thoughts, and a strategy: the complaint thus creates a "mastermind" lurking in some headquarters somewhere. It constitutes a pure construction, i.e., a counter-rumor.

A complaint therefore has no meaning unless it is proclaimed *urbi et orbi:* it is an act of communication. The same is true of official complaints against relays who, in all good faith, believe the rumor precisely because, in their minds, it is not a rumor. In any case, trials take place much later in time, and court decisions can vary. When the suspicious "Villejuif" leaflet was first being circulated, for example, the judges nonsuited the plaintiffs, arguing that the relays had themselves been duped by the initial leaflet, and had acted in accordance with what they believed to be a worthy cause: prevention. (The attitude of the judges has changed since that time).

Offering rewards in the press is also a mythical act. It destabilizes people's perception of the rumor by insinuating that the rumor is not innocuous. In the December 11, 1983, issue of the *Chicago Tribune,* the Stroh Brewery Company bought a full-page ad in which they offered a $25,000 reward to whoever could identify the "person or persons" who had started the rumor that the company was contributing to presidential candidate campaigns. In its denial, Stroh did not specifically mention Jesse Jackson, the candidate alluded to in the rumor. On July 30, 1982, the manager of the Cora supermarket in Wittenheim (in the Haut-Rhin region in France) bought a half of a page in the newspaper *L'Alsace* wherein he proposed a $1,500 reward to whoever had information as to the origin of the rumor of a child being bitten by a snake. This unusual but not illegal procedure reminds us of the legendary reward hunter, whose very presence proved that there was, indeed, a culprit— someone to be nabbed.

It is of little importance whether the Wittenheim rumor was started with the aim of damaging someone's reputation or not (though the particular super-market targeted was the only one to offer a babysitting service): the action depicted in the rumor reproduced the basic plot of grand scenarios that set the imagination afire. The victim took the initiative, and depositioned the rumor: rather than reflecting a real accident, it became a new manifestation of competition between supermarkets.

In the political realm, the mastermind hypothesis is part and parcel of the basic repertory of all replies. In September of 1984, when faced with the rapid circulation of the already mentioned rumor that a thousand immigrants were to be housed in the town of Lorient (by the local office of low rental housing projects), the mayor held an extraordinary press conference in order to "deal a fatal blow to a rumor stemming from pure manipulation," and to stigmatize "those who contributed to making up such lies and who bear full respon-sibility for them". (*Liberté du Morbihan,* November 17, 1984). He then made public the list of new residents at the city's low rental housing project in order to clear up any residual ambiguity.

Generally speaking, by attributing a rumor to someone, some group, or to people with a particular intention (as in Orléans), one is able to able do more than simply refute allegations made by the rumor. Refutation is but a defensive strategy, and the accused always remains a step behind the rumor: the ball is in the adversary's court (whether the adversary is mythical or not).

Announcing the existence of a conspiracy or evil intentions serves a vital function in providing the victim with a way of changing roles. In the case of the British Kentucky Fried Chicken rumor, the owner of a franchise offered a £1,000 reward to anyone "who knows how the rumor started—or who is behind it." Although it did not immediately solve the decline in sales or put an end to emotional pressure felt by the managers and their staff, by proposing a reward, "the onus was on prospective claimants to prove the truth of an illogical and false rumor—if not, the story would be discredited" [243, p. 210].

Counter-Rumors and Disinformation

To postulate a mastermind behind the scenes allows one to win back the lead, or at least create a certain doubt in the minds of those people who no longer know what to think. Generally speaking, counter-rumors mix up the signs. They also amount to a tactic of disinformation. The case of the South Korean airliner shot down by Soviet planes in 1984 provides an especially fine illustration of such disinformation. The Soviet government's representative immediately asserted his conviction that the civilian airliner was, in reality, spying for the CIA, a hypothesis that cannot be *a priori* refuted when one is aware of the close ties between South Korea and the United States. It was thus incumbent upon the Koreans to refute this irrefutable hypothesis (but what facts could ever really deny it?). Here again, reality depends on the source one is willing to believe.

Explaining Belief

Two other approaches can contribute to changing a rumor's image. The first consists in seeking the gross errors contained therein, i.e., the manifest, palpable impossibilities. Alas, that is not always possible: we showed this to be the case in analyzing the limits of denials. The second approach consists in explaining to the public why it believes the rumor. Indeed, most people are unaware of the deeper reasons why they firmly believe a rumor to be true. They believe the adage: "where there's smoke, there's fire." But often the fire is only inside themselves. Belief of a rumor is totally projective. Understanding oneself sometimes sheds new light on the beliefs to which one holds dearly. This approach can be illustrated in a very different context from that of rumors, one in which it is at times necessary to put a stop to persistent impressions: psychological experiments on the simulation of emotions.

How do we know whether we like something or not? How do we know if we are gifted in a certain area? These two questions concern one and the same problem: that of the view we have of ourselves. Cognitive psychology has shown that, in order to know things, we use external, manifest signals. William James had foreseen this process when he said, "We are afraid because we are running and not the other way around." The first experiments [168] done to check whether that is really our way of knowing our own feelings consisted, for example, in presenting male students with a series of photographs of women. An apparatus placed on each student's heart and then hooked up to amplifiers was supposed to allow the student to hear his heart beating, and thus to detect possible accelerations when viewing pictures laden with emotional value. The student had to grade each picture according to his attraction to the female model presented therein. What the student did not know was that the heart beat he heard, complete with accelerations, was not that of his own heart.

The results showed that the grades given to the models corresponded to the cardiac accelerations the students heard. In other words, they relied on *outside signals* in deciding how much they liked any particular picture. The experiment was repeated showing male students pictures of naked men and women, and its results were also convincing.

What relation does this have to denials and rumors? In the second experiment, male heterosexual students began giving good grades to pictures of men. It was thus important to tell them at the end of the experiment that the heart beat had been manipulated. The explanation of the manipulation was considered to be a sufficient denial for them to have no residual doubts about the exact nature of their sexual leanings.

Now similar experiments [257], bearing not on feelings, but rather on the sense of being gifted or not for a certain task, have shown that people to whom false feedback had given the impression of being very gifted continued to believe that they were, despite the ensuing denial. Their impressions thus persisted, despite the head experimenter's explanation that the feedback heard was independent of the errors or correct movements each individual made during the task. Though they understood and believed the denial, the experiment left traces. These experiments are crucial in that they show that, once created, our feelings and impressions become virtually independent of the facts that created them. The negation of the facts did not eliminate feelings and impressions.

Other investigators working on the effects of post experimental debriefings [219] have shown that, in order for this persistency to disappear, it did not suffice to explain the experiment and the mechanism of false feedback. It was also necessary to explain the psychological mechanism of persistence. Returning to the context of rumors, these experiments suggest that a denial cannot be complete without an explanation of the reasons why the public so readily adopted the rumor. What is important is the extent to which the rumor was believed: as the interpretation of dreams is the royal road to the individual unconscious, so the interpretation of rumors reveals the social climate, collective aspirations, and fears [181]. That too must be brought to the public's attention [9]. That is precisely what was systematically done in the United States during World War II, in what was called the "Rumor Clinic."

The Rumor Clinic

During World War II, the well known Boston daily, *The Herald Traveler,* took a step that was quickly imitated by forty widely circulating American dailies, as well as American and Canadian magazines. Between March 1942 and December 1943, *The Herald Traveler* ran a weekly column called the "Rumor Clinic," devoted to refuting current rumors brought to their attention either by their readers or by a group of informers circulating in the population at large who worked for the paper. The refutations were most often based on an interview with virtually indisputable leaders (President Roosevelt, General Eisenhower, etc.) or on a presentation of facts that proved the rumor to be impossible. As every denial also makes the rumor known, many precautions were taken in the writing of the column. The rumor was, for example, always mentioned negatively, being referred to as a joke, hoax, false report, mystification, etc.

Now and then, certain more complicated or malicious rumors received special treatment. With the help of psychologists, the Rumor Clinic presented an interpretation of the reasons why a particular rumor unquestionably fascinated people. The tactic consisted in showing that, if "where there's smoke there's fire", the fire often lies within ourselves and not in some supposed facts. After the creation of an army unit made up of women (the WACs), for example, a whole slew of rumors sprang up. It was claimed, for instance, that many of them were prostitutes, that virgins were not admitted, that they received free of charge a stock of contraceptives as soon as they signed up, and that military personnel found to be seeing WACs had to undergo thorough medical examinations to check for venereal diseases. The newspaper wisely decided not to reply to all of these rumors, but to just one of them, and to thereby eliminate the others, past and future, on the subject. The exemplary rumor they chose claimed that five hundred WACs had had to be suddenly flown back from North Africa as they were all pregnant (illegitimately, obviously).

The Rumor Clinic's article (1) stressed that the number of WACs in North Africa was all out of proportion with the number of pregnancies announced; (2) quoted General Eisenhower's praise for the fine work the WACs were doing; (3) indicated that such rumors could only stem from the enemy; and (4) "psychoanalyzed" the belief. The war brought on physical separations and generally forced soldiers to tone down their sex lives; the public took secret pleasure in contemplating the astounding practices of the WACs, that they could at the same time openly denounce as they in fact corresponded to people's latent desires that had to remain repressed.

It seems that the Rumor Clinic's work was effective, given their published figures. Regular readers believed fewer rumors than did occasional readers. The analysis done showed that this effect was not due to a self-selection of readers: those who never believe such rumors are perhaps more inclined to regularly read the papers, sources in which they have full confidence. In fact, the proliferation of Rumor Clinics not only had curative effects on certain false rumors, but also preventative effects. It became fashionable to play the Sherlock Holmes or Agatha Christie of information, brilliantly proving why a particular rumor was suspect, and seemed to be a false rumor that one should "psychoanalyze." From that point of view, the existence of specialized columns devoted to rumors had an *innoculatory* function. Readers were thus injected with antibodies to make them more skeptical about any rumors yet to come.

But as always, as it is impossible for anyone who hears information by word-of-mouth to say whether it is authentic or false, it is likely that the Rumor Clinics had the pernicious effect of generating greater skepticism about every form of news.

In France, several magazines and papers have columns entitled "Talk," "Rumors," and so on. In those columns, reporters relay or even create gossip and rumors. No paper has a regular column devoted to critical analysis or exegesis of fashionable rumors. Now and then a political editorial will examine the rumor of the day, or a reporter interested in rumor phenomena will pinpoint the absurd rumors going around a nearby region. (Thanks to their work, we have been able to isolate many rumors going around "backwoods" France). Only a few bulletins, with too small a circulation, print remarkable counter-investigations carried out in the field by volunteer experts, intrigued by all kinds of bizarre and apparently unexplained phenomena (flying saucer sightings, helicopter-dropped snakes, etc.) (e.g., the bulletin of the Poitou-Charentes Committee on UFOs, and the Pogonip publications).

20

Preventing Rumors

Introduction

People occasionally wish to discourage the emergence of certain rumors. In the United States during 1960s, for example, authorities in many big cities tried to prevent rumors from circulating that experience had shown would inevitably set off race riots [190]. Obviously, there were rumors because of latent racial tensions, and the attempt to forestall them amounted to curing the symptom and not the cause. Nevertheless at a certain moment in each of these big cities, it was too late to start again from scratch. The concrete, operational problem was an immediate one: how could certain predictable rumors be prevented?

Prevention and Credibility

Most big American cities where there was a high risk of race riots set up specialized information centers starting in 1968, known as rumor control centers [204]. Their goal was to find and disseminate exact information corresponding to the questions city dwellers asked them over the phone. During the first week of its existence, the Los Angeles Rumor Control Center received ten thousand calls. These centers were unfortunately faced with an insurmountable problem: in order to have access to the most exact and recent information, they had to have close relations with local government and police. But by maintaining such relations, they lost a good deal of their credibility in the black community; the latter, in effect, made but a small number of the calls received [155].

As rumors often arise from distrust of official versions, a key to prevention is also the credibility of sources. This trivial recommendation poses, as we shall see, serious practical problems. In order to be considered credible, it is not enough to say that one is; one must have proofs of credibility to back one up, i.e., one must be someone who has always told it like it was [34]. This precept is particularly difficult to apply at moments of crisis, precisely because it often seems preferable not to divulge information or to somehow disguise it.

Two very different men, Winston Churchill and Che Guevara, tried to make themselves that kind of reputation. Throughout the bombings of London by the German air force, rumors about the true gravity of the damage were rare in Great Britain. Winston Churchill had proven that he was willing to call a spade a spade, and reported the exact losses inflicted, even when they were extremely high. In the United States, on the contrary, due to the existence of censorship during the war, many rumors arose after the surprise attack on Pearl Harbor by Japanese bombers. Such rumors proliferated, vying with official figures reported by the ministry of information. Roosevelt himself broached the subject in a press conference held in order to put a stop to the rumors—which it did not do altogether, thereby attesting to the fact that the president had not been able to assuage all apprehension and legitimate anxiety.

In South and Central American countries, regular troops lend credence to the rumors spread by peasants in trying to surmise the nature of the guerillas' progress. Indeed, as they themselves are engaged in combat, they can assess the discrepancy between their knowledge of the facts and official victory statements. Che Guevara was considered highly credible as he refused to dissimulate even the most embarrassing news. To his mind, having a reputation as a noncredible source was, in the long run, more damaging than the publication of such news. And experience shows that such news filters through in one way or another, reappearing thus in the form of rumors. The world leader in photocopies, the Xerox Corporation, can attest to that [165].

Good Faith, Transparency, and Swiftness

In 1978, the Xerox Corporation heard from its British subsidiary that a group of Swedish researchers analyzing the inks and powders used in photocopy machines had found particles in Xerox's ink requiring in-depth investigation because of their potentially carcinogenic effect on animals. Xerox sped its vice-president, H.W. Becker, to Stockholm to find out the exact facts. Hearing that the investigators intended to publish their results in a scientific journal, Becker suggested that the company immediately carry out its own investigation to check for the existence of dangerous particles.

Working seven days a week, the research team especially recruited for this investigation detected particles of nytropyrene—impurities due to the manufacturing process used by one of Xerox's suppliers. When the required corrections were made, analyses of the ink showed no dangerous particles.

In the meantime, a research team in Texas made it known that it had found mutagenic particles in photocopy machine ink used by another company. A newspaper picked up the news, shifting from mutagenic to carcinogenic. As the Xerox Corporation was the best known of the photocopy producers, a rumor went around among the tens of thousands of users, claiming that Xerox ink was carcinogenic. The Xerox telephone operators were suddenly assailed with calls by worried customers. An Australian newspaper even announced on its front page: "Risks run by tens of thousands of people." But the Xerox Corporation was able to immediately announce the results of its own study to the National Agency for Environment Protection as well as to the press.

As we see, the temporal factor is crucial in prevention. One must react very early on, while the rumor is still limited to a certain geographical area. The Saupiquet group reacted in precisely this way: by swiftly putting into practice a policy of transparency, it proved its good faith. Let us recall to mind the facts of the case:

On July 9, 1985, an adolescent was taken to the hospital in Sarrebourg. After having been operated on for appendicitis, the doctors made their diagnosis on July 12: food poisoning. When questioned, the adolescent boy replied that he had eaten some "Graciet" tuna fish. The Graciet brand, number one in France in canned tuna packed in oil, is one of the product lines made by the Saupiquet group. Governmental authorities immediately warned consumers through the press, had all cans from the same series taken off supermarket shelves, and began analyzing them. Thanks to the media's mouthpiece, a red alert rumor about tuna began to spread. The company adopted a three-pronged strategy: not to adopt a position before the results of the analysis were made known, to provide all possible information to reporters and distributors, and to help the investigators so that the conclusions of the analyses would be available as soon as possible.

Instead of adopting a policy of hushing up the event, the company took a positive stance: it calmly asserted its confidence in its product. If the food poisoning were truly due to the Graciet tuna, it would be the first case ever encountered in Europe. On the evening of July 14, the company alerted all of its French distributors. The next day, the sales team went through every warehouse and store to take every can packed on the same day as the suspect can off the shelves. Within three days, every such can had been taken out of circulation.

On July 18, the ministers of consumption and health published a report exonerating Graciet tuna. The company telexed the report to all of its distributors, and was able to get most of the media that had reported the alert to publish a denial. In all, the alert lasted but a week from the supposed diagnosis of food poisoning to the results of the scientific analysis. The rumor did not have the time to get out of hand. This example shows that a certain degree of transparency, while insufficient, is nevertheless necessary in the prevention of rumors. It is exactly what Perrier did in 1990.

Protective Images

As we have already shown, not every rumor targeting someone can succeed. Rumors must first be rendered probable. They actually reveal latent image problems. Conversely, image management is necessary to prevent rumors. No one had ever heard of Procter & Gamble: lacking a corporate image, the firm was decoded as a mere symbol (an anonymous mega-corporation). Sometimes a company's silence, far from being interpreted as a sign of good management and cost-consciousness, may mean that the company has something to hide. Unlike most fast food franchises, Church's Fried Chicken Corporation, for instance, is not fond of advertising. Its advertising budget is one of the lowest in the industry. Although this did not cause the rumor, Church's low visibility surely facilitated the diffusion of allegations in the black community that Church's Fried Chicken was owned by the Ku Klux Klan, and that the white supremacist organization was contaminating the chicken so that eating it would cause sterility in black male consumers.

The Nestles' case offers the best demonstration possible of the value of already having a good image. In March 1974, in London, the War on Want Association published a brochure entitled "Baby Killer." This was the starting point of a worldwide campaign against the multinational corporation, and its massive marketing of baby milk powder in underdeveloped countries where it is well known that mothers cannot afford to boil the water that is mixed into the milk powder. Hence babies that are fed with industrial milk necessarily drink contaminated water. The campaign lasted ten years, at which point an agreement was signed between the Nestles' Corporation and the Boycott Committee. Although the corporation was shaken by this long and not unfounded attack, it was actually helped by its brand image. The world over, Nestles' has become synonymous with "motherhood, gift giving, milk, life, sweetness, etc." This strong and positive stereotype was unable to forestall the attack, but at an unconscious level was able to weaken its effects; the accusation that Nestles' was "killing babies" was too dissonant with people's preexisting credo.

Conclusion

The study of rumors has, up until now, been ruled by a negative conception: rumors have been taken to be necessarily false, fanciful, or irrational. Thus rumors have always been deplored, and treated like fleeting aberrations or momentary folly. Some people even saw in the rise of the mass media an opportunity for dealing a final blow to rumors: television, radio, and the press were expected to do away with rumors' *raison d'être*.

We have shown that this negative view is untenable. On the one hand, it led the study of rumors to a dead end: most aspects of the phenomena remained unexplained, being simply qualified as pathological. On the other, it seemed above all motivated by a moralizing concern and dogmatic prejudice. There is, in effect, but one way to prevent rumors, and that is by stopping people from speaking. The apparently legitimate concern with having only reliable information in circulation leads directly to the control of information, and on to the control of speech: the media would become the only source of authorized information. Thus there would no longer be anything but official news.

Here we arrive at the heart of rumors' *raison d'être*. Rumors are not necessarily "false": they are, however, necessarily unofficial. Marginalized and at times in the opposition, they challenge official reality by proposing other realities. That is why the mass media have not eliminated them.

For a long time it was thought that rumors were substitutes: lacking reliable, controlled media, a substitute or second-best media had to be found. The coexistence of mass media and rumors proves just the opposite: they constitute, rather, a complementary media—that of another reality. This is perfectly logical: the mass media are always part and parcel of a logic of descending communication, from top to bottom, i.e., from those who know to those who know not. The public at large thus only receives what those at the top want it to know. Rumors constitute an alternative source of information, i.e., a source that is perforce uncontrolled.

This absence of control brings to an engineer, technician, or reporter's mind images of defeat in their never-ending battle for information reliability. In the eyes of a politician or citizen, this absence of control means an absence of censorship, a dispelling of secrecy, and access to hidden reality. It must thus be preserved.

The negative conception that associates rumors with falsehood is technological in nature: the only good communication should be controlled communication. Rumors set up another value against that one: the only good communication is unregulated communication, even if reliability thereby suffers. In other words, "false" rumors are the price that has to be paid for those rumors that are founded.

Epistemologically speaking, the study of rumors sheds a harsh light on a fundamental question: why do we believe what we believe? Indeed, we all have a certain intellectual baggage made up of ideas, opinions, images, and beliefs about the world around us. Now the latter have often been acquired by word-of-mouth and hearsay. We are not conscious of this acquiring process: it is slow, occasional, and imperceptible. Rumors provide extraordinary occasions: they recreate this slow, invisible process, but in an accelerated manner. The process at last becomes observable.

And what we find is that altogether unfounded information can circulate in society just as easily as founded information, and has the same mobilizing effects. The few short moments of lucidity provided by the study of rumors make us see how fragile a thing knowledge is. A substantial percentage of our knowledge is, perhaps, unbeknownst to us, totally ungrounded.

Rumors reconfirm something that is self-evident: we do not believe what we know because it is true, founded, or proven. With all due measure we can affirm the opposite: it is true because we believe it. Rumors demonstrate once again, as if it were necessary to do so, that all certainty is social: what the group to which we belong considers to be true *is* true. Social knowledge is based on faith and not on proof. That should come as no surprise: isn't religion itself the best example of a rumor? Isn't religion the propagation of words attributed to an initial Great Witness? It is significant that, in Christianity, this original source is called the Word. Like rumors, religion consists in contagious faith: one expects the faithful to take someone at his word, and to abide by the revealed truth. It is not proofs of God's existence that create faith, but rather the other way around. The intimate convictions that move the peoples of the earth are thus often based on words alone.

References

[1] Abelson, R.; Aronson, E.; McGuire, W. J.; Newcomb, T.; Rosenberg, M.; Tannenbaum, P.H. (1968). *Theories of Cognitive Consistency: A Sourcebook*. Chicago: Rand McNally.

[2] Adams, J. (1973). "Stock Market Price Movements as Collective Behavior." *International Journal of Contemporary Sociology,* 10 (2–3): 133–147.

[3] *Advertising Age* (1982). "Procter and Gamble Rumor Blitz Looks Like a Bomb." *Advertising Age* 53: 68–9.

[4] Allport, F. H. and Lepkin, M. (1945). "Wartime Rumors of Waste and Special Privilege: Why Some People Believe Them." *Journal of Abnormal and Social Psychology* 40: 3–36.

[5] Allport, G. W.; Postman, L. (1946). "An Analysis of Rumor." *Public Opinion Quarterly* 10: 501–17.

[6] Allport, G. W. and Postman, L. (1947). *The Psychology of Rumor*. New York: Henry Holt.

[7] Alter, J. (1982). "Procter and Gamble Sues over Satanism." *Advertising Age* 53: 1.

[8] Ambrosini, P. J. (1983). "Clinical Assessment of Group and Defensive Aspects of Rumor." *International Journal of Group Psychotherapy,* 33 (1): 69–83.

[9] Anderson, C. A.; Lepper, M. R.; Ross, L. (1980). "Perseverance of Social Theories: The Role of Explanation in the Persistence of Discredited Information." *Journal of Personality and Social Psychology* 39, (6): 1037–49.

[10] Anger, K. (1975). *Hollywood Babylon*. New York: Dell.

[11] Arndt, J. (1967). *Word of Mouth Advertising*. New York: Advertising Research Foundation.

[12] Asch, S. (1958). "Effects of Group Pressure upon the Modification and Distortion of Judgments." *Readings in Social Psychology,* E. Maccoby, T. Newcomb, E. Hartley (eds.). New York: Holt, Rinehart & Winston, 174–183.

[13] Ashworth, C. E. (1980). "Flying Saucers, Spoon-Bending and Atlantis: A Structural Analysis of New Mythologies," *The Sociological Review:* 28 (2): 353–76.

[14] Assouline, P. (1985). "Les Complots dans la République." *L'Histoire,* 84: 8–19.

[15] Auclair, G. (1982). *Le Mana Quotidien.* Paris: Editions Anthropos.

[16] Baker, R. L. (1976). "The Influence of Mass Culture on Modern Legends." *Southern Folklore Quarterly* 40: 367–76.

[17] Banta, T. (1964). "The Kennedy Assassination: Early Thoughts and Emotions." *Public Opinion Quarterly* 28: 216–24.

[18] Barloy, J-J. (1985). *Les Survivants de L'Ombre.* Paris: Arthaud Editions.

[19] Barnes, D. R. (1972). "The Bosom Serpent. A Legend in American Literature and Culture." *Journal of American Folklore* 85: 111–22.

[20] Barthes, R. (1957). *Mythologies.* Paris: Le Seuil Editions.

[21] Bascom, W. (1965). "The Forms of Folklore: Prose Narratives." *Journal of American Folklore* 78 (307): 3–20.

[22] Basgoz, I. (1975). "The Tale-Singer and His Audience," in D. Ben-Amos and K. S. Goldstein (eds.), *Folklore, Performance and Communication.* The Hague–Paris: Mouton, 143–205.

[23] Bauer, R. A. and Gleicher, D. B. (1953). "Word of Mouth Communication in the Soviet Union," *Public Opinion Quarterly* 17: 297–310.

[24] Beardsley, R. K. and Hankey, R. (1942). "The Vanishing Hitchhiker." *California Folklore Quarterly* 1: 303–35.

[25] Beardsley, R. K. and Hankey, R. (1943). "A History of the Vanishing Hitchhiker." *California Folklore Quarterly* 2: 13–25.

[26] Beezley, W. H. (1980). "Locker Rumors: Folklore and Football." *Journal of the Folklore Institute* 17: 196–221.

[27] Bellemin-Noël, J. (1983). *Les Contes et leurs Fantasmes.* Paris: PUF.

[28] Bennett, G. (1984). "The Phantom Hitchhiker: Neither Modern, Urban nor Legend?" in P. Smith (ed.), *Perspectives on Contemporary Legend.* Sheffield: Sheffield Academic Press, 45–63.

[29] Bennett, G. (1985). "What's Modern about the Modern Legend?" *Fabula* 26 (3/4): 219–29.

[30] Bennett, G. (1987). "Problems in Collecting and Classifying Urban Legends," in G. Bennett et al. (eds.), *Perspectives on Contemporary Legend*, Volume 2. Sheffield Academic Press, 15–30.

[31] Bennett, G. (1987). *Traditions of Belief, Women, Folklore and the Supernatural Today*, New York: Penguin Books.

[32] Bennett, G. (1988). "Legend: Performance and Truth," in G. Bennett and P. Smith (eds.), *Monsters with Iron Teeth, Perspectives on Contemporary Legend*, Volume 3, Sheffield Academic Press, 13–36.

[33] Bensahel, J. G. (1974). "Should You Pounce on a Poisonous Rumour?" *International Management* 29: 25–26.

[34] Bensahel, J. G. (1975). "Don't Shield Employees from Bad News." *International Management* 30: 49–50.

[35] Bernand, C. (1978). "L'ombre du Tueur." *Communications* 28: 165–85.

[36] Bethke, R. D. (1976), "Storytelling at an Adirondack Inn." *Western Folklore*, 35 (2): 123–39.

[37] Bettelheim, B. (1977). *The Uses of Enchantment*. New York: Vintage. (*Psychanalyse des Contes de Fée*. Paris: Fayard Editions, 1977.)

[38] Bieder, J. (1970). "De l'Homme de Kiev à la Femme d'Amiens." *Annales Médico-psychologiques* 1, 771–75.

[39] Bonaparte, M. (1941). "The Myth of the Corpse in the Car." *American Image* 2: 105–26.

[40] Bonaparte, M. (1947). *Myths of War*. London: Image. (*Mythes de Guerre*. Paris: PUF, 1950).

[41] Bowman, M. (1987). "Contemporary Legend and Practical Joke," in G. Bennett et al. (eds.), *Perspectives on Contemporary Legend*, Volume 2, Sheffield Academic Press, 171–76.

[42] Boyes, G. (1984). "Belief and Disbelief: An Examination of Reactions to the Presentation of Rumor Legends," in P. Smith (ed.), *Perspectives on Contemporary Legend*. Sheffield Academic Press, 64–78.

[43] Brodu, J. L. and Meurger, M. (1985). *Les Félins-mystère*. Paris: Pogonip.

[44] Brunvand, J.-H. (1983). *The Vanishing Hitchhiker*, London: Picador Books.

[45] Brunvand, J.-H. (1984). *The Choking Doberman*. New York: Norton.

[46] Brunvand, J.-H. (1986). *The Mexican Pet, More New Urban Legends and Some Old Favorites*. New York: Norton.

[47] Buckhout, R., (1974), "Eyewitness Testimony," *Scientific American*, 231, (6): 23–31.

[48] Buckner, H. T. (1965). "A Theory of Rumor Transmission." *Public Opinion Quarterly* 29: 54–70.

[49] Byrnes, R.F. (1950). *Antisemitism in Modern France,* New Brunswick, NJ: Transaction Books.

[50] Campion-Vincent, V. (1976). "Les Histoires Exemplaires." *Contrepoint* 22–3: 217–32.

[51] Campion-Vincent, V. (1989). "Complots et Avertissements: Légendes dans la Ville." *Revue Française de Sociologie* 31: 91–105.

[52] Cantril, H.; Gaudet, H.; Hertzog; H. (1940). *The Invasion from Mars.* Princeton, NJ: Princeton University Press.

[53] Caplow, T. (1947). "Rumors in War." *Social Forces* 25: 298–302.

[54] Caritey, J. (1980). "Rumeur et Politique." *La Revue Administrative* 195: 250–52.

[55] Carroll, M. P. (1984). "Alligators in the Sewer, Dragons in the Well and Freud in the Toilet." *The Sociological Review* 32: 57–74.

[56] Carroll, M. P. (1987). "The Castrated Boy: Another Contribution to the Psychoanalytic Study of Urban Legends." *Folklore* 98 (2): 216–25.

[57] Chaiken, S. (1980). "Heuristic versus Systematic Information Processing and the Use of Source versus Message Cues in Persuasion." *Journal of Personality and Social Psychology* 39 (5): 752–66.

[58] Chaiken, S., Eagly, A. H. (1983). "Communication Modality as a Determinant of Persuasion: The Role of Communicator Salience." *Journal of Personality and Social Psychology* 45 (2): 241–56.

[59] Cohn, N. (1987). *Europe's Inner Demons.* St. Albans: Paladin.

[60] Choumoff, P. S. (1985). "Entretien sur les Chambres à Gaz." *L'Histoire* 79: 68–73.

[61] Coleman, L. (1979). "Alligators-in-the-Sewers: A Journalistic Origin." *Journal of American Folklore* 92: 335–38.

[62] Dale, R. (1978). *The Tumour in the Whale: A Collection of Modern Myths.* London: Duckworth & Co.

[63] Dale, R. (1984). *It's True, It Happened to a Friend: A Collection of Urban Legends.* London: Duckworth & Co.

[64] Danner, J. (1972). "Don't Let the Grapevine Trip You Up." *Supervisory Management* 17: 2–7.

[65] Davis, K. (1973). "Care and Cultivation of the Corporate Grapevine." *Management Review* 62: 53–5.

[66] Davis, K. (1975). "Cut those Rumors Down to Size." *Supervisory Management* 20: 2–6.

[67] Debats, K. E. (1982). "A Harmless Sport?" *Personnel Journal* 61: 208.

[68] Defleur, M. (1962). "Mass Communication and the Study of Rumor." *Sociological Inquiry* 32: 51–70.

[69] Degh, L. (1971). "The Belief Legend in Modern Society: Form, Function and Relationships to Other Genres," in W. Hand (ed.), *American Folk Legend*. Berkeley: University of California Press, 55–68.

[70] Degh, L. and Vazsonyi, A. (1974). "The Memorate and the Proto-Memorate," *Journal of American Folklore* 87: 225–39.

[71] Degh, L. and Vazsonyi, A. (1975). "The Hypothesis of Multi-Conduit Transmission in Folklore," in D. Ben-Amos and K. S. Goldstein (eds.) *Folklore, Performance and Communication*. The Hague-Paris: Mouton, 207–52.

[72] Degh, L. and Vazsonyi, A. (1976). "Legend and Belief," in D. Ben-Amos (ed.), *Folklore Genres*. Austin: University of Texas Press, 93–123.

[73] Degh, L. and Vazsonyi, A. (1978). "The Crack on the Red Goblet or Truth and Modern Legend," in R. M. Dorson (ed.), *Folklore in the Modern World*, The Hague-Paris: Mouton, 253–72.

[74] Degh, L. and Vazsonyi, A. (1983). "Does the Word 'Dog' Bite? Ostensive Action as Means of Legend Telling." *Journal of Folklore Research* 20, (1): 5–34.

[75] Delaney, W. (1983). "The Secretarial Grapevine," *Supervisory Management*, 28: 31–4.

[76] Delort, R. (1983), "La Guerre du Loup," *L'Histoire* 53: 6–19.

[77] Delumeau, J. (1978). *La Peur en Occident*. Paris: Pluriel.

[78] Deutsch, E. (1982). "Anatomie d'une Rumeur Avortée." *Le Genre Humain* 5: 99–114.

[79] Dichter, E. (1966). "How Word of Mouth Advertising Works." *Harvard Business Review* 44: 147–66.

[80] Douel, J. (1981). *Le Journal Tel qu'il est Lu*. Paris: Centre de Formation et de Perfectionnement des Journalistes.

[81] Douglas, S. (1988). "Practical Jokes and the Legends Surrounding Them," in G. Bennett and P. Smith (eds.), *Monsters with Iron Teeth, Perspectives on Contemporary Legend*, Volume 3, Sheffield Academic Press, 241–44.

[82] Duhamel, J. (1955), "La Théorie Mathématique des Epidémies et des Rumeurs." *La Presse Médicale* 63 (34): 717–18.

[83] Dumerchat, F. (1985). "Du Nouveau sur le Moine." *Bulletin du Comité Poitou-Charentes des Groupements Ufologiques*, 3: 2–8.

[84] Dundes, A. (1971). "On the Psychology of Legend," in W. Hand (ed.), *American Folk Legend*. Berkeley: University of California Press. 21–36.

[85] Dundes, A. (1987). "At Ease, Disease—AIDS Jokes as Sick Humor." *American Behavioral Scientist* 30: 72–81.

[86] Durandin, G. (1950). "Les Rumeurs." *Polycopié Universitaire, Leçons de Psychologie Sociale,* Paris.

[87] Eco, U. (1985). *La Guerre du Faux.* Paris: Grasset Editions.

[88] Eliade, M. (1961). *The Sacred and the Profane.* New York: Harper & Row.

[89] Elias, N. (1985). "Remarques sur le Commérage." *Actes de la Recherche,* 60: 23–30.

[90] Elms, A. (1977). "The Three Bears' Four Interpretations." *Journal of American Folklore,* 90, (2): 257–73.

[91] Erlanger (1985). *Le Régent.* Paris: Folio-Histoire.

[92] Esposito, J.-L. and Rosnow, R. (1983). "Corporate Rumors: How They Start and How to Stop Them." *Management Review* 72: 44–9.

[93] Favreau-Colombier, J. (1985). *Marie Besnard.* Paris: Robert Laffont.

[94] Festinger, L. (1954). "A Theory of Social Comparison Processes." *Human Relations* 7: 117–40.

[95] Festinger, L. (1962). *A Theory of Cognitive Dissonance.* Stanford: Stanford University Press.

[96] Festinger, L.; Cartwright, D. et al., (1948). "A Study of a Rumor: Its Origin and Spread." *Human Relations* 1: 464–85.

[97] Fine, G. A. (1977). "Social Components of Children's Gossip." *Journal of Communication* 27 (1): 181–85.

[98] Fine, G. A. (1979). "Folklore Diffusion through Interactive Social Networks." *New York Journal of Folklore* 5: 87–126.

[99] Fine, G. A. (1979). "Cokelore and Coke Law: Urban Belief Tales and the Problem of Multiple Origins." *Journal of American Folklore* 92: 477–82.

[100] Fine, G. A. (1980). "The Kentucky Fried Rat: Legends and Modern Society." *Journal of the Folklore Institute* 17 (2–3): 222–43.

[101] Fine, G. A. (1985). "Rumors and Gossiping," in *Handbook of Discourse Analysis, Vol. 3: Discourse and Dialogue.* Orlando: Academic Press, 223–37.

[102] Fine, G. A., (1985), "The Goliath Effect: Corporate Dominance and Mercantile Legends." *Journal of American Folklore* 58 (387): 63–84.

[103] Fine, G. A. (1986). "Redemption Rumors: Mercantile Legends and Corporate Beneficence," *Journal of American Folklore,* 99: 208–22.

[104] Fine, G. A. (1987). "Welcome to the World of AIDS: Fantasies of Female Revenge." *Western Folklore* 46 (3): 192–97.

[105] Fine, G. A. (1988). "The City as a Folklore Generator: Urban Legends in the Metropolis." *Urban Resources.*

[106] Flem, L. (1982). "Bouche Bavarde et Oreille Curieuse." *Le Genre Humain,* 5: 11–18.

[107] Foa, E. B. and Foa, U. G. (1980). "Resource Theory: Interpersonal Behavior as Exchange," in K. J. Getgen et al. (eds.), *Social Exchange: Advances in Theory and Research.* New York: Plenum Press.

[108] Forster, M. (1985). *All the News That's Nuts.* Vancouver: Raincoat Books, 1985.

[109] Fox, W. S. (1980). "Folklore and Fakelore: Some Sociological Considerations," *Journal of the Folklore Institute* 17 (2–3): 244–61.

[110] Gauchet, M. (1985). "Le Démon du Soupçon." *L'Histoire,* 84: 48–57.

[111] Georges, R. A. (1971). "The General Concept of Legend: Some Assumptions to Be Reexamined and Reassessed," in W. Hand (ed.), *American Folk Legend: A Symposium.* Berkeley: University of California Press, 1–19.

[112] Geracioti, F. (1988). *Diaro di una Calunnia,* Roma: Qualecultura, Jaca Book.

[113] Giffin, G. (1975). "The Contribution of Studies of Source Credibility to a Theory of International Trust in the Communication Process." *Psychological Bulletin* 68 (2): 104–20.

[114] Girardet, R. (1986). *Mythes et Mythologies Politiques.* Paris: Le Seuil Editions.

[115] Glazer, M. (1985). "The Traditionalization of the Contemporary Legend: The Mexican-American Example." *Fabula* 26 (3/4): 288–97.

[116] Goldschmidt, B. (1980). *Le Complexe Atomique.* Paris: Fayard.

[117] Gorphe, F. (1927). *La Critique du Témoignage.* Paris: Dalloz.

[118] Goss, M. (1986). "Escaped Snakes and Other Urban Terrors." *Fate,* August: 30–7 and September: 78–88.

[119] Gritti, J. (1978). *Elle Court, Elle Court la Rumeur.* Ottawa: Stanké.

[120] Gross, E. (1968). *Personal Leadership in Marketing.* Madison, NJ: The Florham Park Press.

[121] Hall, M. (1965). "The Great Cabbage Hoax." *Journal of Personality and Social Psychology* 2 (4): 563–69.

[122] Hannah, D. and Sternthal, B. (1984). "Detecting and Explaining the Sleeper Effect." *Journal of Consumer Research,* 11 (2): 632–42.

[123] Harrold, F. B. and Eve, R. A. (1986). "Noah's Ark and Ancient Astronauts: Pseudoscientific Beliefs about the Past among a Sample of College Students." *The Skeptical Inquirer,* 11 (1): 61–75.

[124] Helmreich, W. B. (1984). *The Things They Say behind Your Back.* New Brunswick, NJ: Transaction Books.

[125] Hirschhorn, L. (1983). "Managing Rumors During Retrenchment." *Advanced Management Journal* 48 (Summer): 4–11.

[126] Hobbs, S. (1987). "The Social Psychology of a Good Story," in G. Bennett et al. (eds.) *Perspectives on Contemporary Legend, Vol 2*. Sheffield Academic Press, 133–48.

[127] Holmes, J., Lett, J. (1977). "Product Sampling and Word of Mouth," *Journal of Advertising Research* 17 (5): 35–45.

[128] Hyman, H., and Singer, E. (1968). *Reference Group Theory and Research*. New York: The Free Press.

[129] Jacobson, D. J. (1948). *The Affairs of Dame Rumour*. New York: Rinehart & Co.

[130] Jaeger, M. and Rosnow, R.-L. (1980). "Who Hears What from Whom and with What Effect: A Study of Rumor." *Personality and Social Psychology Bulletin* 6 (3): 473–78.

[131] Jervey, G. (1981). "Entenmann's Fights Moonie Link." *Advertising Age* 52 (November): 33.

[132] Johnson, D. M. (1945). "The Phantom Anesthetist of Mattoon: A Field Study of Mass Hysteria." *Journal of Abnormal and Social Psychology* 40: 175–86.

[133] Jones, E. et al. (1972). *Attribution: Perceiving the Causes of Behavior*. Morristown, NJ: General Learning Press.

[134] Jung, C. G., (1910). "Ein Betrag zur Psychologie des Gerüchtes." *Zentralblatt für Psychoanalyse* 1: 81–90.

[135] Jung, C. G. (1959). "A Visionary Rumour." *Journal of Analytical Psychology*, 4: 5–19.

[136] Jung, C. G. (1969). *Flying Saucers: A Modern Myth of Things Seen in the Skies*. New York: Signet Books.

[137] Kahneman, D.; Slovic, P.; Tversky, A. (1982). *Judgement under Uncertainty: Heuristic and Biases*. Cambridge: Cambridge University Press.

[138] Kapferer, J.-N. (1984). *Les Chemins de la Persuasion*. Paris: Dunod.

[139] Kapferer, J.-N. (1985). *L'Enfant et la Publicité: Les Chemins de la Séduction*. Paris: Dunod.

[140] Kapferer, J.-N. (1986). "Une Rumeur de la Publicité: La Publicité Subliminale," *Revue Française du Marketing* 110 (December): 67–75.

[141] Kapferer, J.-N. and Dubois, B. (1981). *Echec à la Science*. Paris: Nouvelles Editions Rationalistes.

[142] Kapferer, J.-N. (1987). "La Rumeur." *La Recherche* 187 (April): 468–75.

[143] Kapferer, J.-N. (1989). "Les Disparitions de Mourmelon: Origine et Interpréta-

tion des Rumeurs." *Revue Française de Sociologie* (January–March): 81–9.

[144] Kapferer, J.-N. (1989). "A Mass Poisoning Rumor in Europe," *The Public Opinion Quarterly,* Winter, 53 (4).

[145] Kapferer, J.-N. and Laurent, G. (1990). "Movie Star, Illness and Rumor: The Effectiveness of a Broadcasted Public Denial." *HEC-ISA Research Paper.* Jouy-en-Josas: France.

[146] Kaplan, S. (1982). *Le Complot de Famine: Histoire d'une Rumeur au XVIIIe Siècle.* Paris: Armand Colin.

[147] Katz, E. and Lazarsfeld, P. (1955). *Personal Influence: The Part Played by People in the Flow of Mass Communications.* New York: Free Press.

[148] Kindleberger, C. P. (1978). *Manias, Panics and Crashes: A History of Financial Crises.* New York: Basic Books.

[149] Klapp, O. (1975). *Symbolic Leaders* Chicago: Aldine.

[150] Klintberg, B. af (1981). "Modern Migratory Legends in Oral Tradition and Daily Papers." *ARV, Scandinavian Yearbook of Folklore,* 37, 153–60.

[151] Klintberg, B. af (1984). "Why Are There So Many Modern Legends about Revenge?" in P. Smith (ed.), *Perspectives on Contemporary Legend,* Sheffield University Press, 141–46.

[152] Klintberg, B. af (1985). "Legends and Rumours about Spiders and Snakes," in *Fabula,* 26, 3/4, 274–87.

[153] Klintberg, B. af (1989). "Do the Legends of Today and Yesterday Belong to the Same Genre?" in *International Folk Narratives Congress on Modern Storytelling.* Budapest, June 10–17.

[154] Knapp, R., (1944), "A Psychology of Rumor." *Public Opinion Quarterly,* 8 (1): 22–37.

[155] Knopf, T. (1975). "Beating Rumors: Evaluation of Rumor Control Centers." *Policy Analysis* 1 (4): 599–612.

[156] Knopf, T. (1975). *Rumors, Race and Riots.* New Brunswick, NJ: Transaction Books.

[157] Koenig, F. (1985). *Rumor in the Marketplace: The Social Psychology of Commercial Hearsay.* Dover, MA: Auburn House.

[158] Lacouture, J. (1982). "Bruit et Vérité," *Le Genre Humain* 5: 19–29.

[159] Laurent, G. and Kapferer, J.-N. (1985). "Measuring Consumer Involvement Profiles." *Journal of Marketing Research* 22, 41–53.

[160] Le Bon, G. (1965). *La Psychologie des Foules.* Paris: PUF.

[161] Lecerf, Y. and Parker, E. (1987). *L'Affaire Tchernobyl: La Guerre des Rumeurs.* Paris: PUF Editions.

[162] Lecuyer, B.-P. (1981). "Une Quasi-expérimentation sur les Rumeurs au XVIIIème siècle: l'Enquête Proto-scientifique du Contrôleur Général Orry (1745)," in *Science et Théorie de l'Opinion Publique. Hommage à Jean Stoetzel.* Paris: Editions Retz, Bibliothèque du CELP, 170–87.

[163] Lefebvre, G. (1957). *La Grande Peur de 1789.* Paris: Société de l'Enseignement Supérieur.

[164] Lépront, C. (1984). *Une Rumeur.* Paris: Gallimard.

[165] Levy, R. (1981). "Tilting at the Rumor Mill." *Dun's Review* 118 (July): 52–4.

[166] Lienhardt, P. (1975). "The Interpretation of Rumour," in J. H. M. Beattie and R. G. Lienhardt (eds.), *Essays in Memory of E. Evans-Pritchard.* Oxford: The Clarendon Press, 105–31.

[167] London, I. D. and London, M. B. (1975). "Rumor as a Footnote to Chinese National Character." *Psychological Reports* 37 (2): 343–49.

[168] London, H. and Nisbett, H. (1974). *Thought and Feelings: Cognitive Modification of Feeling States.* Chicago: Aldine.

[169] LSA, (1980). "Le Cas Space Dust." *Libre-Service Actualités* 759 (May 23): 56–8.

[170] Lüthi, M. (1976). "Aspects of the Märchen and the Legend," in D. Ben-Amos (ed.), *Folklore Genres.* Austin: University of Texas Press, 17–33.

[171] Mackay, LL. D. (1980). *Extraordinary Popular Delusions and the Madness of Crowds.* New York: Harmony Books.

[172] Maidenberg, J. H. (1980). "Commodities: Rates, Rumors and Facts." *New York Times*, March 3.

[173] Mannoni, O. (1969). *Clefs pour l'Imaginaire ou l'Autre Scène.* Paris: Editions du Seuil.

[174] Marcellin, R. (1985). *La Guerre Politique.* Paris: Plon.

[175] Marchalonis, S. (1976). "Three Medieval Tales and Their Modern American Analogues." *Journal of the Folklore Institute* 13 (2): 173–84.

[176] Marty, M. E. (1985). "Satanism: No Soap," in *Across the Board*, December 19, 8–14.

[177] McConnell, B. (1982). "Urban Legends in Fleet Street." *Folklore* 93 (2): 226–28.

[178] McGregor, D. (1938). "The Major Determinants of the Prediction of Social Events." *Journal of Abnormal and Social Psychology* 33: 179–204.

[179] McSweeny, J. P. (1976). "Rumors: Enemy of Company Morale and Community Relations." *Personnel Journal* 55 (September): 435–36.

[180] Medalia, N. and Larsen, O. (1958). "Diffusion and Belief in a Collective Delusion: The Seattle Windshield Pitting Epidemic." *American Sociological Review* 23: 180–86.

[181] Medini, G. and Rosemberg, E. H. (1976). "Gossip and Psychotherapy." *American Journal of Psychotherapy* 30 (3): 452–62.

[182] Méheust, B. (1988). *Soucoupes Volantes et Folklore.* Paris: Le Mercure de France.

[183] Meyer Spacks P. (1985). *Gossip.* New York: Alfred Knopf.

[184] Morgan, J.; O'Neill, C.; Harré, R. (1979). *Nicknames: Their Origins and Social Consequences.* London: Routledge and Kegan Paul.

[185] Morgan, H. and Tucker, K. (1987). *Rumor,* New York: Penguin Books.

[186] Morin, E. (1969). *La Rumeur d'Orléans.* Paris: Editions du Seuil (*Rumor in Orleans,* trans. by P. Green., New York: Pantheon, 1971.)

[187] Morin, E. (1972). *Les Stars.* Paris: Edition du Seuil.

[188] Mullen, P. B. (1970). "Department Store Snakes," *Indiana Folklore,* 3: 214–28.

[189] Mullen, P. B. (1972). "Modern Legend and Rumor Theory." *Journal of the Folklore Institute* 9: 95–109.

[190] Murphy, R. (1976). "Rumors, Race and Riots." *Contemporary Sociology* 5 (2): 199–200.

[191] Newall, V. (1986). "Folklore and Male Homosexuality." *Folklore* 97 (2): 123–41.

[192] Nicolas, J. (1981). "La Rumeur de Paris: Rapts d'Enfants en 1750," in *L'Histoire* 40: 48–57.

[193] Nicolaisen, W. F. H. (1984). "Legends as Narrative Response," in P. Smith (ed.), *Perspectives on Contemporary Legend.* Sheffield Academic Press, 167–78.

[194] Nicolaisen, W. F. H. (1985). "Perspectives on Contemporary Legend," *Fabula,* 26, 3/4: 213–18.

[195] Nicolaisen, W. F. H. (1987). "The Linguistic Structure of Legends," in G. Bennett et al. (eds.), *Perspectives on Contemporary Legend* 2. Sheffield Academic Press, 61–76.

[196] Nicolaisen, W. F. H. (1988). "German Sage and English Legend: Terminology and Conceptual Problems," in G. Bennett and P. Smith (eds) *Monsters with Iron Teeth, Perspectives on Contemporary Legend* 3, Sheffield Academic Press, 79–88.

[197] Nkpa, N. (1977). "Rumors of Mass Poisoning in Biafra," *Public Opinion Quarterly*, 41 (3): 332–46.

[198] Ojka, A. B. (1973). "Rumour Research: An Overview," *Journal of the Indian Academy of Applied Psychology* 10 (2–3): 56–64.

[199] Park, R. E. "News as a Form of Knowledge." *American Journal of Sociology*, 45: 669–89.

[200] Peters, N. K. (1988). "Suburban/Rural Variations in the Content of Adolescent Ghost Legends," in G. Bennett and P. Smith (eds.), *Monsters with Iron Teeth, Perspectives on Contemporary Legend*, Vol. 3, Sheffield Academic Press, 221–35.

[201] Peterson, W. Gist, N., (1951), "Rumor and Public Opinion." *American Journal of Sociology*, 57: 159–67.

[202] Pichevin, M.; Ringler, A.; Ringler, M. (1971). "Une Approche du Biais d'Equilibre par la Technique de la Rumeur." *Cahiers de Psychologie*, 14 (3): 219–31.

[203] Pomian, K. (1982). "Samedi 19 décembre 1981 à 17 heures: Varsovie." *Le Genre Humain* 5 (Fall): 63–70.

[204] Ponting, J. (1973). "Rumor Control Centers: Their Emergence and Operations." *American Behavioral Scientist* 16 (3): 391–401.

[205] Propp, V. J. (1970). *Morphologie du Conte*. Paris: Le Seuil Editions.

[206] Propp, V. J. (1983). *Les Racines Historiques du Conte Merveilleux*. Paris: Gallimard Editions.

[207] Richins, M. L. (1983). "Negative Word of Mouth by Dissatisfied Consumers: A Pilot Study." *Journal of Marketing* 47 (1): 68–78.

[208] Ricoeur, P. (1967). *The Symbolism of Evil*. Boston: Beacon.

[209] Rogers, E. (1983). *Diffusion of Innovations*. New York: Free Press.

[210] Rojcewiwz, P. M. (1987). "The Men-in-Black Experience and Tradition: Analogues with the Traditional Devil Hypothesis," *Journal of American Folklore* 100: 148–60.

[211] Rose, A, (1951). "Rumors on the Stock Market," *Public Opinion Quaterly*, 15: 461–86.

[212] Rosen, S. and Tesser, A. (1970). "On Reluctance to Communicate Undesirable Information: The Mum Effect." *Sociometry* 33: 253–63.

[213] Rosnow, R. L. (1980). "Psychology of Rumor Reconsidered." *Psychological Bulletin*, 87 (3): 578–91.

[214] Rosnow, R. L. (1988). "Rumor as Communication: A Contextualist Approach," *Journal of Communication*, 38 (1): 12–27.

[215] Rosnow, R. L.; Fine, G. A.; Esposito, J. L.; Gibney, L. (1988). "Factors Influencing Rumor Spreading: Replication and Extension," *Language and Communication,* 8 (1): 29–42.

[216] Rosnow, R. L. and Fine, G. A. (1976). *Rumor and Gossip: the Social Psychology of Hearsay.* New York: Elsevier.

[217] Rosnow, R. L. and Georgoudi, M. (1985). "Killed by Idle Gossip: The Psychology of Small Talk," in B. Rubin (ed.), *When Information Counts: Grading the Media.* Lexington, MA: Heath.

[218] Rosnow, R. L.; Yost, J. H.; Esposito, J. L. (1986). "Belief in Rumor and Likelihood of Rumor Transmission," *Language and Communication,* 6: 189–94.

[219] Ross, L.; Lepper, M. R.; Hubbard, M. (1975). "Perseverance in Self-Perception and Social Perception: Biased Attributional Processes in the Debriefing Paradigm," *Journal of Personality and Social Psychology,* 32, (5): 880–92.

[220] Rossignol, C. (1973). "Le Phénomène de la Rumeur," *Psychologie Française,* 1 (18): 23–40.

[221] Rotbart, D. (1984). "Anatomy of a Rumor on Wall Street," *Wall Street Journal,* October 26.

[222] Rouquette, M.-L. (1975), *Les Rumeurs.* Paris: PUF.

[223] Rouquette, M.-L. (1979). "Les Phénomènes de Rumeurs." Doctoral Dissertation, Université de Provence.

[224] Rowan, R. (1979). "Where Did That Rumor Come from?" *Fortune* 100 (August): 130–31.

[225] Rysman, A. (1977). "How the Gossip Became a Woman," *Journal of Communication* 27 (1): 176–80.

[226] Sabini, J. and Silver, M. (1982). *Moralities on Everyday Life.* New York: Oxford University Press.

[227] Saintyves, P. (1987). *Les Contes de Perrault et les Récits Parallèles.* Paris: Robert Laffont Ed.

[228] Sampson, S. (1984). "Rumours in Socialist Romania." *Survey,* 28 (4): 142–64.

[229] Sanarov, V. I. (1981). "On The Nature and Origin of Flying Saucers and Little Green Men." *Current Anthropology* 22: 163–67.

[230] Sanderson, S., (1969), "The Folklore of the Motor-Car." *Folklore* 80 (Winter): 241–52.

[231] Sapolsky, H. M. (1986). *Consuming Fears: The Politics of Product Risks.* New York: Basic Books.

[232] Sauvy, A. (1985). *De la Rumeur à l'Histoire.* Paris: Dunod.

[233] Schachter, S. and Burdick, H. (1955). "A Field Experiment on Rumor Transmission and Distortion." *Journal of Abnormal and Social Psychology* 50: 363–71.

[234] Schmitt, J-C. (1985). *Precher d'Exemples: Récits de Prédicateurs du Moyen-Age*. Paris: Stock Editions.

[235] Séguin, J.-P. (1975). *Nouvelles à Sensations, Canards du XIXème siècle*. Paris: Armand Colin.

[236] Sheatsley, P. and Feldman, J. (1964). "The Assassination of President Kennedy," *Public Opinion Quarterly* 28: 189–215.

[237] Sherkovin, Y. and Nazaretyan, A. (1984). "Rumors as a Social Phenomenon and as an Instrument of Psychological Warfare." *Psikhologicheskii Zhurnal*, 5, (5): 41–51.

[238] Sheth, J.N. (1971). "Word of Mouth in Low Risk Innovations." *Journal of Advertising Research*, 11 (3): 15–18.

[239] Shibutani, T. (1966). *Improvised News: A Sociological Study of Rumor*. Indianapolis: Bobbs Merrill.

[240] Simpson, R. (1981). "Rationalized Motifs in Urban Legends." *Folklore* 92 (2): 203–7.

[241] Slotkin, E. M. (1988). "Legend Genre as a Function of Audience." in G. Bennett and P. Smith (eds.), *Monsters with Iron Teeth, Perspectives on Contemporary Legend*, 3, Sheffield Academic Press, 89–111.

[242] Smith, P. (1983). *The Book of Nasty Legends*. London: Routledge and Kegan Paul.

[243] Smith, P. (1984). "On the Receiving End: When Legend Becomes Rumour," in P. Smith (ed.), *Perspectives on Contemporary Legend*, Sheffield: Sheffield Academic Press, 197–215.

[244] Smith, P. (1987). "Contemporary Legend and the Photocopy Revolution." in G. Bennett et al. (eds.), *Perspectives on Contemporary Legend*, 2, Sheffield Academic Press, 171–76.

[245] Snyder, M. and White, P. (1981). "Testing Hypotheses about Other People: Strategies of Verification and Falsification," *Personality and Social Psychology Bulletin*, 7, 39–43.

[246] Soriano, M. (1977). *Les Contes de Perrault: Culture Savante et Traditions Populaires*. Paris: Gallimard Ed.

[247] Stein, H.-F. (1980). "Wars and Rumors of Wars: A Psychohistorical Study of Medical Culture." *Journal of Psychohistory*, 7 (4): 379–401.

[248] Stewart, S. (1982). "The Epistemology of the Horror Story." *Journal of American Folklore*, 95 (375): 33–50.

[249] Stiebing, W. H. (1984). *Ancient Astronauts, Cosmic Collisions and Other Popular Theories about Man's Past*. Buffalo: Prometheus Books.

[250] Thorne, T. (1976). "Legends of the Surfer Subculture." *Western Folklore* 35 (3): 209–17 and 35 (4): 270–80.

[251] Tubiana, M. (1985). *Le Cancer*. Paris: PUF.

[252] Tudor, H. (1972). *Political Myth*. London: Pall Mall Editions.

[253] Turner, P. A. (1987). "Church's Fried Chicken and the Klan: A Rhetorical Analysis of Rumor in the Black Community." *Western Folklore* 46: 294–306.

[254] Tybout, A.; Calder, B.-J.; Sternthal, B. (1981). "Using Information Processing Theory to Design Marketing Strategies." *Journal of Marketing Research* 18: 73–9.

[255] Volkoff, V. (1986). *La Désinformation*. Paris: Julliard.

[256] Walster, E. and Festinger, L. (1962). "The Effectiveness of Overheard Persuasive Communications." *Journal of Abnormal and Social Psychology* 65: 395–402.

[257] Walster, E. et al. (1967). "Effectiveness of Debriefing Following Deception Experiments." *Journal of Personality and Social Psychology*. 6: 371–80.

[258] Wason, P. C. (1965). "The Contexts of Plausible Denial." *Journal of Verbal Learning and Verbal Behavior* 4: 7–11.

[259] Watzlawick, P. (1976). *How Real Is Real? Communication, Disinformation, Confusion*. New York: Random House.

[260] Wegner, D. M.; Coulton, G. F.; Wenzlaff, R. (1985). "The Transparency of Denial: Briefing in the Debriefing Paradigm," *Journal of Personality and Social Psychology* 49 (2): 338–46.

[261] Wegner, D. M.; Wenzlaff, R.; Kerker, R. M.; Beattie, A. E. (1981). "Incrimination through Innuendo: Can Media Questions become Public Answers?" *Journal of Personality and Social Psychology* (40) 5: 822–32.

[262] Weinberg, E. (1978). "Fighting Fire with Fire." *Communication Quarterly*, 26 (3): 26–31.

[263] Williams, N. (1984). "Problems in Defining Contemporary Legends," in P. Smith (ed.), *Perspectives on Contemporary Legend*. Sheffield University Press, 216–28.

[264] Wyer, R. S. and Unverzagt, W. H. (1985). "Effects of Instructions to Disregard Information on its Subsequent Recall and Use in Making Judgments." *Journal of Personality and Social Psychology* 48 (3): 533–49.

[265] Yandell, B. (1979). "Those Who Protest Too Much Are Seen as Guilty." *Personality and Social Psychology Bulletin*, 5: 44–47.

[266] Zillmann, D. and Bryant, J. (1985). *Selective Exposure to Communication*. Hillsdale, NJ: Lawrence Erlbaum Associates.

Index